Steppingstones

to

Curriculum

A Biblical Path

Steppingstones

to

Curriculum

A Biblical Path

Harro Van Brummelen

Alta Vista College Press
Seattle, Washington

for Wilma

whose constant example of
unconditional love for children
of all ages has added a much-needed
dimension to my thinking

ISBN 1-886319-05-7

Published by Alta Vista College Press
P.O. Box 55535, Seattle, Washington 98155

Scripture quotations are taken from *The Holy Bible: New International Version.* Copyright 1973, 1978, 1984 International Bible Society. Used by permission of Zondervan Bible Publishers.

Preface

In this book I consider what a Biblical worldview implies for curriculum theory and practice. I first describe the worldview and values that underlie common approaches to curriculum. I then sketch the basis for an alternate approach. The second part of the book builds on this foundation by discussing a Biblical view of knowledge and its implications for the curriculum as a whole as well as for some specific subject disciplines. The third part of the book shows how we use what we know about knowledge and pedagogy as we go about planning curriculum for the classroom and beyond. The last chapter sums up the role of Christian teachers with respect to curriculum in both Christian and public schools.

The book has several intended audiences. It is a textbook for curriculum and instruction courses in Christian post-secondary institutions. It will also serve as a guide for Christian teachers as they plan their day-to-day classroom and school curriculum. While the content will be useful particularly for teachers and leaders in Christian schools, it will also help Christians in public schools think anew about the direction of the programs they design and implement.

A few explanations are in order. This book will be used in various jurisdictions and countries. Rather than explaining grade level categorizations each time, I have used the term kindergarten to designate the first year of school for five-year-olds. "Primary" refers to the three years of schooling after kindergarten (often called grades or years 1, 2, and 3). "Intermediate" refers to grades 4, 5, and 6; "middle school," grades 6 to 8 or 9. Instructors and discussion leaders using this book may find that there are more situations and questions for discussion than can be analyzed in detail; I have done so to provide some choice in particular situations. Also, I have found that teaching Part III of this book concurrently with rather than after Parts I and II helps students to integrate their own theory and practice.

I dedicate this book to my wife. Our combined classroom experience ranges from teaching four-year-old kindergartners to post-graduate students in their sixties. It is especially her insights into teaching young children that has complemented my experience at the secondary and university levels. Our discussions over the years are reflected in the content of this book.

This book would not have been possible without the cooperation of many classroom teachers in Alberta, British Columbia, Washington, and Australia. The examples they described and allowed me to observe give a special flavor to the book. All examples with names are real examples. A list of schools and teachers that were involved is given in an appendix. My thanks to all, not only for your time, but also for sharing your valuable insights!

I thank Trinity Western University in Langley, British Columbia, for granting me a sabbatical during the 1993-94 academic year. This leave enabled me to write this book and undertake several other projects. A grant from the Social Sciences and Humanities Research Council of Canada covered my expenses for visiting classrooms during the year.

Three persons spent a great deal of time to give me feedback on drafts of each chapter. My thanks to Curtis Gesch, Albert E. Greene, and Robert Koole for their thoughtful and helpful reactions and suggestions. The final product is, of course, my own responsibility.

I wrote this book because I am deeply concerned about the superficiality of modern culture. Our school curriculum can do much more than it does now to counter the self-centeredness and lack of commitment that plagues our society. I believe that God demands Christian educators to do so. I pray, then, that this book will help teachers and prospective teachers implement programs that encourage their pupils to become responsive and responsible disciples of our Lord Christ Jesus.

Harro Van Brummelen

TABLE OF CONTENTS

PART II: KNOWLEDGE AND CURRICULUM   85

4 VIEWS OF KNOWLEDGE
AND MODES OF KNOWING   87

5 ORGANIZING CURRICULUM CONTENT   115

6 TEACHING AND LEARNING

THE ASPECTS OF REALITY   143

PART III:

PLANNING AND   IMPLEMENTING CURRICULUM   176

7 PEDAGOGICAL CONTOURS FOR CURRICULUM 177

8 PLANNING CURRICULUM

FOR THE CLASSROOM   203

9   SHAPING CURRICULUM

OUTSIDE THE CLASSROOM   231

10   THE TEACHER'S ROLE IN CURRICULUM   256

PART I:
Worldviews and Curriculum

Our social context shapes our students, ourselves, our schools. That context differs substantially from that of my schooling in the 1950s. Basic human nature and the nature of knowledge do not change. But our shifting social environment requires us to rethink and refashion our school curricula.

When I think of the social currents of the last fifty years, I do not think in the first place of the information revolution, important as it has been. Photocopiers, fax machines, and computers bury us daily under an information avalanche. People find it difficult to distinguish the significant from the insignificant. Nor do I think primarily of the increasing contrast between rich and poor in North America. Even many recent college graduates take the only available, low-paying, service industry jobs, overqualified as they may be. Closer to the heart of change is the fact that the Judeo-Christian values that still unified North American society in the 1950s have been replaced, on the one hand, by individual ethical relativism, and, on the other, by what is currently viewed as "politically correct." I can also point to changes in the structure and integrity of the family, the role of religion, gender relations, and increasing violence.

The foregoing changes have contributed to an attribute that, I believe, poignantly characterizes today's society. What marks every aspect of our culture today is a *lack of trust*. We do not trust politicians. Too often they break their promises of jobs or fairer taxes. We do not trust the media. They often seem little more than their advertisers' handmaidens. We do not trust large corporation or union directors. Too frequently their self-interest in profits or power overshadows the positive effects their actions may have on society-at-large. We do not trust environmentalists. They show more interest in publicity than in living the causes they espouse. We do not trust our neighborhoods. We install alarm systems and no longer walk alone after dark. We do not trust the stranger entering a school building. We do not trust God; most of the eighty percent of the population who believe in His existence totally neglect Him in their daily life.

The Enlightenment faith in ongoing progress, still strong in the 1950s, has all but disappeared. Our society is distrustful, skeptical, uncertain of its future. This climate contributes to the self-centered individualism of our age. It leads to a lack of compassion for those with whom we live. It undermines ethical integrity by encouraging short-sighted personal and communal hedonism. We decry violence and pornography. Yet we watch movies and videos that prompt both. We say we are concerned about our environment. Yet we live in large homes with countless gadgets. Our economy can function only if those who have well-paying jobs buy far more material goods than they need. Advertising aims at making our wants our needs. We are reluctant to make long-term commitments. We walk away from marriage without seriously trying to restore the relationships.

What does all this have to do with schools and their curricula? First, our social context affects all of us. We are part of our cultural milieu. Analyzing what is happening, however, helps us to understand the cultural baggage with which our students enter our schools. That, in turn, allows us to construct a framework for schooling and curriculum to prepare pupils for meaningful, responsible roles in today's culture.

Further, our cultural dynamics underscore the need to examine where we ourselves stand on important value questions. What do we hold dear? What does this mean for the aims of schooling? How we can help students become committed to those values we hold to be crucial for a compassionate and just society? Our answers to such questions will say a great deal about the curricula we develop and implement in our classrooms.

A curriculum cannot be neutral. Indeed, even curricula that attempt to be scrupulously neutral or objective hold to certain values that leave a "value residue" in the minds and hearts of students. For one, they suggest that thinking rationally about facts and concepts is more important than accepting in faith certain matters of morality and belief. For another, the choice of curriculum content shows students what educators hold to be important. If a unit on trees emphasizes classification, it promotes human rational thought as something to be valued. If the unit stresses how forest ecosystems can be destroyed or preserved, students will be more likely to learn to value human care of the environment.

In teaching we need to be fair to various value positions. But fairness does not mean neutrality. We must not indoctrinate in the sense of being one-sided in our presentations or discouraging students from asking probing questions or from disagreeing with us. But our students need to hear from us what we believe about the important issues in life—and why. Only then will they learn to make and act on value commitments essential for a compassionate, just, and principled society.

A worldview is a way of perceiving the meaning of life. It is based on one's explicit and implicit beliefs, and leads one to make choices and act in certain ways. Part I shows how worldviews affect approaches to curriculum planning and implementation. The first chapter discusses four major curriculum orientations and their basic premises, none of which are specifically Christian in their worldview perspectives. The second chapter delineates a Christian worldview and what that means for school curriculum. Finally, the third and last chapter in Part I considers how Biblical values provide an alternate base for curriculum development.

Chapter 1
Orientations to Curriculum

- Three days before the start of the 1993 school year, British Columbia's premier Mike Harcourt announced the end of the government's trailblazing *Year 2000* program. "To put it bluntly, the report card on *Year 2000* is in and it's failed the grade. There are going to have to be some quite substantive changes." Eleven days later, he fired his Minister of Education. He instructed his new one to provide a "good, basic education" with high standards to help students function in a more competitive economy.

  The *Year 2000* program, based on recommendations of a 1988 Commission on Education, had been hailed as an innovative program that would successfully launch students into the 21st century. Students progressed at their own rate through individualized programs in cross-grade settings. Teachers "facilitated" learning by interactive and self-directed learning activities, cooperative learning, making available suitable resources, and so on. Learners "constructed" their own knowledge through investigations. Using anecdotes, evaluation described what students actually accomplished in social, aesthetic, physical, and intellectual development and in social responsibility. Integrated thematic approaches replaced isolated subject content.

  When Harcourt announced his changes, the program had operated for three years in B.C.'s primary grades. Several months earlier, it had been given a resounding vote of approval by a panel of experts from around the world. Draft versions for other grade levels were also being tried out. Many millions of dollars had been spent on developing and implementing the program.

  What caused the program's sudden official abandonment? Political reasons played a prominent role. Parents were up in arms, blaming politicians as well as teachers. They believed their students were not learning basic skills. In group work, they claimed, one or two students did the actual work, with most no longer able to achieve on their own. Report card content had become a mystery for them. They wanted to know how their children's progress compared to that of other students, rather than receive a vague description of what their children "can do." They saw the open-ended approaches lead to a lack of discipline and standards. They complained about the vague curriculum guidelines and the lack of emphasis on proper spelling. Although the program had been introduced in only a few scattered experimental classrooms beyond grade 3, the new program became the scapegoat for all the perceived shortcomings of the schools. Newspaper columnists, feeding on public discontent, wrote time and again that classrooms were in crisis. Their writing contributed to a poll that showed that only twelve percent of the adult population believed it was getting good value for its education tax dollar.

The controversy involved more than politics, however. One proponent of *Year 2000*, an education professor, correctly pointed out in a radio interview that the program represented "a whole different way of looking at life that goes much beyond education." A few days later another professor agreed but claimed that it was impossible to get *Year 2000*'s advocates to listen to research calling into question its approaches. They hold such strong presuppositions about education, he said, that they dismiss all evidence that contradicts their basic beliefs.

What quickly became clear was that the shift back to more structure mirrored other pendulum shifts in discussions about schooling in the twentieth century. Such shifts reflect conflicting, deep-seated convictions. Ultimately, the basis of *Year 2000* was Jean Jacques Rousseau's view that children are fundamentally pure and should develop freely and naturally on the basis of their own experience. When Harcourt axed the program, he distanced himself from Rousseau and positioned himself more closely to the Greek philosopher Plato. Schools are to pass on wisdom and knowledge so that all persons can take on their appropriate roles in society. Schools are to prepare students in the basics, not only to become lawyers and psychologists, but also technicians and craftspersons. Schools serve the needs of society, and currently we particularly need practical, job-related skills.

This case study raises several questions. Are there conflicting worldviews that govern school curriculum? If so, does the curriculum necessarily continue to swing between progressive and traditional poles? Or do schools haphazardly move from one location to another on a spectrum of curriculum alternatives? Who should have the authority and power to make curriculum changes—the government, school boards, community leaders, teachers, parents, or students? If a school's curriculum does not reflect parents' beliefs about education, whether these are valid or not, is the curriculum ultimately doomed? If there are certain views of the person and of knowledge that frame the official curriculum, can an individual teacher with a different perspective still teach comfortably in that school system or school? Can you think of other questions regarding this case? How would you answer these questions?

Different worldviews lead to different views on education and to diverse approaches to curriculum theory and practice. Not all teachers have delineated an explicit, clearly-defined worldview. In fact, classroom practice over the years changes less than discussions about education would have us believe. Yet what teachers believe, perhaps implicitly, about the nature of the learner, their role as teacher, and "relevant" content will affect how they implement a curriculum.

In this chapter, I will discuss four distinct orientations to curriculum that have affected our schools during the past fifty years. Each bases itself on certain presuppositions that its proponents accept as self-evident. These four orientations are the academic traditionalist, the technical, the deliberative, and the constructivist orientations. Few schools or teachers fit precisely into any one of the categories. Yet most tend to lean more in one direction than in another. This chapter introduces the basic tenets of these orientations and gives some examples of how these affect classroom practice.

All four orientations have strengths as well as deficiencies. As will become clear later, it is not enough just to adapt one or a combination of these orientations in order to teach Christianly. Therefore I develop a fifth, distinctly Christian orientation to curriculum, one based on a Biblical worldview. Chapter 2 describes the contours of such a worldview and some of its implications for school curriculum. Later chapters explore the implications of Biblical views of values, knowledge, and the person for planning and implementing curriculum.

WHAT IS CURRICULUM?

■ How do you use the word "curriculum"? Before reading this section, formulate and write down your own definition for "curriculum." After reading what follows, compare your definition with the four definitions given in this section. Then revise your own definition so that you feel comfortable with it.

In medieval times, curriculum as it applied to schooling meant the length of time needed to complete a program of learning. Gradually, its meaning shifted to the content that was to be taught. This was likely the result of Protestant church reformers wanting more control over the content of schooling in order to bolster the knowledge of the common person. Today, dictionaries define curriculum the way it is most commonly used, as the course of study in a school. Most people assume that such a course of studies outlines the content to be taught.

For more than 100 years, however, educators like Montessori and Dewey have stretched this definition by addressing not only course content but also teaching methods. In other words, "How?" questions became as much part of curriculum discussions as "What?" ones. In fact, most education writers stipulate a broader definition for the concept of curriculum than that found in dictionaries. Such definitions often reflect the authors' beliefs about education in general and about planning for learning in particular.

■ Consider the following four definitions of curriculum.

1. Curriculum is what is taught, particularly the subject matter of a school's course of study.

2. Curriculum is an organized set of documented, formal educational plans intended to attain preconceived goals.

3. Curriculum is a dynamic, ever-changing series of planned learning experiences.

4. Curriculum is everything learners experience in school.

What do the definitions have in common? How do they differ? With which one would you feel most comfortable? Least? Why? Can you suggest what type of classroom learning each definition implies?

The first definition parallels the dictionary one. It emphasizes subject content. Academic traditionalists and most of the general public use or assume a definition similar to this. Academic traditionalists plan curriculum by dividing the program of study into subjects, and then listing the content to be taught by topics and sub-topics. Implicit in the definition is the belief that the overall aim of education is to transmit a body of knowledge.

The second definition embraces a more technical conception of curriculum. It holds that curriculum planners must first decide goals or objectives, and then develop a series of precise prescriptions for teaching and learning. Teachers use the resulting detailed, sequenced documents to plan day-to-day teaching and learning activities. They then carefully monitor whether they have attained the pre-specified learning outcomes. One value implicitly promoted in this model is the importance of efficiency. With this definition, a basic curriculum question becomes, ''How we can reach our objectives in an efficient manner?'' To do so, the teacher and ultimately the curriculum planner must take full control of all learning situations.

The third definition holds that teachers must plan learning activities, but must adapt them to each situation. Even as teachers implement activities, they (or the learners) may change them because of new circumstances. Teachers, in other words, do not consider learners to be just objects to whom they apply the curriculum. Rather, learners are subjects whose background and reactions teachers must carefully consider as teaching and learning take place. While the curriculum may suggest topics and methods, these are not cast in stone. The particular situation will affect how learning proceeds.

Finally, some definitions of curriculum state that it encompasses anything and everything that happens in schooling. Some even go beyond the school setting and suggest curriculum involves all possible ways of thinking about human experience. The implication is that while teachers may plan some activities, we cannot know what pupils will learn as a result. The school influences students in different ways, some planned, many unplanned. Pupils, it is held, construct their own personal knowledge and meaning as a result of learning experiences.

Most persons endorsing this last definition do not want to define curriculum content too precisely. They delineate some general guidelines and some skills that need to be taught. They leave much latitude for teachers to decide, however, what works best in their particular circumstances. A few even argue that developing a curriculum plan in a document undermines their belief that pupils should be totally involved in planning their learning experiences (McLaren 1986, 229).

Note that all four of these definitions are based on certain views of education. The four, in order, typify the academic traditionalist, the technical, the deliberative, the constructivist curriculum orientations. After discussing each of these orientations, I will then show how a Christian worldview also leads to a way of looking at curriculum.

THE ACADEMIC TRADITIONALIST ORIENTATION
TO CURRICULUM

■ List some features of schools called "academic" or "traditionalist." Based on your list, deduce what would be some basic beliefs about education that an academic traditionalist would espouse. Do you agree with these beliefs? Why or why not?

When a school is known as an academic or a traditional one, you probably envision one that prefers subjects like literature, history, and mathematics to broad thematic approaches such as minicourses on the environment or on clothing and style in the 21st century. You also think of a classroom where the teacher transmits a great deal of knowledge and emphasizes basic literacy and numeracy skills. Teachers structure learning carefully and check the level of mastery with regular tests.

In the introduction of this chapter, I quoted politician Harcourt to say that schools need to return to basic education and high standards. He likely did not base this on a theory of education he had carefully considered. He was reacting to public opinion. Yet he used the language and ideas of an approach to education called essentialism.

Essentialism holds that schools must systematically teach basic knowledge and not be afraid to stress hard work and discipline. Knowledge consists of facts, concepts, and skills that must be mastered through memorization and drill. By learning many facts about plants, for instance, students will develop knowledge schemata and generalizations that will enable them to apply their knowledge. Similarly, by focusing on specific elements of phonics students have the best opportunity to become fluent readers.

Teachers, according to essentialists, generally know better than students what knowledge is significant for living and working in society. Therefore, teachers make the decisions on what to teach, possibly using lists of topics and skills in curriculum documents to guide them, but without taking students' interests into account. Teachers as professionals best know curriculum content and sequence. They should apply the research that states that direct, well-sequenced large group instruction most effectively helps students grasp subject matter (Wittrock 1986, 360-62). Further, they should tell both students and their parents exactly how well pupils achieve on tests when compared to their classmates. Students need to get used to living in a competitive world in which some do better than others.

Academic traditionalists believe that to achieve the intellectual purposes of education requires effort and discipline. A curriculum consisting of carefully structured basic subject matter disciplines does so best (Lucas 1976, 14). The focus of the curriculum is to transmit and assimilate a prescribed body of basic knowledge.

Not all academic traditionalists are essentialists. Another group, called perennialists, came to the fore again with Mortimer Adler's *The Paideia Proposal* (1982). Perennialists believe that the basic feature of humans is their ability to reason. Learning to use higher mental processes and cultivating rationality and reflection becomes the main thrust of education. The content of the curriculum therefore needs to offer students the best thinking humans have done through the ages. As soon as they can, students read and study primary source material written by great intellects. Memorization and tests emphasizing recall are, once the students are ready, complemented by in-depth reasoning and analysis about the materials studied. A common core curriculum for all students develops critical understanding of the values embedded in significant writings. Perennialists favor a general education for all students, one that emphasizes our common cultural heritage. That is more important than teaching vocational skills or allowing students to choose from many electives.

For perennialists, schools prepare for life, and developing rationality prepares in the best way possible. Ultimately, they hold that rationality needs no justification. Humans are the measure of all things through their reasoning ability. They can discover knowledge in general, and truth, beauty, goodness, and justice in particular, through reason and reflection. Thinking sets the stage for and therefore is more important than doing, and the school curriculum is designed accordingly. Great writings of the past transmit shared cultural ideals and are important as examples of reasoned thought about universally valid truth.

■ At the elementary level, the curriculum favored by essentialists and perennialists may not differ much, since perennialists look at those years as ones where pupils learn the basic tools. At the secondary level, however, there would be some significant differences. On a chart, show the similarities and differences in a secondary curriculum designed by an essentialist and a perennialist. In what ways are both "academic tradition-alists"? Which of the two approaches do you prefer? Why?

THE TECHNICAL ORIENTATION TO CURRICULUM

■ We usually consider technology to be a positive feature of our society. Being able to do your banking by telephone and having bank machines in different local and foreign locations simplifies life. In schools, the use of word processing programs improves writing.

Yet, there is another side to technology. The French philosopher Jacques Ellul has said that "technology has two consequences which strike me as the most profound in our time. I call them the suppression of the subject and the suppression of meaning" (Ellul 1981, 49). For education, his ideas suggest that a technical orientation is so concerned with *how* we teach and learn that we lose sight of *why* we live and what we want our students to become. Thus, it suppresses values and meaning of ultimate significance.

A technical approach to curriculum, Ellul would argue, treats pupils (and to a lesser extent, teachers) as objects to be processed rather than as responsible subjects. Certainly a technical approach does emphasize efficiency in planning and implementing teaching and learning. Ellul would also counter the technologist's claim that knowledge can be objective and value-free. If God made the creation with the specific intention of revealing Himself (Romans 1:20; Job 42:5-6), is not all knowledge filled with meaning and value?

Is Ellul right? Or is he overstating his case? First list the advantages of a technical approach to curriculum. Then, reflecting on Ellul's claims, think about the disadvantages this approach might entail. Why would it be that the technical approach dominated curriculum writings during most of the twentieth century?

Academic traditionalists use beliefs and values to justify curriculum decisions. Technicists, on the other hand, use the results of empirical research about the effects of certain methods on learning outcomes (L. Darling-Hammond and J. Snyder in Jackson 1992, 41). They want to control and manage the curriculum, the teacher, the learner, and the learning environment. They emphasize the question, "How can we most proficiently accomplish what we want to do?" They find efficient means to reach predetermined, detailed, and measurable ends.

Technicists regard knowledge as an objective, impersonal, value-free commodity to be grasped. Consequently, mastery of knowledge can be measured. Technicists begin with specific objectives for which they can assess student attainment. They then develop and sequence learning experiences that will achieve the objectives. If evaluation shows a less than satisfactory degree of student success, they revise the learning experiences (and possibly the objectives). This linear process of planning curriculum has been popular since the efficiency movement championed by Franklin Bobbitt early in the 20th century. It is the basis of this century's most popular curriculum publication, Ralph Tyler's *Basic Principles of Curriculum and Instruction* (1949).

Let me give two examples of the technical approach. In the 1970s behavioral objectives became popular. Such objectives, sometimes also called performance objectives, are precise statements of purpose whose specific outcomes are measured. For example, "The student will demonstrate knowledge of multiplying three-digit numbers by two-digit ones by successfully completing 8 of 10 such problems on the accompanying worksheet within the indicated time." Such objectives, technologists believe, give a clear focus to teaching and learning and enhance accountability. For each lesson, they construct several objectives. Then, as much as possible on the basis of empirical research, they carefully design activities to maximize student mastery. Some designers have even used the term "teacher-proof curriculum" since teachers would be technicians whose task was solely to follow the step-by-step instructions in their manuals.

In the 1980s, several large corporations jumped into the educational fray in the United States. They promised school districts that they would raise average standardized testing results by a certain number of points if the school districts would sign a time-limited contract. The corporations would use scientifically designed curricula as well as computer technology to improve learning and raise standards.

Today, we hear little about either initiative. Why not? Is it a mistaken assumption that all learning can be broken down into specific objectives? Are there many more components involved in reading effectively than we can ever list as behavioral objectives? Is it worth teachers' time to write out lists of behavioral objectives when they already have a good idea of what they want their students to accomplish? Do we miss what is really important by focusing on what is easily measurable? Do technologists neglect the spiritual, ethical, and aesthetic dimensions of education? Do many important values, attitudes, and dispositions become evident only long after we have taught a particular lesson? Further, isn't learning so complex and aren't learners so different that a formula-like approach to lesson design is not likely to work in the long term? Even if we know valid general approaches, doesn't their applicability depend on many factors in particular classroom settings?

Despite such questions, the technical approach to curriculum has been and continues to be a popular one. It is attractive to be able to follow some uniformly applicable steps in planning a program, and to have procedures to assess its effectiveness. Some specific, scientific research results on teaching success, such as Rosenshine's steps for direct instruction, may be tempting to apply in curriculum planning. Today, technicists use this to promote "performance objectives" and "outcome-based education."

A danger with this approach is that such instruction tends to neglect long-term aims and deeper value considerations. Curricular technicists need to answer Ellul's concerns. Is Ellul right when he claims that their technical orientation *ipso facto* treats students as less-than-human objects? Does it neglect basic value questions in education? Does it by default accept and therefore promote the values that dominate our western society? Does it just train technically competent "cogs" interested mainly in doing their work efficiently in order to make money to buy pleasurable things in life? Does it contribute to schooling an individualistic generation that lacks the commitments needed to foster a just and compassionate society?

■ This section describes how technicists go about curriculum design. But it doesn't say much about the content they favor. Before continuing, reflect on the basic premises of the technical orientation and then list some content that technicists would want to include in a school program.

You likely listed the natural sciences, technology, mathematics, and computer literacy. Technicists ask which skills and knowledge have been shown to be useful in today's society. They emphasize content that prepares students for the world of work. The social sciences are important to help students function as citizens in society. Of course, basic reading, writing, and communication skills are also essential, but the humanities and the arts are not as directly applicable and therefore are given less emphasis.

In the nineteenth century, Herbert Spencer asked what has become one of the most famous curriculum questions, "What knowledge is of most worth?" One hundred and fifty years later, the debate continues. Is the "most worth" found in enculturation to our heritage so that students consider and become committed to values on which we can build a just society, as the perennialists believe? Or do we emphasize knowledge that helps students with everyday living skills and with finding a productive job, as technicists argue? Where do you stand? Or do the questions imply a false dichotomy? If so, how would you answer Spencer's question? Justify your answers.

THE DELIBERATIVE ORIENTATION TO CURRICULUM

■ Educators agree that curriculum content must be relevant. Relevance, however, is one of those words that at first has a solid ring about it but that, on closer examination, rings hollow. Should content be relevant for students' immediate interests or for their long-term ability to cope in society? Who should decide what is relevant: governments, parents, teachers, or students themselves? Essentialists believe that relevant content consists primarily of the "basics," the three R's. For perennialists, relevance means critical thinking about the best writings of the past. Technologists hold that content is relevant only if students can use and apply it in their technological environment. In short, the meaning of "relevant content" depends on your view of education.

What curriculum content is relevant? Educators favoring the deliberative and constructivist orientations do not answer this question as quickly nor as precisely as those already described in the academic traditionalist and technical orientations. Deliberators and constructivists see knowledge as more than a product that has to be mastered. Students, they believe, must interact with the world around them and interpret it. What is relevant content for them will depend on many factors: the social and economic contexts of schools, students' background experiences, their particular aptitudes and abilities, their reactions to learning activities, the availability of resources in the community and in the school, and so on.

Consider the following example. Suppose a grade 10 mathematics teacher plans to teach a six-week geometry unit. She would like to explore the historical development of geometry, having her students weigh the effects of the Greek emphasis on theoretical reasoning. Some of her students are artistic and she knows they would be excited if she based her geometry unit on its use in art and architecture: the Golden Rectangle, perspective, geodesic domes, and so on. She also has available a computer program that shows how three-dimensional geometry is applied in drafting in general and in new car design in particular. Developing the unit around such applications might encourage some students to become interested in technical design, an area with good job prospects. She does not have time to do justice to all three approaches, particularly if she makes sure she teaches all the concepts in her curriculum guide. Her students have a wide range of abilities and interests. She wonders whether she should define a core that she teaches to all students, with optional modules for groups of students.

At the same time, her school board in three months time will evaluate basic mathematics skills for all grade 10 students in the district. She knows that her students will do best on the geometry part of the tests if she carefully follows the textbook page by page. She would then teach the concepts sequentially and spend no time on the other approaches. How well her students do on the tests will affect her stature as a teacher--and her freedom to design her courses in the way she thinks best. The local press is playing up the importance of the tests for maintaining high standards, and her principal is putting pressure on teachers to prepare the students well.

The teacher has to make some choices. In the allotted time, she cannot do everything she would like to do. What advice would you give her? In her situation, how would you define the content that would be most relevant for the students? Why?

Technicists see teachers as technicians who follow certain predetermined procedures and standards. Persons in the deliberative orientation ("deliberators") disagree. They believe that curriculum planners and teachers must consider the uniqueness of each situation and help students interact with knowledge. They point out that in curriculum planning most groups do not follow specific steps in order. They may not even construct objectives until the end of their work, and then may do so primarily to express their purpose to teachers. Walker has shown that the starting point for curriculum planners often is a set of commonly held beliefs about schools, students, teaching and learning, and content. The planners then try to judge the best course of action by applying such beliefs to the situation in question, weighing all the available evidence. In short, they *deliberate* (Walker and Soltis 1992, 60).

As they develop curriculum, academic traditionalists first ask, "What have thinkers found out about our world?" Technicists ask, "How can we achieve our objectives efficiently?" Curriculum deliberators ask different questions. "What should be the overall aims of education?" "How can education help humanity achieve a just and compassionate society?" "What does this mean in our specific educational situation?" In short, "What *ought* we to do? What is the *right* thing to do?"

Deliberators start with their beliefs about life and then make practical decisions about curriculum and promising courses of action in the classroom in light of available educational theory. Not only curriculum specialists but also teachers, students, and parents are involved in this process. Deliberators consider a curriculum situation. They pose and define the problem. Then they apply both theoretical principles and practical experience and judgment in making curriculum decisions. Such decisions or resolutions are temporary ones in that new evidence or a new situation may call for a revised solution (Walker 1990, 169ff.). In other words, they use critical interpretation or what they call hermeneutics to understand the meaning of a situation and its related theory. Reflective judgement leads to the implementation of a resolution. This, in turn, sheds light on the theory and leads to further self-understanding.

Teacher-technicists use their skills to implement the requirements of syllabus documents, and then evaluate their success based on the degree to which students have achieved the document's stated objectives. Teacher-deliberators consider the syllabus to be a proposal or general guide that informs their judgments. They consider their class and provide appropriate learning experiences, continually adjusting them on the basis of classroom interactions. What ultimately guides their decision-making process is what they consider to be the basic meaning of and norms for human life (Grundy 1987, 62-63).

Deliberators see human beings as subjects rather than as objects. Both teachers and students must exercise judgment on the basis of understanding. Rather than "mastering" knowledge, students establish meaning for their lives through understanding and interpretation. As such, curriculum involves interaction between teachers and learners, between learners and learners, between learners and curriculum content. The focus of teaching is more the making of meaning through learning than the transmission of concepts and skills. Teachers and students are reflective practitioners.

The deliberative approach has appeal. It appears to alleviate Ellul's concerns about the treatment of humans as objects and the disregard of questions of meaning and purpose. It also recognizes that no one planner or teacher has a corner on the whole truth. It admits that human nature and human learning situations are so complex that each must be considered on its own, even when research suggests some general guidelines. Curriculum documents are no more than guides, with teachers using professional and considered judgement in determining what is best for a particular situation. In the deliberative orientation, theoreticians and curriculum specialists work with school-based people to find courses of action for context-based problems.

Yet here, too, questions remain. For one, if schools and teachers deliberate about each and every curriculum issue little time would be left over for teaching and learning. Deliberation, if taken seriously, is a time-consuming process. It is not helpful, for instance, for minor decisions, nor for situations where the participants have deep-seated disagreements.

The first author to describe deliberation in curriculum was the late Joseph Schwab. He glossed over the fact that diverse views of the purpose and meaning of life and of education within a curriculum planning group make it difficult to arrive at specific decisions or recommendations. Schwab said that agreeing on ideals would be easy, and that groups should quickly focus on solving practical problems (Schwab 1978, 315). He failed to recognize that our basic faith commitments are at the basis of all our interpretation and search.

Deliberator Decker Walker is more realistic than Schwab. He states that even comprehending each others' views is a long, difficult intellectual and emotional process. To reconcile conflicting points of view is even more arduous, if possible at all (Walker 1990, 206). Whether a group can arrive at a mutually acceptable compromise will depend to a large extent on the compatibility of their outlooks on life and on educational principles. What deliberators should recognize is that religious views, in the sense of beliefs about matters of ultimate significance, provide a framework for all curriculum deliberation.

Deliberators hold that a curriculum plan only informs a teacher's judgement. This is so because the classroom curriculum must be directly related to the needs, interests, experiences, and capabilities of the students. The students must personally interpret and respond to knowledge. Therefore deliberators promote interactive curriculum planning as well as interactive pedagogy in the classroom. They want to include content that deals with human values and meaning, sometimes in broad themes rather than in specific subject disciplines. Still, proponents within a deliberative planning group may have very different views about the content of the curriculum. On the whole, the deliberative orientation does not address the type of content to be taught and learned. That means, in effect, that deliberators with different views on the meaning of life will suggest different curriculum content.

■ The term hermeneutics means procedures for critical interpretation or explanation. Usually it refers to interpreting Biblical text. More recently, partly as the result of the work of French philosopher Paul Ricoeur, it has been applied to curriculum and its context as the "text" to be interpreted. Ricoeur suggests three stages in his hermeneutic "arch." First, you read a "text" naively, grasping its apparent meaning (a text can be any written passage or videotape dealing with education or an actual classroom situation). Secondly, you consider a deeper structural explanation, based on analyzing the presuppositions and the context. Thirdly, you grasp for a fuller understanding of the text or situation in its cultural context and of yourself as you reflect and react (Reynolds 1989, 44ff.).

Re-read the situation the geometry teacher faced as she has to make some curriculum decisions about her geometry unit (pp 12-13), or choose another situation you know that involves difficult curriculum choices. With two or three other persons, use Ricoeur's three hermeneutic steps to deliberate about the situation and reach a "temporary decision" about what she should do. Do you now understand the scenario and your response to it more fully than before? What are the advantages and disadvantages of a deliberative hermeneutic approach?

THE CONSTRUCTIVIST ORIENTATION TO CURRICULUM

■ The *Year 2000* primary program that became so controversial in British Columbia reflected a constructivist curriculum orientation. It was based on the following premises:

»Students are unique, also in their learning styles, and they need to develop their abilities primarily for self-improvement.

»Pupils are innately good. They are self-directing, autonomous individuals, themselves the source of their own truth and freedom. Their capacity to think critically will lead to an ever-improving society.

»Teachers facilitate learning by providing positive learning environments that stimulate active, self-directed learning.

»Learners actively construct knowledge and assign their own meaning to whatever they learn.

»Evaluation should report only what students "can do," and students should determine the method and timing of assessments themselves.

Consider and evaluate each of these premises. Which ones do you accept? reject? Give reasons. Change the premises with which you disagree to statements that you believe will provide a sound basis for curriculum planning.

Constructivism stands at the opposite point of the curriculum spectrum from academic traditionalism. For constructivists, learning is a continuous and active process. Pupils do not just absorb information handed down by teachers or fill their minds with concepts transmitted by printed or audiovisual resources. Nor do they just become acquainted with worthwhile works of the past and think about them. Rather, true learning involves active construction of meaning and knowledge. The teacher is a facilitator who provides suitable experiences and resources. All humans, including pupils, use their experience to construct their own individual meaning of reality. Through social and environmental interactions pupils "progressively build up and restructure their own schemes of the world around them," thus making sense of events (Driver 1989, 85). The aim of constructivist education is personal autonomy.

Many, though not all, constructivists believe that human knowledge serves the organization of the experiential world, rather than reflecting the discovery of reality. Scientific concepts like electrons, for instance, are imaginative constructions not abstracted from but brought to bear on the world (Bishop and Carpenter 1993, 149-50). Constructivism thus involves a shift in how we look at knowledge. For "radical constructivists" (which is the position I will discuss since the term is now used so broadly that its meaning is becoming more difficult to discern), there no longer is an objective, factual "body of knowledge" to be transmitted. Rather, the curriculum emphasizes the *process* of pupils learning to construct and interpret for themselves. Many feminist curriculum theorists add that besides knowledge being provisional, it is also relational. In other words, it is affected by and depends on how we relate to others as we learn (Luke and Gore 1992, 7).

The process of writing about one's personal feelings and reactions, for instance, becomes a vital, integral part of the curriculum. The study of literature is important mainly to provide examples of the process of human creativity, not a way of learning to understand and react to the human condition portrayed in books. History is not learned to understand the roots of our culture but to be able to see how change comes about and to write personal interpretations of events. Mathematics is a human way of thinking and solving problems that helps us make sense of the world. Science confronts students with evidence that contradicts their non-scientific conceptions so that by changing their conceptions they may bring order to their world.

A basic tenet of constructivism is that "as we assimilate and use knowledge in independent, thoughtful, and purposeful ways, we become able to shape our lives and the future of our world" (*Primary Program* 1990, 57). To ensure that such a curriculum is relevant for learners in their specific situation, however, neither the procedures of curriculum design nor the curriculum content can be stipulated. Which problems need to be posed and how they are to be explored depends on each situation. This will involve some risk taking by both teachers and their pupils. Teachers and students negotiate the content of the curriculum, with learners ultimately having the power to decide whether or not to engage in the learning situation. Rather than entering the classroom with lists of objectives, content or skills, the teacher enters the classroom with one or two potentially big ideas which the students investigate—perhaps for a whole year (Brooks 1990, 69).

One group of educators who would agree with the foregoing but are usually referred to as critical theorists rather than as constructivists are those influenced by the Brazilian educator Paulo Freire. Freire opposes "banking education" and "narration sickness" by which teachers deposit information into the passive minds of their pupils. Learners, according to Freire, should not only be active participants, but in doing so should develop critical consciousness. For that, we need a critical pedagogy in which teachers and pupils pose problems about real life experiences and relationships. In this way, they become critically discerning and, since they learn to control knowledge, can liberate themselves. Action and reflection form a dialectical movement that Freire calls *praxis*. Such praxis involves constructing meaning and reconstructing the social world of the learner. Learning in this sense recreates and therefore leads to empowerment and emancipation, not only of individuals but also of groups of people who share critical insights into the nature of their lives in culture (Freire 1970). Freire's main concern has been the poor and powerless in the Third World who need to be emancipated from oppression.

Critical theorists thus add to constructivist theory the belief that teachers and students should together develop critical consciousness in order to understand and eventually displace the subtle forces that exploit them. Educators like Michael Apple and Henry Giroux have extended Freire's thinking to the North American scene. They hold that technical control and certainty in school curriculum reproduce and prolong the striking inequalities of race, gender, and class in our cultures. For them a key curriculum question for both teachers and students is, "Whose interests are being served?", a question rooted in their belief that our present society cannot be equitable or provide an unprejudiced school system (Eisner in Jackson 1992, 314-15).

For critical theorists, the basic criterion will be whether what is analyzed, interpreted, and constructed leads to critical consciousness on the part of the student (Grundy 1987, 121-27). However, for them to offer curriculum guidelines "would belie the very commitment to democratic participation and organization" since these "must be worked out *collaboratively* with those teachers, administrators, community members, and students with whom most of us interact every day" (Beyer and Apple 1988, 10).

As for other curriculum orientations, certain aspects of constructivism are appealing. Constructivist pedagogy incorporates action as part of knowing. It rejects the view that pupils are empty "piggy bank" objects into which teachers just deposit "coins" of information. It treats students as human subjects who are actively engaged in their learning by conceptualizing and interpreting their classroom experiences. It has shown deep respect for personal purpose, and, in the case of critical theorists, for social purpose as well, especially for freedom, equity, and social justice. The probing questions critical theorists have asked about everyday classroom education have revealed the myth of neutrality in curriculum planning and practice.

The key questions that undergird the constructivist orientation have a built-in bias, however. This is true especially for critical theorists who ask questions such as, "How is control of [curriculum] knowledge linked to the existing and unequal distribution of power, goods, and services in society?" (Beyer and Apple 1988, 5). They argue that schools, rather than allowing critical consciousness to develop, perpetuate class and gender inequalities. They vigorously uncover and attack the negative aspects of today's schooling, but then claim that giving positive guidelines would undermine their philosophy. They criticize eloquently without constructing alternatives. As Elliot Eisner says, "Most critical theorists do not plant flowers; they pull weeds" (Eisner in Jackson 1992, 315). Freire has done much practical literacy work in various parts of the world. The prolific writings of North American critical theorists, however, have had little direct effect on North American classrooms.

Other constructivists have been more successful in influencing school programs in the English-speaking world. Some of the pedagogical insights of such constructivists overcome the narrow view of the person as little more than an object to be processed by schools. But a basic assumption of persons philosophically committed to constructivism is that since pupils differ from each other in how they construct their own knowledge and meaning, reality is relative and subjective. There is no ultimate truth. The most we can say is that some personal constructions may be more viable than others at a certain time and in a particular context. Thus radical constructivists reject the idea of an underlying order in reality, an order that humans may discover. Instead they hold that persons construct and interpret their own lifeworld, one that is always subject to revision. Knowledge is "true" if it works, and therefore pupils also must be helped to clarify and choose and modify their own values. In the end, one model of reality or one set of values is as good as another, if defensible on the basis that it "works" and promotes individual autonomy.

Note, finally, that the boundary between the deliberative and constructivist orientations is not always clear-cut. Deliberators emphasize the importance of reflecting about life's meaning and interpreting situations and knowledge. More so than deliberators, constructivists stress that ultimately "the student is the final authority regarding the authenticity of the knowledge." For them, "the power to engage or not in the learning situation should reside with the learner (Grundy 1987, 126-27). Nevertheless, the views of deliberators and constructivists often overlap since both may stress human dignity and freedom.

■ Now go back to the five premises undergirding the *Year 2000* program listed at the beginning of this section. Which of the five propositions could be held not only by proponents of the constructivist but also of the academic traditionalist orientation? the technical? the deliberative? Why?

Your answer probably led you to reaffirm that there is an overlap in the premises and thinking within these four orientations, and that diversity also exists within any particular orientation. Further, the units of a classroom teacher may not always consistently "fit" one specific orientation. When planning a grade 8 science unit, for instance, teachers may well have a whole section of investigations that encourage students to reexamine their previously-held beliefs about everyday phenomena (the constructivist orientation). They may also have some tightly controlled, step-by-step instruction of basic concepts, with daily quizzes and feedback (the technical). Then they may conclude the unit with readings and presentations that deal with an historical overview that the students analyze and summarize (the academic traditionalist).

Even my division of the curriculum field into four orientations is not sacrosanct. Other writers have given different classifications, with as few as three and as many as six categories. It could be argued, for instance, that constructivists and critical theorists should be separated: while they share a similar view of knowledge, they have different political agendas. Yet, despite the difficulties and dangers of "pigeonholing" individuals too precisely, we need to be aware of different ways of approaching curriculum issues. Our presuppositions do influence what happens in classrooms. If we are not aware of the basic thinking behind different orientations, we tend to be eclectic in our approach. That is, we use every new idea that seems attractive without recognizing that it may not fit our own beliefs and theory of education. It would be worthwhile here to review the main points of each orientation. Reconsider and justify your own reactions to the points.

SUMMARY

ORIENTATION/ METAPHOR	BASIC QUESTION	KNOWLEDGE & LEARNING EMPHASIS	REPRESEN- TATIVES
ACADEMIC TRADITIONALIST: curriculum as conveyor of information and ideas	What content do students need most? (transmission)	Basic skills and best thinking of past; gaining knowledge in the subject disciplines	M. Adler A. Bloom E.D. Hirsch
TECHNICAL: curriculum as efficient process	How can we do it most efficiently? (control)	Investigating, collecting, and applying objective data in small, manageable parts	F. Bobbitt R. Gagne R. Tyler
DELIBERATIVE: curriculum as reflective interpretation	What ought we to do? (understanding)	Reflection, interpretation, and response to promote "right" action through exercise of judgment	J. Schwab L.Stenhouse D. Walker
CONSTRUCTIVIST: curriculum as active construction	How can we construct our own reality? (formation and transformation)	Personal, critical, and autonomous production and negotiation of meaning	R. Driver F. Smith ———— P. Freire D. Purpel

REFLECTING

1. Which of the following would you consider to be part of "school curriculum"?
   »a mathematics curriculum guide
   »a list of recommended novels for middle school literature
   »a teacher-made plan for a unit on transportation
   »a class discussion about plans for a field trip
   »an on-the-spur decision by a teacher to discuss a hot air balloon a student has spotted through the window
   »a spontaneous classroom demonstration of conflict resolution
   »a peer-counseling program involving twenty students
   »students learning the baseball "pecking order" by playing it informally at lunch time
   »a voluntary extra-curricular band program taking place before school three times per week
   »a set of social studies textbooks on a classroom shelf
   »a teacher posting the five best reports on her bulletin board
   »a school selecting the best academic student as valedictorian
   Take the ones you rejected and those of which you were unsure and compare them with your own definition of curriculum developed earlier in the chapter. Is your definition an operational one? In other words, did your choices reflect your definition?

2. Consider Spencer's famous curriculum question, "What knowledge is of most worth?" Think back to your schooling. What are the three or four things you learned that have benefited you most? If you had designed an "ideal" curriculum for the schools you attended, what changes would you have made? Why? What does that say about what knowledge you consider to be of most worth?

3. Christian educators have not always agreed on their approach to curriculum. Many have favored an academic traditionalist approach, fearing that other orientations contribute to cultural impoverishment and ethical relativism. Consider the teaching of Jesus, sometimes called the Master Teacher, in the Biblical gospels. In what ways did His teaching illustrate an academic traditionalist approach, if any? What aspects of the other three orientations came out in His teaching? Are there any implications for the way in which Christians should plan and implement school curriculum today? Why do you think it is possible to identify Christian curriculum thinkers within each of the four orientations described in this chapter?

Chapter 2
A Christian Worldview as a
Basis for Curriculum

■ Followers of Jesus Christ share a common faith. They believe that God created people as His images but that humanity has fallen into sin. Therefore, they know they need Christ's redemption for personal salvation. They also believe that the Bible is God's authoritative Word for life. Thus the Old and New Testaments of the Bible, they hold, provide a framework not only for the spiritual dimension of life, but also for the ethical, aesthetic, economic, social, psychological, and physical aspects of life. The basic norms of Scripture guide their thoughts, words, and deeds, even if the implications of those principles are not always clear in the complexities they face in our modern society.

Christians are far from united on the meaning and, even less, on the implications of Biblical norms, however. Even a simple command like "You shall not kill" leads to searching questions. Christians disagree whether this command applies to very young human fetuses or to punishing murderers. For bringing up children, some Christians hold that an injunction to tell the next generation God's praiseworthy deeds and His laws (Psalm 78) applies to the family and church but not to the school. They see schools as places where students from diverse backgrounds learn to live together while studying an objective curriculum that is largely neutral religiously and morally. Other Christians, however, believe that Christian schools are necessary if they are to fulfil the intent of this injunction. These Christians usually reject the possibility of moral and religious neutrality.

Even Christian school supporters differ about the aims of schooling and how to implement them. They share the basic tenets of the Christian faith and the belief that God calls them to live in society according to His purposes. Nevertheless, they have diverse views about those purposes and how Christians ought to interact with their surrounding culture. Let me give examples of three Christian schools with three different approaches to this issue.

The *Bethel Christian School* leadership sees an unbridgeable chasm between Christian beliefs on the one hand and human achievements and customs of our secular society on the other. It therefore views the Christian life mainly as a personal life of righteousness and winning souls. Until Christ returns, God calls Christians to redeem the time in our decadent society by living lives of personal moral integrity and bringing our neighbors to Christ. The school shelters children as much as possible from the secular influences of society. The board selects teachers to a large extent for their personal faith and how they model a Christian life-style. The teachers promote character traits and good manners as an essential aspect of the Christian life.

Bethel Christian School bans unacceptable ideas from the classroom. When those occur in books, teachers skip the selections rather than discuss them in class. As much as possible, the school uses textbooks and curricula developed specifically for Christian schools. It chooses selections that emphasize personal conversion, uprightness, and obedience to authority. The school bans any books or selections not promoting personal godly living. If unavoidable, it warns that the material is to be used solely for reference to factual material or for comparative study with Biblical truth. The school's curriculum advances the view that Christians should lead personal lives of faith, witness, and integrity but that the gospel has little to say about social issues and concerns (Van Brummelen 1989, 15-22).

The *St. Francis School* has a very different approach. Christian beliefs, it holds, have influenced and benefited society's moral underpinnings. Its chapel services usually emphasize the importance of high moral standards, as does its religious studies program. Such courses include Biblical history, an overview of world religions, and units on ethics. But beyond that the school does not believe that Christian faith has much relevance for the curriculum. So the remainder of its program follows curriculum guides and textbooks recommended by the government. The school sometimes cannot find suitable teachers who are Christians. It then does not hesitate to employ well-qualified specialists who are not Christian for subjects considered to be secular (e.g., mathematics, science, French, art). The school's curriculum prepares its students to lead ethically responsible lives. By default the curriculum suggests to the students, however, that Christian faith is not relevant for most school subjects and for issues in society.

Trinity Christian School bases its curriculum on the conviction that Biblical guidelines apply to all of life. Therefore, they are relevant for all school subjects. The school holds that Biblical faith directs the Christian community to work at influencing all aspects of culture, including science, politics, the media, health care, and the arts. The school designs its curriculum around units that emphasize Biblical themes. Three of such units deal with responsible stewardship of creation's resources, the promotion of righteousness and justice as a task of government and its citizens, and the role of the arts and literature in advancing responsive discipleship. The school's Christian teachers use mainly secular resources, but try to address the issues raised within a Biblical framework.

Each of these three schools calls itself a *Christian* school. Yet each has a differing view of what its curriculum ought to be. Each view is based on a different perception of the role Christians play in a post-modern, secular society. Such a perception, in turn, depends on the worldview held by the leaders in each school.

A worldview is a set of basic beliefs and assumptions about life and reality. It answers what a person believes about the nature of life in our world. It provides meaning and guides and directs the thought and action of its adherents. The three schools described in this section share some aspects of their worldviews, but differ in other ways. List in what respects the worldviews of the three schools are similar. Then write down some points in which they differ. Which approach do you prefer? Why?

A worldview is a comprehensive framework of basic convictions about life. Our professed worldview may not always be our actual operative one; our actions rather than our words sometimes demonstrate what we ultimately believe. Nevertheless, the framework of beliefs to which we ultimately (even if implicitly) hold plays a decisive factor in our lives and in how we view and conduct schooling. Worldviews are usually described by addressing, in turn, what we believe about the nature and purpose of reality, of human beings, of knowledge, and of life in society.

A Christian worldview is shaped by God's revelation in His Word: His Word in creation, His Word in the Bible, and His Word Incarnate, Jesus Christ. The Bible makes clear that reality is God's creation. God created, upholds, guides, and rules His world. He sustains the laws of nature. He also provides us with the norms for human culture and society that enable and call us to be His co-workers in unfolding God's work. God's norms for human life include love, faithfulness, compassion, righteousness, integrity, justice, responsible stewardship, and peace.

Humankind's fall into sin, however, perverted God's good creation. Sin distorts all of human life—personal morality, marriage, and family life, political systems, economic, and environmental practices, the use of technology, the fine arts, agriculture, health. Sin is foreign to God's order for creation, and it is through Christ's death that redemption and restoration have become possible. The task of Christians in society is to proclaim the Good News of Jesus Christ by discipling others and to call and work for a restoration of all aspects of culture according to God's creation norms. Christians recognize, at the same time, that God's creation will be restored fully only when Christ returns. Until that time, nevertheless, God calls us to erect signposts for His Kingdom in all aspects of life.

The foregoing principles undergird my thinking about education and curriculum. It reflects the ideas in books on Christian worldview by Greene (1990), Holmes (1983), Walsh and Middleton (1984), and Wolters (1985). Note that I have been careful to say "a" Christian worldview, since my introductory example shows that not all Christians agree on all features of their worldview. My own worldview is closer to that of Trinity Christian School than those of the other two schools described. But there are occasions, nevertheless, when Christians have to shun corrupted aspects of our society.

To present the details of a responsible, Biblical worldview is beyond the scope of this book. Instead, I present four important obligations that result from such a worldview, and how these relate to education. I then consider some resulting aims for the school curriculum. I include some of the goals of the Pentecostal Assemblies (Public) Board of Education in Newfoundland, a system that has deliberately worked out the implications of a Biblical worldview for its schools. I revisit the four curriculum orientations discussed in the previous chapter, and conclude by sketching an orientation based on a Christian worldview.

THE BIBLE AND EDUCATION

A Christian worldview takes as its starting point that the Bible is God's authoritative Word for life. Scripture is God's inspired self disclosure that calls for obedience and response. That does not mean that the Bible gives us detailed formulas whose applications solve all current issues. God created us as human beings. As such, He calls us to think through and act on the principles for life that He reveals to us in Scripture, in His creation, and in the person of Jesus Christ. As we respond, we continue to work out our salvation with fear and trembling (Philippians 2:12). In other words, once converted, God calls believers to continue to understand God's Word of life and apply it in a more responsible way.

God's written Word, the Bible, provides guidelines and wisdom for answers to basic questions about the sort of world we live in and our role in it (Psalm 119:105, Romans 16:25-27). Our culture has privatized Christian faith. Consequently, a Christian voice in society has become marginalized. Society around us assumes that Christian faith has little to say about life in a pluralistic society. Yet, the Bible takes a very different approach, claiming that the Christian faith is all-encompassing. It calls not just individuals but whole nations to obedience. We are called to be imitators of God, full of love and sacrifice, not just in church, but everywhere in life (Ephesians 5:1).

If the Bible is relevant for all of life, then it is also relevant for education. If the Bible makes clear that God demands a life of love and sacrifice, then classrooms should be places where teachers encourage and help pupils to be responsive disciples of Jesus Christ. If the Bible says that people are created in God's image, then classrooms should encourage pupils and teachers to unwrap their talents and gifts to God's honor and to the well-being of their fellow humans. If Scripture expects Christians to share each other's joys and bear each other's burdens, then classrooms should stimulate teachers to seek shalom—God's peace and righteousness—for and with their pupils, their communities, their nation, their world. If teachers believe a Christian worldview is relevant, then they should strive for that kind of classroom, each day again, as they prayerfully plan and guide learning activities for their pupils. They would do this even when sin thwarts their best efforts to have those pupils think and behave as responsive disciples.

This chapter considers the relevance for education of four Biblical charges or "great injunctions" that are essential to a Biblical worldview. These are the Great (Cultural or Creation) Mandate, the Great Commission, the Great Commandment, and the Great Community. I use these injunctions to explore what the gospel says about the calling of Christ-confessors in a post-modern society, particularly of teachers and students who strive to be responsive and competent followers of Jesus Christ.

These four injunctions, of course, overlap. They are not discrete. All relate to Christ's injunction to seek first His Kingdom and its justice and righteousness. All require us to conform to the image of Christ in all areas of life. All challenge us to understand, evaluate, and transform the world from the foundation of God's unchanging values. Despite their overlap, however, it is useful to consider each in turn, deducing some of their implications for a classroom based on a Biblical worldview.

THE GREAT MANDATE

■ Read Genesis 1:26-28 and 2:15 and their contexts. These verses have been called the *cultural mandate* or, more accurately, the *creation mandate*. Also read Psalm 8. What do these passages say about the task God has given people in His created reality? What are the implications for schooling? Does this mandate still apply after the fall into sin? Why or why not? (See, for instance, Ephesians 2:8-10.)

Psalm 19 says a great deal about God's creation and our place in it. "The heavens declare the glory of God; the skies proclaim the work of His hands. Day after day they pour forth speech; night after night they display knowledge" (Psalm 19:1,2). Created reality continually reflects God's handiwork. We gain awe, understanding, and insight from the way God speaks to us in His creation order. We may not leave God at home when we do an experiment or when we discuss the properties of wood in a science class.

But God's law for life goes beyond the physical laws that He created to govern our world. As our covenant God Yahweh, He also gives us trustworthy laws for our everyday lives. These laws provide strength, comfort, and discernment for the immature (Psalm 19:7-8). We thank God for both the nature He made and for the principles of obedient living He spoke. Note that the laws of nature directly govern the earth as created by God. The impact of the precepts or norms that God gives to govern culture and society, however, depends on whether and how people apply those norms (Wolters 1985, 36). Nevertheless, the laws of nature and the laws for obedient response belong together. All truth is God's truth. There are no separate secular and sacred realms, with God having little to do with the former. Rather, God calls us to use His marvelous physical gifts within the guidelines He gives us for ethical, aesthetic, social, and economic life.

How do we then respond? Psalm 19 concludes with a simple yet profound prayer: "May the words of my mouth and the meditation of my heart be pleasing in your sight, O LORD, my Rock and my Redeemer" (Psalm 19:14). *The words of my mouth*: everything I think and say must honor God's laws. Then God will "put a new song in my mouth," giving me a firm place to stand even when "poor and needy" (Psalm 40: 2,3,17). *The meditation of my heart*: what lives deepest inside me, the source of my emotions, motivation, and action, must be pleasing to God. God accepts this when His law is written in my heart (Psalm 40:8).

In other words, when we acknowledge all laws, whether physical, social or moral, as God's laws, and use them responsibly in His service, He will give us strength and redemption. God complements His faithfulness in upholding His creation structure with upholding the cause of the oppressed. That, in turn, also becomes our task (Psalm 146). The fear of the Lord, including submission to the commands of His Law-word, is the beginning of wisdom, of knowledge, of discernment, of the Christian life (Psalm 111).

It is within this context that we listen to what has been called the creation mandate or, as I here call it, the Great Mandate. Before the fall into sin, God told Adam and Eve to be fruitful, to rule over the earth, and to work and take care of the Garden God gave to them (Genesis 1:28, 2:15). To subdue and rule over the earth meant, as the King James version said, to have dominion or lordship over all of life. In Scripture, ruling and leadership always involved service; God gives authority to serve. Similarly, the word "lord" in English originally hailed from "loaf-keeper," that is, the one who is the protective guardian of the bread that makes life possible. To have dominion over the earth meant to form and serve for the benefit of others. Jesus' life embodied perfect lordship. He has all authority. Yet He gave up His life to redeem even those who fail Him.

The Great Mandate thus has two aspects. First, creation is not something that remains static. God calls people as His images (Genesis 1:27) to develop and unfold its possibilities, to be co-regents with a loving, dynamic God. Human history is not outside God's plans for the world, though sin has distorted and ravaged God's intentions (Wolters 1985, 38). God intended that people would develop the creation and be culture formers.

Second, God required Adam to work and take care of the garden. "Taking care" literally meant "to guard the sanctity of." The Garden was a place God had given humans to keep holy in that everything in it should fulfil its intended function to God's glory. God called people to preserve His earth, to be protective guardians, to be responsible stewards of God's gifts so that all living creatures would benefit. Our authority may not be exercised without our servanthood (Walsh and Middleton 1984, 58-59). God entrusts us with His creation in all its complexity. The fall into sin has not negated that call, though we need to recognize that until Christ returns sin will continue to undermine our efforts to be obedient.

What does that mean for the classroom? Our pupils need to be imbued with a sense of God calling them to be royal servants as they play and discover and work in His world. Because of sin, the earth reflects its royal createdness only dimly. Even those who commit their lives to God do not always see the implications of their commitment for their work in a culture permeated with evil. But a classroom that takes the Great Mandate seriously values the students' daily contributions in being stewardly cultivators of the God-given gifts within and around them. The students experience and learn about and apply and value mathematical and physical and biological objects and theories and laws. Moreover, they experience how God-given norms can promote compassion, integrity, and justice in communication, economics, social interaction, the arts, government and law, and family living. Such classrooms support pupils to exercise godly image bearing, with levels of responsibility appropriate to their levels of maturity. They encourage the students to be and become committed to Kingdom service, and to act accordingly.

In this chapter I am going to illustrate my main points with some examples from physics. Why did I choose physics, when most prospective teachers studiously avoid the subject in high school and university? In part, because modern physics has some fascinating stories to tell. And in part, because if you can see that a Christian worldview affects the teaching of physics, you will likely agree that it touches other subjects as well.

Let's consider the history of the theories of relativity and quantum mechanics. Einstein showed that the element of chance was not inescapable in a physical description of the universe, as quantum mechanics claimed in the 1930s. At the same time, he discovered that there was some form of communication that was faster than light. This was a result that opposed his own theory of relativity. Einstein called it telepathy. In 1964 John S. Bell proved Einstein's discovery mathematically. In 1972 Bell's proof was verified experimentally.

Why was this so important? Well, Einstein and Bell gave back to physics the correlation between cause and effect at a deep and awesome level. Information between sub-atomic particles somehow gets around faster than the fleetest photon. There is something beyond light. Just like an onion has many layers that we can peel off one by one, there appear to be multiple levels of reality (Owens 1983, 106ff.).

The essence of this history is not difficult to understand and is enlightening, with implications far beyond physics. We learn, for instance, that human knowledge is limited: we see through a glass darkly, also in physics. What we discover is but a pale, superficial reflection of God's infinitely rich creation. "The impression of design is overwhelming," says physicist Paul Davies (*Time* Dec. 28, 1992, 39). Like many modern physicists he considers recent discoveries to be a path in the search for God (Davies 1983, ix). Christians would say that the underlying design reveals God's power, faithfulness, and love (Romans 1:20). What is significant is that these discoveries have once again sparked the flames of awe and wonder in physical scientists.

But the main point of this history becomes, I believe, that it helps pupils to look at knowledge in the light of Scripture. This story undermines, first, the positivist view of knowledge (i.e., the only reality is that which you can observe). This view, still the basis of school science programs, rejects as knowledge anything that cannot be demonstrated empirically. The existence of God and of God-given absolute norms for life is relegated to beliefs that do not have the weight of actual knowledge. This view assumes that we can solve humankind's problems through the observation-based scientific method. If one ethical approach is observed to work, it must be valid, at least in that circumstance and at that time. The foregoing story of modern physics, however, makes clear that much exists beyond that which we can observe.

Secondly, this story rejects the now-common constructivist view of knowledge (i.e., the only reality is the meaning that you construct). Even non-Christian physicists agree that "the universe seems calibrated for life's existence" (*Time* Dec. 28, 1992, 34). Yet, as we saw in the previous chapter, recent curriculum documents in Canada hold that each individual *constructs* his or her own reality and meaning. The resulting curriculum holds process to be all-important and neglects content, including enculturating students to our heritage and civilization. As autonomous beings, pupils choose their own meaning, not only for works of fiction but also for their values and their way of life. The chronicle of modern physics shows that while we discover, conceptualize, and interpret reality and its meaning, we do not construct it. Even when reading literary fiction, we do not create but we interpret and expand its meaning.

Thirdly, the story contradicts fatalist/nihilist views (i.e., everything depends on chance; there is no meaning in reality), something that until now has influenced philosophers more than educators. Physicists are concluding that "the overarching pattern . . . of 20th century science [suggests] there is more to the universe than meets the eye, something authentically divine about how it all fits together" (*Time* Dec. 28, 1992, 36).

This story in physics—and I could have chosen other stories in other fields—underscores how a Biblical view of knowledge is the only one that makes sense. We find comfort in that God governs all things in His sovereignty and faithfulness. All knowledge depends on revelation. God reveals Himself in His Word of creation, in His Word in Scripture, and in His Word Incarnate in Jesus Christ. So we may peel away layer upon layer of meaning in God's created reality, also in the classroom. Our theories, conclusions, and applications will always be limited and imperfect. As Agur already said in Proverbs 30, we never understand fully; we never reach the "core" of the onion. Yet we may use the knowledge we gain to God's glory, recognizing that we should do so in obedience to His norms for human life. That is the essence of the Great Mandate.

The story of creation and Psalm 19 make clear that we do not have to believe arrogantly that we personally *construct* all knowledge and meaning. That is a scary thought, if we consider the nature of human beings. A Biblical view of knowledge allows us to recognize that our observations and theories and applications are limited and imperfect. They do not necessarily lead to truth. Yet they enrich our lives. Our interpretations and extrapolations and applications take place within the bounds of our faith parameters. God calls us to explore scientific phenomena so that we can understand and disclose and use His creation. We also depend, however, on the overriding interpretive and applicatory framework of Scripture, God's special revelation to us. We may then use our results in obedience and service to God and to each other, even when we recognize that all scholarship is tentative and flawed.

If we obey the Great Mandate, then, we respond through what we know in obedience and service: knowing has purpose that brings joy and peace to our lives. And, as Psalm 19 makes so abundantly clear, such laws of creation include both the physical ones and the social/economic/ethical ones that govern wholesome human culture.

■ This section did not give a detailed analysis of the Bible's view of knowledge (that comes in chapter 4). It does show that the Bible rejects both a scientific-empirical, a constructivist, and a nihilist view of knowledge. Describe how a Biblical view of knowledge differs from the other three. Then choose a topic in science and discuss how the topic would be taught based on each view. How would the way based on a Biblical view promote the Great Mandate?

■ Teacher Margaret Barlow takes the Great Mandate seriously in her high school English classes. Her tests, for instance, require much more than recall information. They challenge students not only to explore the implications of the Great Mandate but to exercise it as they write them. For a study of Shakespeare's *Macbeth*, for instance, the students get two or three periods to write a story. "Imagine," Margaret tells her class, "that you come home and your parents ask you the standard question, "What did you learn today?' You answer, 'Well, I learned from Macbeth that there is universal truth.' But your parents want to know more. Your test assignment is to write a story for them which illuminates the universal truth of Macbeth, using the characters and issues of the play."

Margaret suggests several possibilities for the framework of students' stories. A student might imagine that she is a psychologist who travels back in time and reacts to and analyzes what happens in *Macbeth* from her twentieth century perspective. Or a student might suppose that he is Sherlock Holmes who investigates the murder of Duncan. Students use and develop their creativity and imagination, their thinking and writing skills, and their insight into "universal truth" as they complete this exam. In what ways do Margaret's students examine and follow the Great Mandate?

THE GREAT COMMISSION

■ Christians usually think of the Great Commission in terms of witnessing personally to those who do not believe in Christ. That is an important aspect of the Great Commission. But read Matthew 28:18-20 again with fresh eyes. Why does Jesus Christ start by saying that "all authority in heaven and on earth has been given to me"? Why does He enjoin us to make *disciples* (not just converts) of all *nations* (not just individuals)? And what does it mean to teach them "to obey everything I have commanded you"? Discuss what implications these phrases may have for schooling.

God assigned the Great Mandate before the fall into sin. The fall did not revoke that mandate, but it did make it impossible to fulfil in the way that God originally intended. By God's grace in Jesus Christ, however, we still may be co-heirs with Christ and fellow workers of God, still tending His earth in a loving and responsible way (Romans 8:17; 1 Corinthians 3:9). Jesus himself spent much more of His life fulfilling the Great Mandate as a carpenter in out-of-the-way Nazareth than He did preaching the Good News directly. Similarly, our role as Christians is not limited to personal evangelism. Teachers who help students gain knowledge, learn skills, and develop positive attitudes toward meaningful work are doing their part to obey the Great Mandate.

The fall into sin and Christ's work of redemption made it necessary, however, for Jesus to add His Great Commission of Matthew 28:18-20 to the Great Mandate:

> All authority in heaven and on earth has been given to me. Therefore go and make disciples of all nations, baptizing them in the name of the Father and of the Son and of the Holy Spirit, and teaching them to obey everything I have commanded you. And surely I am with you always, to the very end of the age.

This Great Commission does not replace the Great Mandate but complements it. Indeed, obeying the Great Commission contributes to exercising the Great Mandate in a secular society. Jesus Christ here reminds us that through His death and resurrection He has all authority and is always with us. That is why Paul can say that we are co-heirs with Christ and God's fellow workers. That is what makes it possible for us to make disciples of all nations, teaching them what Christ has commanded us. Discipleship begins with a personal commitment to following Christ, and with baptizing those who make such a commitment.

But there is more that we need to note here. First, being a disciple does not mean following blindly. It means we base our thinking, words, and deeds on the principles Jesus taught us, but we work this out responsively and responsibly in our own lives and in our environment, thus in turn influencing others. Second, discipleship is not just a personal call. Christ commands us to make disciples of *nations*. He calls us to disciple not just individuals or even whole communities but whole nations! If an entire nation recognizes what it means to serve God, the resulting conditions will set the stage for a more loving, just, and joyful implementation of the Great Mandate. Third, note that Christ emphasizes that we teach *everything* that He commanded us, not just the first principles of repentance and conversion.

What are Christ's injunctions that we ought to teach? The gospel of Matthew, the gospel of the Kingdom of Heaven, is clear. Be meek and humble, merciful, peace-making, seeking justice and righteousness (wherever the gospels use righteousness it can also be translated as justice). Be persons of integrity, with compassion and forgiveness even for those who oppose you. Be faithful to your marriage partner. Don't care for earthly riches. Be thankful for and enjoy God's blessings, giving generously to the needy, and be responsible in your business ventures. Use your God-given gifts in meaningful ways. Live according to the principles of Scripture, but avoid legalism and hypocrisy. Believe that the Kingdom of Heaven is ever-renewing and all-powerful, but remember that its current manifestations will be beset by sin until Christ returns.

Missionary Lesslie Newbigin sums up such discipleship as follows:

Christian discipleship is a following of Jesus in the power of his risen life on the way which he went. That way is neither the way of purely interior spiritual pilgrimage, nor is it the way of realpolitik for the creation of a new social order. It goes the way Jesus went, right into the heart of the world's business and politics, with a claim that is both promising and vulnerable. It looks for a world of justice and peace, not as a product of its own action but as the gift of God . . . Such discipleship will be concerned equally in the private and in the public spheres . . . It will provide occasions for the creation of visible signs of the invisible kingship of God. (Newbigin 1983, 37)

Elsewhere, Newbigin (1989, 121) asks why Paul in his letters fails to tell his readers to be active in mission. The main reason, Newbigin suggests, is that Paul is first of all concerned that the church be faithful to its Lord. Once Paul had preached the gospel where Christ was not known, Paul left. His work was finished when he could leave behind communities who believed the gospel and lived by it (Romans 15:20, 23). Once the power of God's Kingdom was present in this way, people would take notice and begin to ask the questions to which the gospel provides answers.

Therefore, Newbigin continues, the heart of our mission is (1) to give God the service of our lives, (2) to be part of communities whose members are deeply rooted in Christ, and (3) to invite all people to consider and accept our beliefs. We tell the story of salvation and at the same time act on its demands, as Christ made clear in His charge to the disciples in Matthew 10. We not only announce but also embody the presence of the reign of God. A community enabled by the Spirit to live in Christ will challenge both individuals and the powers and principalities (e.g., the structures of society such as global consumerism). Both our words and our deeds can then promote justice and peace, though we need to remember that no human endeavor is free from the corrupting power of sin. Our words are empty unless our daily activities reflect them in all our involvements (Newbigin 1989, 119-139).

Before we consider what this means for classroom learning, we should note that obeying both the Great Mandate and the Great Commandment depend on God having created us as His images. Exegetically we cannot dissociate being images of God from our mandate to rule and subdue the earth (Hall 1986, 71-72). If we believe that God is a serving, loving, and suffering God, we are images of God in our response to such qualities. And response is possible only if we recognize that our being depends on our relationship with God.

The possibility of a restored relationship is possible through Christ's redemption. Only if God reaches out to us through Christ and we accept His grace can we begin to understand what it means to image God and consciously seek to establish God's shalom on earth. Only then can we image God in our relationships with other people and with God's creation. God created us for relatedness-in-love with Himself, with others, and with His world. We image God in loving (Hall 1986, 132). We image God as Christ reincorporates us into the stewardship of God's world through His grace and faith (Hall 1986, 200). We image God in suffering with Christ and our fellow beings as we lament the absence of God's shalom on earth. That makes us responsive, responsible, and accountable creatures who walk with Jesus Christ as their caring companion, their tutor, their personal Redeemer and Lord.

This understanding of what it means to be images of God leads to the conclusion that, since the fall, the Great Commission and the Great Mandate are flip sides of the same coin. At our conversion, the image of God and therefore our relationship with God begins to be restored in us. This also makes it possible for us to restore our relationships with people around us and to obey both the Great Commission and the Great Mandate.

The first letter of Peter is instructive in how living as God's image relates to these two mandates. Peter writes that God gives us new life and hope through the resurrection of Jesus Christ (1:3). It is our loving relationship with Christ that gives us salvation (1:8-9) and faith and hope in God (1:21). This relationship makes it possible for us to prepare our minds for action (1:13), live holy lives (1:15, 2:1), and grow up in our salvation as we deepen our relationship with Christ (2:2-8; the Great Mandate). Since we now belong to God, He calls us to be a royal priesthood, interceding for humans before God and representing God to humanity (the Great Commission).

In everything we do, Peter continues, God calls us to live as His servants (2:16; the Great Mandate), and, as such, live such good lives that our good deeds teach others (2:12; the Great Commission). This applies to how we live as wives and husbands (3:1-7). If we live in harmony, compassion, and humility, repaying insult with blessing (3:8-9, the Great Commandment), then we can in good conscience and with gentleness give an answer to everyone who asks us to give the reason for the hope that we have (3:15, the Great Commission). We should use whatever gifts we have received to serve others (4:10, all four "great injunctions"). All this also sums up what Paul means when he speaks of "having the mind of Christ." The Christian mind is the crux of our personhood as images of God. It includes our reason, emotions, attitudes, feelings, and will as we stand in relationship to God (Greene 1990, 7).

What does all this mean for classroom learning? First, Christian teachers make clear that our whole life and being depend on our relationship with God (Acts 17:28). Teachers therefore do not hesitate to lead students to a personal relationship with God when students ask questions about their source of hope and peace—that is part of the Great Commission. They also model a life of joyful obedience so that their students, too, will begin to understand what it means to put their lives into His hands.

The Great Commission has more implications for classroom learning and teaching, however. The definition of self-actualization will be very different for Christian teachers from the normal one, for instance. Usually, curriculum guides assume that critical thinking and self-motivation that lead to autonomy are the crux of self-actualization. By themselves, however, these lead to death, not life. In classrooms that take into account the Great Commission, teachers recognize Christ's authority and know that He is always present. That leads them to exercise their calling as God's images who practice compassion, self-sacrifice, justice, righteousness, and truthfulness, albeit in a way limited by our sinfulness, and encourage students to do so also. Teachers also choose curriculum content that reveals how people have responded obediently and disobediently to God's mandate. To understand the influence of sin and explore Christian responses, it will be necessary sometimes to discuss controversial, anti-Christian materials such as modern rock music videos. Failure to do so may mean students blithely accept what they read, hear, and see, instead of learning to apply Christian principles to personal and societal life issues.

Teachers who follow the Great Commission strive to teach students all the norms that Christ has taught us. They will build relationships with the students so that together they can explore the implications of such norms in our secular society. They model and cherish the fruits of the Spirit as they structure their classrooms and plan their curricula—love, self-sacrifice, peace, integrity, justice. The calling of pupils is to practice these fruits while they become enculturated to our Christian traditions and the ideals and follies of our Western society. Simultaneously, they begin to search out how the fruits of the Spirit have a bearing on the affairs of daily life. What does it mean to be an ambassador of Christ wherever God puts us? That is a tall order in a society drenched in secularism. Nevertheless, teachers imbued with the importance of the Great Commission will carefully design units and choose literary selections and structure their assignments so that students will learn everything Christ has commanded us.

Consider physics once again. "Blessed are the meek, for they will inherit the earth . . . Blessed are the peacemakers, for they shall be called children of God." Physics classes may never just unfold theories and applications of physics. Also there, God calls us to obey the Great Commission. Blessed are the meek, also the meek physicists who recognize their limited understanding of their theories and, even more so, of the implications of their applications. How can we use physics to promote peace and justice? What are the moral and religious dimensions of how we use physics? Sometimes there are no easy answers. The jet that contributes to the deterioration of the ozone layer also sends Bible translators to Papua New Guinea. Yet pupils should grapple with issues of stewardship and justice if they are to know how to obey everything that Christ taught us. Only then can they live as God's images who, as they grow in their relationship with Him, are granted the grace to erect signposts to the Kingdom of Heaven here on earth.

■ I quickly referred to a Biblical view of the person, but left a more complete consideration until chapter 7. Look up text references to the nature of human beings (e.g., Psalm 8:6-8, Isaiah 42:5-7, John 13:12-17, Acts 17:28, Romans 12:1-8, Ephesians 4:22-24). Make a list of the characteristics the Bible assigns to human beings. Then give, with examples, some implications for curriculum structure and content.

■ As one element of a theme on communities, Inge Maier's grade 2 class has discussed what it means to be part of the Body of Christ. She has a large cut-out of a person on the bulletin board made up of segments of different colors, each piece with the name of one of her students. After a discussion about the role of the church in the community, the children write a story about their church with an accompanying drawing. The stories include sentences such as: "We go to church and prays God. My church looks better than my house. In my church I usually go to Sunday School boring. My grampa does the offering. I sing in choir. We have communion." Discuss how Inge could continue this unit so that her students begin to understand the scope of the Great Commission. Include ideas related to the customs of different ethnic communities (her own students are from many different church and ethnic backgrounds).

THE GREAT COMMANDMENT

■ The Great Commandment emphasizes one dimension of the Great Commission, for loving God and neighbor is an important thing that Christ taught us (Matthew 22:37-39). The second half of the commandment is found, in one form or another, in all religious traditions. It is a universal law without which a society finds it impossible to function. But Scripture says that the greatest commandment is to love the Lord your God. Again, this points out that our lives cannot image God unless we first have a restored relationship with God. What are some concrete ways in which the curriculum can help students to love God above all and their neighbors as themselves?

"Love the Lord your God with all your heart and with all your soul and with all your mind. This is the first and greatest commandment. And the second is like it: Love your neighbor as yourself" (Matthew 22:37-39). This Great Commandment, of course, is not separate from the Great Mandate or the Great Commission. We cannot rule over the earth responsibly without loving God and our neighbor. And it was certainly Jesus' intent that this commandment, as the greatest one He taught us, would be part of obeying the Great Commission.

Yet, it is worthwhile considering the Great Commandment as a separate mandate. First, note that the word Jesus used for love, *agape*, does not mean friendly or sentimental affection, but a self-sacrificial love, love even for the "unlovable." *Agape* love embodies a total commitment, a deliberately chosen devotion. It is the gist of Christ's easy yoke and light burden (Matthew 11:29). It is a yoke and a burden that can be carried out joyfully because Jesus bears it with us. Jesus emphasizes that love for God involves the core of our whole being, our hearts. It begins with our innermost commitment and faith, our souls. It consumes all our strength: strength of conviction, strength of character, strength of will (Mark 12:30). And it includes our whole mind: to love God, we ought to have the mind of Christ. Perhaps Jesus added "mind" to the commandment found in Deuteronomy 6 because of the split between heart and mind found in Greek culture. The Christian life is empty unless it is based on such all-encompassing love for God.

The second point to note is that Jesus here brings together two familiar passages of the Old Testament Scripture that until His time had been widely separated. Love for neighbor, Jesus emphasizes, is not separate but flows naturally out of love for God. Dualism has all too often divided life in the Christian community into two sectors. Christians operating the St. Francis school at the beginning of this chapter, for instance, promoted a personal Christian love for God. They failed to see, however, that love for God and neighbor are integrally connected and encompass all of life, and therefore all of the curriculum. The St. Francis school, while serving God in its chapel program and general atmosphere, may well have served the god of rational autonomy or the god of individualism or the god of material prosperity elsewhere in its curriculum. As Jesus points out in Matthew 6:24, no one can serve two masters without eventually serving one more than the other. Historically, God has usually lost out during the last two centuries of Western culture and education.

A Christian approach to curriculum rejects such dualism. It is based on loving God and neighbor in an all-encompassing way. The curriculum is based on the principle that whatever we do is done in the name of the Lord Jesus. That is true whether we are pastors or missionaries or computer programmers or nurses or bankers or janitors. God calls all

Christians to full-time Christian service. The work of Jesus as a carpenter was part of His earthly service to God. There is no sacred part of life that can be separated from a secular part. What we do for our neighbor in our occupation or as citizens or as family members is all part of obeying the Great Commandment.

A school curriculum helps a student develop Christian alternatives and be a Christian cultural witness only if it sees both parts of the Great Commandment as an essential, integral foundation for all schooling. The school curriculum should make clear, for instance, that Biblical norms for stewardship say a great deal about how we run our businesses. Those norms reject the notion of Christian businessmen who say that their faith has nothing to do with their business affairs. As Walsh and Middleton point out, Christian faith should transform our vocations, whether that be in medicine or in agriculture or in business (1984, 97-98).

Love God above all and your neighbor as yourself. I don't think you can read the final chapters John's gospel without being overwhelmed by the omnipresent love of God, and by our need to offer our lives in return, wholly and wholeheartedly, in love for God and neighbor. We must be willing to wash each other's feet, and, indeed, lay down our lives for our friends. Only through total love of God may our joy be complete. As teachers we serve our pupils by loving them as we love ourselves. Only if our *agape* love for God and His Kingdom drives our teaching can we feed Christ's lambs. Love for God and neighbor is the key to being transformed by the renewing of our minds so that we no longer conform to the pattern of this world (Romans 12:2, 9ff.).

Such Biblical love characterizes classrooms that are alive. That does not mean classrooms with lots of warm, fuzzy feelings. Rather, it means classrooms filled with a mutuality of care and respect, with constructive and fair relationships, with teachers driven by a deep desire to do everything possible to help children be and become what God wants them to be. It means providing a spectrum of learning activities suited for students with diverse learning styles. It also means using assessment and evaluation practices with such variety that every student can shine in at least one or two types. It means giving students meaningful responsibilities and trusting that they will fulfil them unless contrary evidence suggests they need help and direction. It means choosing curriculum content that deals with issues of strategic importance to our Christian community and to our culture, issues where our love can make a difference.

We face obstacles as we try to implement the demands of the Great Commandment. Alasdair MacIntyre (1982) argues convincingly that moral precepts have lost their function in our society. Nicholas Wolterstorff adds that "if the school offers merely prudential reasons for acting in the manner of the citizen, then it is not moral character that it develops but prudential alertness, not ethical sensitivity but pragmatic shrewdness" (Hauerwas and Westerhoff 1992, 20). In other words, even the second part of the Great Commandment no longer serves as a base for living in today's society.

Our society no longer shares commitment to even the most basic Biblical values. David Purpel claims that schools contribute to this societal malaise. How we structure schools and what we teach, he shows, replaces a sense of a loving community based on shared values with a self-gratifying and egocentric individuality. An arrogant faith in individual achievement and success, intellectual certainty and reason undermines values such as mutual support and care, humility and self-sacrifice—all necessary for a loving, compassionate society (Purpel 1989, 28-64). We therefore deliberately structure the school curriculum to convince students that commitment to the Great Commandment is a necessary condition for our society to function with compassion and justice.

Let me return to my physics classroom example. The structure of physics classrooms, like all classrooms, should reflect Biblical *agape* love for God and neighbor. I say more about that in chapter 7 on pedagogy. Loving our neighbor as ourselves also includes discussing how physics has led to a technology that enslaves us. Consumption rather than stewardship has become the norm in industrial nations. We are on our way of becoming a two-class society of "haves" and "have-nots" as the middle class is slowly disappearing. We still live on the edge of nuclear disaster, with aging and poorly maintained nuclear reactors and weapons in the former Soviet Union, as well as likely proliferation of nuclear expertise. Our Western technological genius combined with greed for profits arm nations around the world to the teeth, with the arms suppliers who profited greatly then having to intervene to stop the agony to which they contributed.

Physics classrooms that obey the Great Commandment, moreover, investigate how we can use technology to live more with less. They model how this can be done in the classroom, the school, and the community. They emphasize how loving our neighbor as ourselves means that we use technology to provide a respectable living for people across the world. They contrast this approach with that of our present economic system that enslaves us with its demands for material greed. Loving God above all and our neighbor as ourselves is Christ's mandate that provides a practical guideline for planning school curriculum.

- This section briefly discusses the problem of *dualism*. Dualism has resulted in many Christians living a personal life of devotion to God, but failing to see how their faith affects their work place or their education. The result: faith is no longer allowed to have a public presence and is relegated to the private dimension of life. But Scripture tells us that God requires us "to act justly and to love mercy and to walk humbly with your God" (Micah 6:8). That applies to all of life. The prophet Micah addresses corruption and injustice in society. He says that bowing down before God and giving Him offerings is not the heart of loving Him. Worship and praise in church are important, but more crucial yet is that we love God by dealing with life's issues with justice and mercy. Develop a curriculum theme to help students see how Christians can do this in concrete ways.

■ How does an elementary school of more than 400 students enable pupils to understand and experience the Great Commandment? For one, says principal Henry Contant, the school has to provide opportunities for service. One thing his staff has done is to give the grade 7s (the highest grade level in the school) meaningful areas of responsibility. In a kick-off retreat one September afternoon and evening, the students (joined by their parents later in the evening) brainstormed possible areas of service and chose the ones in which they wanted to serve.

The students identified sixteen areas. These included refereeing and keeping records for the school's intramural program, supervising the computer room at noon while helping primary students type stories on the computer, arranging for all audiovisual equipment to be set up and taken down at teachers' requests, and organizing and maintaining the school's recycling program. Each teacher trained students in one or two of the sixteen areas, and maintained contact with the students during the year. Each student volunteered for at least one area and signed a service pledge. The school also held regular team-building events such as pizza and swimming parties. In the future, Henry plans to branch out beyond the school with an "adopt a block" program to keep the school neighborhood clear of litter, and also involve the grade 6s.

What effect has this program had? First, it has affirmed students, especially those not academically inclined. They feel good about serving others. They usually fulfil their responsibilities better than what teachers expect. They almost always make responsible choices when they decide themselves, for instance, when they can leave class to set up equipment for a videotape presentation in another room. Teachers appreciate students' willingness to help the school function more smoothly on a regular basis. They have gained more faith and trust in their students. The grade 7s also interact frequently with the other grade levels. As a result, overall interpersonal relationships in the school have become more respectful and caring.

Henry Contant considers this program a significant and strategic part of the grade 7 curriculum. In what ways does the program realize both parts of the Great Commandment? Can you suggest improvements to the program? Do you agree with Henry Contant that this is part of the school's *curriculum*? Why or why not?

THE GREAT COMMUNITY

■ The Bible does not mention the Great Community (or communion) directly. Nor, like the Great Mandate, can we point to one or two Bible verses that encapsulate the Great Community (although chapters like Ephesians 4, Romans 12, 1 Corinthians 12 and 13 have much to say about it). In Galatians 6, Paul says that we must carry each other's burdens, share all good things, and do good to all people, especially to those who belong to the family of believers. Paul here first addresses the church communion. In what ways would this apply to the school context as well? Can you suggest ways to structure a classroom in which students and their teacher experience a community based on these principles?

Christ and Paul both emphasized and reemphasized the importance of communion in community. Christ is our model for finding worth in all persons and using their gifts despite their flaws and sins. Jesus used a despised and dishonest tax collector to author the first Gospel, the one that so clearly expounds the Kingdom of Heaven. He related to an ethnically-shunned and loose-living Samaritan woman, and to other women with questionable pasts. He made an impetuous and rude fisherman, who denied Him three times, the rock on which He built His church. Paul similarly enjoined the Roman Christians to accept and serve each other, and at the same time valued them for their goodness and knowledge (Romans 15). In Ephesians, he expanded on this by urging the Ephesians to bear with each other in love, using their unique gifts for building up the Body of Christ (Ephesians 4).

Similarly, each of us, and each of our pupils, has a holy calling to have communion with God. God calls us to be co-heirs with Christ and co-workers with Himself. God created us as unique individuals with the capacity to work out, in a particular way, our own God-given abilities and talents. However, in contradiction to the pervasive doctrine of individualism, we always do so for the benefit of the communities in which God places us. Christ exemplified what Paul later wrote about building the Body of Christ. He used and developed the diverse gifts of His followers. Very soon He sent them out for the upbuilding of the whole community. He treated all those with whom He came in contact as important. He encouraged and allowed each to be a fellow learner who had something unique to contribute. He spoke the truth in love, encouraging us to do likewise. He emphasized the importance of personal responsibility, of personal choice. But He also showed appropriate and effective methods of working together, to build communion and community.

Lesslie Newbigin describes how a community true to its Christian calling will understand and display a gospel framework for life. It will be a community of praise and thanksgiving that lives by the amazing grace of a boundless kindness. It will be a community of truth that is modest and realistic but also skeptical of modern propaganda. It is a community that has deep concern for its neighborhood rather than living for and focusing on itself. It is a community of priests that offers sacrifices of love and obedience as it exercises its diverse gifts in the public life of our society. It is a community of mutual responsibility. In that sense, it provides a foretaste of a social order where God's peace and justice are evident. Finally, it is a community of hope, one that rejects the false technological optimism of Western culture but also the nihilism and despair of modern Western literature (Newbigin 1989, 227-33).

What does that mean for our classrooms? Praise and thankfulness will be both implicit and explicit parts of its program. Rather than insisting on personal rights, teachers and students will together observe personal and communal gratitude for God's gifts of grace. The school's curriculum will pose problems and raise questions about life and cultural issues. It will analyze them from a Biblical perspective and help students discern the spirits of the age without assuming that Christians have all the answers (or even always know which questions to pose). It will not avoid dealing with the effects of sin in society, but it will also proclaim hope in the future because God remains faithful forever (Psalm 146). It will include service projects in the school and community, allowing the school community to celebrate diverse gifts as it helps those within and without the school. The school will set realistic but high expectations for all members of its community. It will give meaningful and suitable responsibilities and hold each one accountable for agreed-upon commitments. The school will promote conflict resolution, peer support, and evaluation methods that promote Biblical peace, justice, and the responsive use of gifts.

Let's consider the physics classroom once again. Physics is a practical science that can be taught in a way that can excite a wide spectrum of students. More than any other high school science, it can explore both the benefits and harm caused by scientific thinking and technology. We teach physics as a course for the intellectually elite only. Yet it is a subject where students with theoretical and practical bents can learn to work together and share their gifts. In other words, it provides good opportunities for practising the Great Community to which God calls believers.

We might, for instance, restructure our physics courses so that all students would take a core that is not very mathematical. Mathematically-inclined pupils could then opt to take more theoretical sections within each unit while others explore much more practical ones. Such classrooms could build community, particularly if we deliberately develop a sense that the theoretical and practical complement each other, instead of one standing above the other. Such classrooms also have much potential for collaborative learning where theoretically-oriented students can explain basic concepts and ideas to small groups of students. Others can take leadership in doing experiments and building models. Still others can exhibit the work of their group to the class. Students need to learn to appreciate each other's gifts and learn to support each other: *that* is an essential ingredient of the Great Communion in Christ for which we strive.

But all this leaves an unanswered question. In Christ we may be part of His great worldwide communion, particularly as it comes to expression in our local churches. What then is our vision of life in a society that, by-and-large, does not want to be part of that Great Community? In a pluralistic society, the church neither can nor should try to regulate the affairs of government or business. Rather, its role is to proclaim the Gospel of Jesus Christ, call people to repentance, and encourage members of Christ's Body, Christ's Great Community, to base their thought, word, and deed on Biblical principles. All domains of life are subject to the direction of humans, and all Christians should personally submit to the demands of Christ. The church reminds Christ's followers of their task to bring glory to God as they fulfil the Great Mandate, the Great Commission, and the Great Commandment.

How we fulfil that role will depend on our circumstances. Joseph and Daniel did not try to change the secular government structures for which they worked. They were witnesses to righteousness, justice, and stewardship through their personal faith and integrity. Today, some Christian politicians similarly establish a credible witness in a secular setting by being as wise as serpents and as gentle as doves as they address political issues within a framework of Biblical norms. Abraham and Moses led groups of people out of secular environments so that their followers would be a communal witness to the peoples in their immediate environment (not always successfully!). Various Anabaptist groups have similarly often lived as communities of Christ that witnessed and helped others toward economic and social justice. Christian schools can similarly be seen as places where students experience the Great Community so that later they can better share and demonstrate what it means to build a community where Christian virtues are evident (Pentecostal Education Council 1991, 65-66).

Such efforts may be the best and sometimes the only possible way for the Christian community to reach out with the power of the gospel. God in His sovereignty and grace does sometimes allow the Christian community to take one additional step, however. Christians alive with the Holy Spirit also may be involved in building culture and society. Subject to the Truth of Christ in which all things cohere, Christians also address the structural problems in society and erect signposts to the Kingdom of God. They do so while recognizing that the forces of evil will continue to influence our culture until the return of Christ. Nevertheless, by being discerning of the sinful deviation from what God intended His creation to be they may work at calling for a more Biblical direction. Through the renewing power of salvation in Jesus Christ they may restore aspects of family life, law making and enforcement, business, music and art, the use of technology, academic scholarship, and so on. For that, Christians also should work closely together in communion with each other. We need networks of Christian businessmen, Christian doctors, Christian lawyers, Christian musicians and artists who communally explore what it means to reclaim and re-form strategically important areas of life.

The curriculum, then, may begin the process of Christians together asking and experiencing what it means to live as Christ's Great Community. Schools can deal openly with their students about the tension caused by Christians being in the world but not of it. They can address those areas of life from which we may have to withdraw as a Christian community. It is hard to see, for instance, how we can currently redeem the profit-driven and thoroughly secular film production industry without becoming swept away by its tide. The best we may be able to do is discuss the dangers with students, model our own refusal to consume certain types of programs and advertising, and help students to consume and produce alternative programming.

The curriculum should use content and learning approaches that help students be responsive disciples of Christ wherever God places them. The curriculum helps them unfold their gifts to serve others, to share each other's joys, and to bear each other's burdens. Teachers and students together celebrate and bring about God's shalom where it is possible to do so, and lament its absence where the power of sin prevails. Such a curriculum is most likely to succeed where a fellowship of Christians works together in the unity of the Spirit, thus exemplifying a Christ-like community.

■ Dietrich Bonhoeffer wrote:

In a Christian community everything depends upon whether each individual is an indispensable link in a chain ... It will be well, therefore, if every member receives a definite task to perform for the community, that he may know in hours of doubt that he, too, is not useless and unusable. Every Christian community must realize that not only do the weak need the strong, but also that the strong cannot exist without the weak. The elimination of the weak is the death of the fellowship. (1954, 94).

Discuss Bonhoeffer's intent and the implications of his views for the classroom as a community and for the way we structure curriculum.

■ Today the main factor that still allows people to function as a community is their tolerance of other views. This is one difficulty with maintaining one uniform public school system in a pluralistic society. Paradoxically, as soon as tolerance of all viewpoints becomes a leading value in society, any view that holds that there are absolutes that guide life is considered intolerant and therefore not acceptable in the public sphere. Does this mean that Christians have little opportunity for obeying the Great Commission the Great Commandment in the public school setting? Why or why not? In what ways would the curriculum necessarily differ for Christians in public and those in Christian school settings?

■ Teacher Curt Gesch has designed teaching aids for a high school course called *Conservation and Outdoor Recreation Education* (Gesch 1993b). He expects completion of all work, cooperation, and a 50% average for a passing grade. Optional enrichment assignments chosen by the students themselves allow them to get a "B" or higher. The course focuses on what it means to live in community with other humans and with animals in recreation activities such as hiking, fishing, and hunting. Students explore issues that go much beyond outdoor recreation: how laws and regulations protect community; what it means that something has to die for other things to live; the moral standards which almost all civilizations have upheld; why it is important to be courteous, considerate, and cooperative; and how people go about reaching a consensus or compromise when they have conflicting goals, preferences, or ethics. In what ways can a course such as this contribute to building communion in community in a Christian school? a public one? Because of the issues raised, is such a course more important than, say, a grade 11 mathematics or Spanish course? Why or why not? Does Curt's grading method contribute to or detract from building community? Give reasons.

THE AIMS OF THE CURRICULUM

■ Aims, goals, and objectives for schooling have been formulated and categorized in many different ways. In my book *Walking with God in the Classroom* I formulated the aims of Christian schooling as follows:

The general aim of Christian schools is to help and guide students to be and become responsible disciples of Jesus Christ (1). This involves maximizing God-given personal abilities (2) in order to build Christian relationships in the community (3) and the disposition to participate in our culture in a Christian way (4):

A. To unfold the basis, framework, and implications of a Christian vision of life (5), encountering the contours of a Christian worldview and its relevance for living in today's society (6).

B. To foster the development of concepts, abilities, and creativity (7) that (a) proclaim the marvel and potential of God's creation, even in its fallen state (8), and (b) enable students to walk in God's way by using their God-given talents in service to God and their neighbors (9).

C. To let students experience the meaning of living out of a Christian worldview (10), in order that they may be able and willing to (a) make personal and communal decisions from a Biblical perspective (11), and (b) develop values and practice dispositions in harmony with Christian principles (12).

D. To encourage students to commit themselves to Jesus Christ and to a Christian way of life (13), willing to serve God and their neighbors (14).

Look at each of the 14 numbered clauses. Which of the four great injunctions (the Great Mandate, the Great Commission, the Great Commandment, and the Great Communion) does each clause emphasize? In terms of the four dimensions, is the set of aims a balanced one? What revisions, if any, would you make?

You could argue that this statement of aims applies to any Christian agency that nurtures children, including the home and the church. However, each agency is distinctive in the degree to which it emphasizes each aim. Which one(s) would be emphasized most by the home? the church? the school? Does that mean that the school should also emphasize one or two of the four great injunctions more than the others? What are the implications of your answer for school curriculum?

Teachers who are reflective practitioners check whether a unit they plan to teach helps attain at least some aspects of their overall aims. After developing a set of general aims, most school jurisdictions formulate more specific objectives that form a bridge between the general aims and the planned learning activities.

Al Greene (1984) has given five criteria for statements of objectives for Christian schools. First, the statement is understandable and simply stated in terms which grip everyday life in the classroom. Second, it agrees with Scriptures and recognize the world in terms of creation, fall, and redemption. Third, it reflects a Biblical worldview, with everything in life seen in the light of Christ. Fourth, it is livable and practicable, influencing lesson planning, playground activity, sports events, staff and parent meetings, and so on. Last, it is accepted, used and practiced. To ensure that such a statement does not stay in the archives, he suggests that it be the result of community consensus, and be visible everyday in the school.

Greene proposes the four overall objectives shown below. You may want to compare this statement with the example given at the beginning of this section. What are the advantages and disadvantages of each?

Would either set meet Greene's five criteria for an effective statement?

1. *To see Christ formed in the students.* We want the world to see Him in their walk, their talk and their ways. We want them to show the fruits of having come to Him, taken His yoke on them, and learned of Him (Galatians 4:19 and Matthew 11:28-30).
2. *To advance the Kingdom of God.* We must bring our faith to bear on all areas of life today, transforming them in His name.
3. *To confront the idols of our times.* Our students must learn to "discern the spirits" and recognize idols such as statism, materialism, technicism, scientism, and other "isms" where faith is placed in something other than God.
4. *To change culture.* The Bible shows clearly that the Church has always changed the culture when it was in touch with the Spirit of God, and that part of our responsibility has not been rescinded.

Greene then develops twenty-three more specific objectives in four categories: *commitment* (to God and neighbor), *awareness* (of creation, God's presence, Christ's redemption, our calling), *ability* (literacy and numeracy skills, thinking clearly, shaping and using creation, serving God and fellow humans in all areas of life), and *responsible decision making*.

Newfoundland's Pentecostal Education Council coined 149 objectives for its denominational public school system, including 61 dealing with school operations, 45 "pervasive goals," and 43 curriculum objectives (Pentecostal Education Council 1991, 103-120). I first list four pervasive goals with curriculum implications, and then a subset of curriculum objectives relating to social studies.

Teachers are to help students
2.1.7 Apply Christian principles to life issues.
2.6.1 Assume their role as citizens in response to God's cultural mandate.
2.6.6 Develop the critical, creative, reflective thinking, and decision-making skills necessary to resolving societal issues.
2.7.1 Recognize that career decisions are an integral part of their Christian commitment to God and service to society.

The Christian school is responsible for preserving and extending the cultural heritage of the society that it serves. It is expected to help students to
3.2.1 Develop an appreciation for that which is excellent and honorable in their cultural heritage.
3.2.5 Understand interrelationships between people and their environment.

3.2.6 Understand how our social, political, and economic structures have evolved from structures of other times and places.

3.2.7 Value the prudent use of natural resources so that they can be enjoyed by future generations.

3.2.8 Understand and appreciate the vital role that family, school, and church play in the life of the community.

3.2.9 Understand the essential role of government and law in human affairs.

3.2.10 Recognize that humanitarian service to others, regardless of ethnic, cultural, social, or linguistic background, is a Christian responsibility.

3.2.11 Understand that the quality of life rests not only upon the economic well-being of society but also upon the spiritual, moral, and social conditions.

3.2.12 Understand and appreciate the influence of Judeo-Christian values on Canada's cultural heritage.

3.3.8 Prize integrity, patience, gentleness, and similar positive elements of character.

3.3.13 Appreciate their privileges and responsibilities as members of their family and community.

■ Do these objectives, taken as a group, adequately encompass the four "great injunctions"? Are there any objectives that you would delete? add? What are the implications of these objectives, taken as a group, for a school's social studies curriculum? How would the resulting social studies program differ from ones with which you are familiar?

REVISITING THE CURRICULUM ORIENTATIONS

■ Chapter I described four common curriculum orientations: academic traditionalist, technical, deliberative, and constructivist. The main reason that persons in one orientation seldom convince others of their point of view is that they hold different worldview presuppositions. Review the orientations by listing two or three of the basic beliefs that undergird each one.

The four Biblical mandates described earlier in this chapter delineate some contours for a Biblical worldview and, hence, some overall guidelines for school curriculum. We know from the Great Mandate, for instance, that as stewards of God's creation we have servant leadership rights and responsibilities for which we prepare our students. One emphasis of the Great Commission is that we teach our students the nature of a Christ-like life of discipleship, including modeling and emphasizing values such as compassion, self-sacrifice, and integrity. The Great Commandment and Great Communion enjoin us to choose curriculum content and structure our schools so that students understand and experience what it means to love your neighbors and bear their burdens, both within and outside the school. All this is not easy to do in a cultural context that promotes individual consumerism and hedonism.

A curriculum based on a Biblical worldview has a greater chance of accomplishing this than the four curriculum orientations of Chapter 1, however. The "basics" of the academic traditionalist orientation, for instance, are not the Biblical basics. The Bible says that basic knowledge does not primarily mean knowing how to read or having insight into the history of Western democracy. Of course, students need literacy and numeracy knowledge and skills to function in society. Schools neglect this important aspect of education at their peril. Also, perennialists are right when they claim that if we do not enculturate students to their heritage they will lead impoverished lives, and, indeed, our whole civilization will suffer. In the Bible, however, a lack of basic knowledge means not acting justly and not loving mercy—that is, ignoring Biblical norms (Hosea 4:6; Micah 6:8). Knowledge is in the first place an affair of the heart.

Perennialists in the academic traditionalist have correctly pointed out that the ability to think critically about life's issues is an aptitude that too few people develop. Yet, as Nick Wolterstorff points out, authentic Christians ought to ensure that their religious beliefs function as control beliefs for their thinking (Wolterstorff 1976, 72). Reason always functions within the bounds of faith assumptions that determine one's stance toward life. In Biblical terms, it is our "heart" knowledge/commitment that governs our minds, our intellect. The faith assumption of academic rationalists is that reason itself is the ultimate human value and can answer life's basic questions. Yet it is precisely this faith assumption that has resulted, for one, in the failure of such moral education initiatives as values clarification and Kohlberg's moral reasoning approach.

The technical curriculum orientation has brought to the fore the importance of giving careful consideration to curriculum goals and how such goals can be implemented effectively. In the process, however, the orientation has focused on efficiency to such an extent that it has often neglected more important but less easily measurable goals. Also, in concentrating on the success of the stated objectives, this orientation has overlooked other, perhaps more significant, effects of a particular approach. Rosenshine's direct instruction method may well improve students' short-term long division skills, for instance. It is unclear, however, whether those effects can be maintained for a long period, or whether its narrow emphasis on individual students solving the algorithm in isolation may inhibit other abilities or applications. The technical orientation emphasizes narrowly-defined conceptual and skill knowledge and does little with the Biblical values embedded in the "great injunctions."

The deliberative orientation poses basic questions that need to be asked: "What is the right thing to do?" This orientation does not specify, however, on what ground this question is to be answered, or what to do when educators give very diverse answers to the direction in which they want to go. Persons favoring this orientation could promote the Great Mandate and the Great Commandment, but could just as easily reject them. Nevertheless, if a curriculum team shares common beliefs and values, a deliberative orientation with its emphasis on hermeneutics as a tool for extending understanding and meaning yields a more thoughtful approach to curriculum planning than the technical one.

Finally, while a constructivist orientation encourages children to use their gifts to the fullest, ultimately it promotes a self-centered individualism. It does not recognize that God has created a reality that we care for and unfold, but holds that we create reality and meaning in and of ourselves. Its emphasis on personal construction of knowledge and meaning neglects the cultural embeddedness of knowledge and the shared communal values we need to function as a caring society. Its belief in the innate goodness of all people leads it to assume that students will choose not only their own useful and constructive values but also their own preferred modes of work with little or no habituation or focused skill development. Constructivists will allow students themselves to adopt or reject the "great injunctions." As such, constructivists reject the notion that there are universally binding mandates.

In short, persons holding to any of these four views have seen something about education that is important. By absolutizing certain assumptions, however, they have adopted approaches that at best are limiting, and at worst distort schools into institutions where students will have difficulty serving as stewardly, loving, responsible, and responsive images of God.

TOWARD A BIBLICALLY-GROUNDED CURRICULUM ORIENTATION

This book develops the framework and implications of a Biblical curriculum orientation. In this chapter I describe some Biblical groundings for curriculum. In particular, I develop a guiding vision for life and education that undergirds much of what follows. Also, I consider the purpose of schooling. In this section I take another step and list some ingredients of a Christian orientation to curriculum. I develop these further later in the book.

The overall aim of Christian schooling is to help students understand and exercise personal and communal responsive discipleship. To do so:

1. The *role of teachers* is more than that of facilitators. They are religious craftspersons who use and develop their teaching skills reflectively within a well-defined philosophical/religious framework. This framework enables them to guide their students. Such guidance takes place through unfolding curriculum content that advances a Christian worldview. It also occurs by implementing classroom structures through which students experience the four great Biblical injunctions. Teachers do not indoctrinate students by demanding unthinking regurgitation or uncritical compliance with specific views. Rather, they help students attain a knowledge and skill background that allows them to grapple with important issues and concerns. Teachers witness to a Christian view but accept their fallibility and do not attempt to force adherence to particular interpretations (Gesch 1993a, 8). Thus they enable students to take on life's tasks capably and responsibly.

2. *Learning strategies* are based on students being unique images of God called to serve each other in the Great Community. The rhythm of preparing, presenting, practising, and responding in learning allows all students to exercise their gifts to the fullest at some point during any unit. A mixture of individual, whole group, and small group learning helps students see the need to develop their gifts in order to obey the Great Mandate. They then also see how they can contribute their gifts to the classroom community for the good of the whole.

3. The *content of the curriculum* is based in students' own experiences of God's created reality. Teachers choose content related to students' experience in the past, or they allow students to consider and explore an aspect of God's creation at the beginning of a unit or topic. The teacher then helps students to analyze, develop, and respond to the concepts and issues in a more formal and abstract way, at a level appropriate to their age. At least four criteria govern the choice of content. First, the students are able to recognize the content's significance in their own lives and in society-at-large. Second, the content acquaints students with the strengths and weaknesses of their cultural heritage and explores questions of significance to our nation and culture. Third, the content helps students develop the skills necessary for functioning effectively in society, including the ability to weigh various viewpoints and interpretations. Fourth, it develops attitudes, values, dispositions, and commitments based on a careful consideration of the worldviews affecting culture. In this way, the content encourages them to consider and adopt a Christian vision of life that affects their decisions about personal and social phenomena and issues.

4. The *evaluation procedures* promote student and teacher growth. As such, there is a wide range involving formative assessment by the teacher, self- and peer-evaluation, and reflection on the degree to which teachers and students attain pre-set personal teaching and learning goals. We evaluate students in terms of our goals and standards, not just for their intellectual progress, but also for their spiritual, moral, aesthetic, social, emotional, and physical growth.

5. The *curriculum planning process* is based on clear intents and goals relating to a Christian worldview: "How are we going to tackle this topic in faithfulness to Scripture?" The designers and implementers continually ask about the effects of curriculum plans and their implementation on teachers and students. Consequently, any curriculum plan is implemented flexibly, with schools, teachers, and students revising the plans constantly as particular needs become clear.

SUMMARY

A Christian school that promotes a Biblical worldview will recognize that while Christians are not of the world, God does call them to be in the world. It encourages the positive engagement of Christians in society on the basis of four great injunctions. It does not see Christian faith as something that provides icing on top of the cake of secular, objective scholarship. All its learning takes place within the context of God's faithful provision of laws by which we can live—physical laws as well as what Scripture calls God's precepts.

A Christian school will, in short, consciously ask whether all aspects of the content and structure of its curriculum contribute to helping students be and become responsive disciples of Jesus Christ. The curriculum develops "knowledge-that" (concepts), "knowledge-how" (skills), and creative talents. But it does not do so as an end in itself. Through these concepts, skills, and experiences, the curriculum develops values, dispositions, and commitments that reflect God's calling for our lives: to obey the Great Mandate, the Great Commission, the Great Commandment, and the Great Community.

REFLECTING

1. Marxists, followers of Islam, and secular humanists, to name just three, have seen clearly that their worldviews affect school curriculum. They have all established schools based on their beliefs. Consider a non-Christian worldview with which you are familiar. How would the curriculum of a school based on its principles differ from a public school in your area? How would both differ from a Christian school curriculum based this chapter's worldview?

2. Read the thematic statement and four objectives for a unit dealing with Canada's aboriginal people. In what ways do these reflect the Christian worldview described in this chapter? What changes, if any, would you suggest to ensure that the unit deals explicitly with all four of the great injunctions?

The aboriginal people of Canada have responded to God's creation in unique ways and have formed a distinct culture that differs substantially from the European way of life. In this unit students will investigate how the Haida people and members of a local tribe have expressed and experienced their vision of life. The students will examine how aboriginal and European interaction has affected the aboriginal way of life, and how aboriginal people live today. They will consider personal and communal obligations that would provide justice for aboriginal people and allow diverse cultures to live responsibly in God's world.

»to compare and contrast the Haida vision of life with Western humanist, pantheist, and Biblical ones.
»to explore how Canada's aboriginal people have enriched our nation.
»to foster a sense of empathy and responsibility toward aboriginal Canadians and their communities and families.
»to examine how Christians (aboriginal and others) can exercise their responsibilities with respect to local aboriginal peoples.

3. Make a one-page outline of points you would include in a statement that describes your personal curriculum orientation. Save this outline and update it each time after you read the next three chapters.

Chapter 3
Values and
the Curriculum

■ "What makes your junior high school unique?" I asked Doug Monsma, assistant principal of the West Edmonton Christian School. "It has to do with our fundamental convictions," he answered. "We constantly ask why we do things. The notion of *servanthood* is at the basis of everything that goes on. At a staff retreat we pledged to help our students experience discipleship as a lifelong calling. This includes teaching thematic units that make students critically aware of God's complex world. It also means building a school community that heals brokenness through frequent acts of restoration, also in our discipline. As a school community we constantly try to stress 'us' over 'me.' It helps that our homeroom teachers usually spend at least half the school day with their class, even in grade 9.

"We try to develop spirituality and involve our students in service projects. We encourage them to speak up about their faith. We set up cross-grade prayer families. Students lead our biweekly assemblies. The other day they role-played and discussed how some classmates get hurt when others form a tight-knit clique. Our students also volunteer in a thrift store and arrange food hampers for needy families. Older students help younger ones with reading or supervision. We seek to foster a servant attitude throughout the school. We stress that servanthood puts the needs of others first without looking for recognition.

"At least once per year we also have a junior high theme week that includes all students and teachers. Here we break cross-age barriers in experiential settings. We've chosen the topics carefully to tie in with servanthood: world hunger, our environment, celebrating our creativity. Our last one we called 'Can you still see the tiger?' We considered those parts of childhood that are worth hanging on to: imagination, wholesome laughter, child-like faith, love of stories, risking art and drama, creating games—in other words, the ability to see the imaginary tigers in the oil company ads. The students ate it up because they could respond and be genuine without worrying about peer pressure. And they also learned much about how children develop.

"We try to provide units with real life settings where learning is done as part of discipleship training. Students, as much as possible, learn through experience. They react to real situations. We emphasize their responsibility to discover and share their gifts, and relate this to a Christian lifestyle. But for any subject matter to be meaningful, it must be taught and learned in a community that is inclusive, accepting, and celebrative. Our peer support program has become an integral part of our curriculum—a powerful health course! It has changed our teaching styles to more experiential ones. It generally also creates a better tone in the classroom. It overcomes, for instance, awkward partner and grouping situations that can occur with cooperative learning.

"The program involves sixteen girls and five boys this year (one out of five students). There's good sampling from different social groups and types of students. The applicants we accept go on a two-day team-building and training retreat. They then have weekly sessions on Biblical servant leadership in a school setting. The students themselves decide their goals and activities each year. Last year's group, to strengthen the school as a community of learners, set up a student-run tutoring system during lunch hours. They also became daily 'hallway walkers' who modeled and encouraged positive talk and behavior, and resolved conflicts. They did so without other students realizing that this was part of the program. Finally, they were available for friendship and informal conversation about situations fellow students faced. We train them to be 'listening ears' but to refer rather than solve problems. Significantly, theme units such as *Taking Care of God's Earth* take on additional meaning as students learn to care for each other."

List the values that Doug, his principal and the staff set out to teach their students. How do these relate to the Great Mandate, the Great Commission, the Great Commandment, and the Great Community? Is Doug Monsma right when he claims that schools should plan programs like peer support ones as part of the curriculum just as they do regular subjects? Or does the school then usurp the role of the home or church? Are initiatives like this necessary only in an age of weak family nurture? Or should this type of emphasis be part of any school? Why or why not?

NURTURE AND INDOCTRINATION

Schools cannot function without instruction. Instruction, however, is a means to an end, not an end in itself. Instruction helps students learn essential concepts and skills. Yet instruction in ecological stewardship may result in students who know all about such stewardship but who are not inclined to apply this in their lives. Instruction introduces students to concepts and skills. But the nurturing dimension of schooling goes beyond this. Nurture sets out to develop attitudes, foster the acceptance of values, instill dispositions, and encourage commitments in harmony with an underlying worldview.

Some argue that such nurture is unwarranted indoctrination. They hold that education must first of all develop individual rational autonomy. Such autonomy enables persons to justify and choose their own values on the basis of their own reasoning. Therefore they claim that religious "autonomy" to stand up and be counted for values in which a person believes is not real autonomy. Such "autonomy," they point out, depends on faith assumptions and a community ethos accepted in trust—not just on rational justification. Thus educational nurture rooted in religious or other faith values undermines real autonomy. It promotes a priori submission to specific moral precepts.

This objection to nurture as a task of the school is not tenable, however. First, education always involves initiation and socialization. Although these lessen as persons mature, they are necessarily based on certain value assumptions (Thiessen 1993, 253). Besides, if indoctrination means teaching a point of view without giving reasons or evidence, then rationalists are also guilty of indoctrination. They hold that rationality needs no justification and assume that reason alone gives us ultimate answers. This is an a priori value position in itself.

Of course, indoctrination that plans to withhold or misuse evidence has no place in education; nor does indoctrination that fails to develop normal rationality or independence, or that deters students from examining all sides of controversial issues (Thiessen 1993, 240). Such indoctrination takes place when sex education programs fail to give the physical, emotional, and social benefits of abstinence before marriage. It also occurs when history books deliberately suppress religious motives and causes. Some Christians similarly skew evidence—they unfairly label many fantasy novels as "New Age."

However, allowing students to reach their own decisions about the values they adopt is also a form of indoctrination. This approach conceals the difficulties and consequences of individuals personally choosing values in society. It minimizes the importance of common value threads that weave our cultural tapestry into an operative one. It also withholds the historical evidence that cultures decline if they fail to uphold a commonly-held ethos that includes honesty and respect for others. Clearly, indoctrination occurs in both public and Christian schools, and that some of it is unwarranted.

Aristotle claimed that students develop rationality best only after families and schools have habituated them into life's important values. Critics of values-based nurture have yet to disprove that claim. At a young age students learn a great deal about life from adult role models, by reacting to values embedded in stories and by experiencing and practicing virtues. They have an intuitive sense of what is right and wrong. It is only gradually, however, that they learn to develop full-fledged arguments for value positions they hold or reject.

Schools cannot avoid indoctrinating students in the early years of schooling. Kindergarten classes cannot function without teachers initially insisting that some behavior is desirable (e.g., punctuality) and some is unacceptable (e.g., speaking out of turn). Kindergarten teachers may instruct their five-year-old pupils how to resolve interpersonal conflicts. By that they implicitly indoctrinate them to value the principle that conflicts ought to be dealt with in open, loving, and peaceful ways. Wise teachers give reasons for their actions and involve their classes in making decisions about classroom procedures and curriculum choice. But only much later can students stand back and in a formal way think through the validity of value positions.

Therefore teachers need to consider with their parent communities which values their school structure and programs ought to foster. For Christians, both the instruction and nurture components of schooling are rooted in the four Biblical injunctions described in chapter 2. The Great Mandate shows the importance of responsible stewardship as we unfold the potential of God's creation. The Great Commission encourages personal and communal discipleship based on righteousness and justice. The Great Commandment values unselfish love for God and neighbor. The Great Community upholds the value of using our gifts to serve others and our communities. All these are desirable ideals and qualities for Christians and for society-at-large.

■ Mark Holmes writes that "the word [indoctrination] is usually confined, in talk of education, to those situations where it is deemed unacceptable, without much consideration being given to those situations where it is assumed to be acceptable" (Holmes 1992, 90). He goes on to say that if indoctrination implies rejection of any authority other than empirical evidence or personal rationality, then indoctrination occurs not only in religious education but also when teachers teach the desirability of safe sex or of narrow forms of environmentalism (91). He adds that even in science we indoctrinate. We teach many assumptions as truth when they "are really no more than generally accepted theories (and sometimes not even that)" (93). Give some examples of indoctrination that you have experienced in school. Was the indoctrination legitimate or not? Why or why not? On what basis did you decide?

■ Robert Irvine Smith claims that classroom practices that stem from a commitment to objectivity actually promote a cluster of substantive values. First, teachers who implement such practices are committed to the overriding importance of rationality, the moral autonomy of each person, and respect for other persons. Despite their commitment to impartiality, however, they also tend to have predictable views on issues such as media censorship, apartheid, gender discrimination, bigotry, and authoritarianism—some of which are less rational than others (Smith in Tomlinson and Quinton 1986, 83). If it is impossible for teachers to be neutral or impartial, how can they be fair-minded? To what extent and at what point should teachers' own views on issues become known to their students?

VALUES EDUCATION

Values education refers to everything schools do that affects or intends to affect students' attitudes, tendencies, conduct, decision-making, or commitments. Values are more than rules. Rules, though often based on values, are specific and transitory. Values, on the other hand, are general and long-lasting. They are conceptions of ideals or desirable guides for living deemed to be important. They set direction in life, giving it meaning and purpose. Because values are often "caught" rather than taught, schools should carefully consider how they affect students' values, both implicitly and explicitly.

Educators often use the terms *values education* and *moral education* interchangeably. Values education, however, is broader than moral education. Values include but go beyond personal moral values such as honesty, forgiveness, and fidelity. The overarching Great Commandment to love God and neighbor enjoins us to recognize the dignity and worth of all persons as images of God. Within that scope, schools need to uphold many other values.

Spiritual values include the worth of life-affirming faith as well as devotion and piety. Political values that schools nurture are justice, respect for authority, and the importance of balancing personal and communal rights and responsibilities. Aesthetic values include beauty and harmony. Economically, school programs promote stewardship in managing resources. Socially, schools foster respect for others, cooperation, trusting and unselfish relations, kindness, faithfulness, and loyalty. They also value clear, eloquent, and authentic communication. In the logical domain, schools uphold respect for truthful reasoning and the ability to develop lucid and convincing arguments. Psychological values that we nurture are emotional balance, sensitivity to others, self-control, perseverance, and prudential courage. Key biological and physical values are respect for life and physical things. All these point back to one or more of the four great Biblical injunctions.

The way we plan and implement curriculum is rooted in specific values. We cannot but help but foster values in our students. If we teach a fact it is God's truth and as such has value. By teaching it we are also telling the students that we ourselves or our culture considers it to be important—a value in itself. Often our curriculum teaches the value that empiricists hold dear, viz., that what is important in life is neutral knowledge based on empirical observation. Empiricists draw a sharp (but untenable!) boundary between facts and values. They hold that facts are objective truth; values, subjective opinion based on feelings and beliefs. As such, values are relative and private. Schools should deal only with objective truth. Both this narrow cognitive emphasis and ethical relativism have prevented schools from doing their part to instill universal values.

Thomas Lickona says that schools may not continue to abandon their role to transmit society's values. School programs often imply that students (or communities) may choose whatever values they deem best. In other words, truth is what works for you at a particular time; there are no absolutes. Yet, Lickona points out, to survive and thrive, society needs basic values such as justice, honesty, civility, dependability, democratic process, and a respect for truth. He adds that the two most important questions we face are: "How can we live with each other?" and "How can we live with nature?" (Lickona 1991, 20-21). To help students face these questions, schools should consciously base their structures and programs on well-defined values. Not to do so undermines the task of educators to nurture children as loving, principled, and contributing members of society.

Enculturating children to Biblical values is not easy. Schools need to enculturate students to be followers of Jesus while acculturating them to function in a society that adheres to few of His values. Consequently, helping students exercise their gifts as apprentices of the Christian life is difficult, particularly in an environment that promotes individualism, aggression, and consumerism (Hauerwas and Westerhoff 1991, 269-273).

We live in a world where, as I write this, armed conflict has killed 1.5 million children under fifteen, and left six million physically disabled in the last decade. We live in a world filled with addiction to substance abuse, to violence, to pornography and illicit sex—all of which, as former sex addict Jack Nittel put it, "dissolve the hard boundaries of a jangled world and grants, for a moment at least, the illusion of kinship with God" (*Vancouver Sun*, Dec. 18, 1993, D11). Our pervasive and dominating media generally oppose Biblical values. Our society glorifies reaching materialistic ends by whatever means possible. There will be tension as schools nurture students to be in the world but not of it (John 17:14-18). But in our present situation nurture in Biblical values and norms is critical.

Most students accept and act on Christian values only if their general environment supports such values. Research since the 1920s consistently shows that by themselves neither didactic methods nor learning to reason about value questions have much lasting effect on students' value dispositions. Analyzing and considering values formally must be accompanied with creating a positive school ethos and moral climate (Kilpatrick 1992, 226). The values that operate in the students' home and church communities also need to be consistent with what the school teaches. If a wide gap exists, a school's explicit curriculum will have little effect on students' behavior, values, and commitments.

Nevertheless, with concerted effort, schools can make a difference in children's lives. Thomas Lickona (1991) describes how the California Child Development Program has made measurable and lasting differences in children's moral thinking, attitudes, and behavior. Without affecting academic learning, students in this program cooperate, help, and encourage more spontaneously. They show more concern toward others without becoming less assertive than students in control groups.

How does the Child Development Program accomplish this? Students experience and discuss diverse prosocial situations such as building community as they set rules cooperatively. They participate in helping relationships such as cross-age tutoring. They regularly learn cooperatively in groups. Schools use developmental discipline that foster self-control. Teachers use children's literature deliberately to develop empathy and understanding of others. Moreover, a home program ensures that parents not only understand and support the initiatives but also implement the same goals at home. Family homework, for instance, includes discussing reading selections about common family situations (Lickona 1991, 25, 29, 112, 402-04).

To be effective, schools need to plan moral and values education comprehensively. Curriculum content alone has little long-lasting effect. Schools should implement a total program of nurture that goes beyond the direct instruction of values. The whole school milieu should lend itself to recognizing and addressing ethical and unethical thought and behavior. Teachers should help students develop wholesome and operative commitments. A trust relationship with their students is essential for teachers to foster action based on responsible value decisions.

■ Think about the point of view taken in the following three quotes. If you agree, suggest some curriculum implications. If you disagree, formulate your own alternate value position and describe its implications.

»Concerning the secular program of study felt necessary in American schools to allay charges of indoctrination: "Exclusion of religious perspectives is anything but neutral or fair. Students need to learn that religious and philosophical beliefs and practices are central to the lives of many people. Omission of discussion about the religious and philosophical roots of developments in history, economics, literature, and other subjects gives the student the false impression that only nonreligious ways of seeing the world are valid." (Haynes 1993, 32)

»Concerning a proposal to meet the needs of the mathematically weakest in designing curriculum and allocating staff and material resources: Is it fanciful to suggest that such a reordering of priorities by mathematics educators would accord with a Christian framework of values? Christians have always to give special care to the poor, usually taken to mean the poor in wealth. In modern western society, the poor in mathematics and the poor in wealth are frequently the same . . . In today's schools, the poor in mathematics rapidly become the poor in spirit, and an education based on Christian values would give their needs priority over the needs of their more able contemporaries. (Bryan Wilson in Tomlinson and Quinton 1986, 107)

»Concerning "forming" Christians in a Christian school: "Worship would be at the heart of [the Christian school's] life. . . . In the place of singing the national anthem and saluting the flag, the community would pray for the nation and its leaders. While supporting athletics, there would be no spectator sports, and non-competitive, non-aggressive games would be encouraged. Students would be awarded for cooperation and other Christian values. Communal projects would dominate over individual ones. . . . Faculty would be expected to set an example in terms of simplicity of life, compassion and service to those in need, prayer and meditation, and the stewardship of life and resources. . . . The school would be concerned about how people treat each other and would encourage relationships between blacks and whites, rich and poor, young and old, wise and simple, and males and females that make friendship possible. Groupings based on age and ability would be avoided." (J. Westerhoff in Hauerwas and Westerhoff 1992, 279-280)

VALUES EMBEDDED IN CURRICULUM RESOURCES

Textbooks often frame classroom learning experiences. As such, they play an important role in transmitting the economic, social, and moral views of political and educational leaders. To gain market acceptance, today's textbook authors try to be objective and avoid controversy. However, as I showed in a study of Canadian elementary textbooks (Van Brummelen 1991), authors generally promote those values currently held by persons responsible for making decisions about textbook use. The texts chosen influence both teachers' and students' beliefs, values, and attitudes (Klein 1985, 14).

Value bias in individual selections is often easy to discern. One story in the widely-used *Impressions* reader describes a girl wondering about Christmas. Since a wise woman did not want to tell her, she goes out to search for it. Eventually, she finds a green glass bottle that she fills with branches of red berries and pine: ''And lo! it was Christmas!'' The last line, in script, is: ''*Christmas is not only where you find it; it's what you make of it*'' (Trina Schart Hyman in Booth 1985, 170-184).

This selection fosters several values. First, wise adults do not tell you about important things in life. It is best to find out values and meaning yourself through experience and exploration. Second, whatever value you assign to an object or event, that will be its value for you. You alone choose and assign meaning. Community or cultural values are unimportant. Third, it is up to you alone to make something of whatever you face in life. Here the individualistic and existential values are clear.

In my study, I went beyond identifying biases of specific selections, however. I teased out underlying values that pervade textbooks as a group. I described, for instance, how Canadian textbook authors promote the idea that our technology and our economic system guarantee continued progress. Such progress centers on an ever-improving consumer lifestyle, not on social justice or moral integrity. The authors also foster the notion that personal courage and persistence are the basic ingredients of success and happiness. Families are arbitrary groups of people who band together for common advantage. Although authors avoid obvious sexism and racism, they neglect the existence of unjust social structures and barriers. Overtly they favor multiculturalism. Yet throughout the books they give the implicit message that to be content all citizens should fit into the dominant individualistic, materialistic, western way of life.

Textbook authors do foster certain traditional moral values. Do unto others what you would have them do to you. Avoid personal dishonesty, theft, and greed. Hard work and ingenuity lead to personal gain. Yet the authors avoid discussing moral dilemmas, giving students few opportunities to consider moral value problems. Nor do they deal with the need for making long-term value commitments. They uphold obedience to rules and laws but only to prevent procedural hassles. They fail to give any rationale or ethical basis for what the founders of Canada called "peace, order, and good government." As such, they do not encourage students to consider or analyze communally-held values that undergird life in a democracy. By their almost universal absence, except when discussing aboriginal cultures, the authors also imply that faith and religion are irrelevant.

In short, textbook authors attempt to conform students to a narrow, consumer-oriented, individualistic autonomy: "Everything is possible when I am me." Such influence goes beyond textbooks. *Channel One* shows daily ten-minute news programs in many American schools that includes two minutes of commercials. Research indicates that students who watch the program regularly are more likely than those who do not to agree that money is everything and that wealthy people are happier than the poor. They also say more often that designer labels make a difference and that they want what they see advertised (Greenberg and Brand, 57). Note two points. First, what schools teach does influence students more than commercials watched at home (in the case of *Channel One*). Second, most public school texts and resources promote values at odds with those of Christianity, the religion to which the majority of English-speaking people in the West at least formally adhere. Impartiality is notable for its absence.

VALUES EMBEDDED IN CURRICULUM ORIENTATIONS

Not only textbook authors but all curriculum planners develop and implement programs based on deeply-held value presuppositions. Educators in each of the four curriculum orientations described in the first chapter promote certain values. Academic traditionalists foster faith in absolute truths, hard work, respect for authority, and the power of reason. Technicists teach students that what is most important in life is learning concepts and skills as efficiently as possible, and accepting willingly the social control that leads to such efficiency. Persons in the deliberative orientation do not all agree on what "good" they should promote. Often, however, their writings recognize the importance of human freedom, justice, compassion, personal response to knowledge, and creativity and imagination (see, for instance, James B. Macdonald in Pinar, 101-13 and 156-74). Constructivists promote human worth, autonomy, and the capacity to create knowledge and meaning.

These values differ significantly in some ways. Yet, as C. A. Bowers points out, the underlying theories share some common assumptions that are rooted in the western liberalism of the Enlightenment. The first assumption is a faith in rationality as the sole arbiter of the affairs of everyday life. Second, human nature is good or at least can become so through education. Third, it follows that change is inherently positive. Finally, the individual is the basic social unit "within which we locate the source of freedom and rationality" (Bowers 1987, 2).

Thus all four curriculum orientations teach students to view themselves as autonomous, self-directing individuals. Academic traditionalists emphasize the importance of a general knowledge background so we have content on which we can exercise our power of rationality. Technicists hold that students can master our world as long as we provide the right environment and procedures. Most deliberators believe that personal interpretation and reflection will fulfil students' quest for meaning. Constructivists say that individual learners create patterns, guidelines, and rules to exercise and fulfil their personal independence. Even neo-Marxist critical theorists posit that individuals through personal critical reflection can work toward emancipation and empowerment (Pinar and Bowers in Grant 1992, 181). That is why David Purpel in his book *The Moral and Spiritual Crisis in Education: A Curriculum for Justice and Compassion in Education* (1989) in the end concludes that humans can construct a world of love, justice, and joy through their own creative powers.

The dominant emphasis on individual autonomy in all four curriculum orientations has led to value judgments made personally and subjectively. Little sensitivity remains that freedom requires restriction of the self for the sake of others. Strangely, rights and freedom are held to be independent of goodness and responsibility. As a result, says John F. Alexander, our culture has produced a billion free and prosperous but empty people. He adds that our society is playing with FIRE, that is, it has dedicated itself to the self, to *my* Freedom, *my* Individualism, *my* Rights, and *my* Equality. And *my* opinion on any subject is just as good as everyone else's (Alexander 1993, 202-04). Individual selfishness has replaced mutual servanthood.

Particularly in the latter half of the twentieth century, commercial interests have exploited the FIRE assumptions that most proponents of the four orientations share. The consequence is that for a large proportion of our population, the pursuit of material self-interest is the ultimate goal of individual freedom, a pursuit that ultimately enslaves. At the same time, the focus on the self-realization of the individual has undermined responsible mutual concern, weakened social commitments, and made the outlook for maintaining wholesome community and civic life "increasingly problematic" (Bowers 1987, 23; Lickona 1993, 6).

■ List, together with strengths and weaknesses, the main values advanced by each of the four curriculum orientations. On this basis, define and justify the values you believe the school curriculum should nurture. Suggest how you could promote these values for a specific curriculum topic.

BIBLICAL VALUES AND THE CURRICULUM

■ Read the following three descriptions of learning situations. For each, decide which values the students are learning, both directly and indirectly. Consider to what extent these reflect a Biblical value perspective. Would you make any changes to foster the values you want to advance in the curriculum?

»Teachers Bruce Hildebrandt and Paul Smith plan an election simulation for their school's seven, grades 4-7 classes. Each class represents one riding and has candidates for three parties with pre-determined platforms on public works, the environment, curriculum content, criminal justice, arts and entertainment, social services, and taxes. The Leafy Green Party, for instance, will give each student a job to do at lunch or recess, allow them to choose their assignments, let the girls choose physical education activities for the whole class, insist on reusable lunch containers (with offenders doing several hours of public service work), have a subsidized canteen for everyone, and provide a free entertainment video—but also have a high tax levy on all students. The party that forms the government is to carry out the policies for one school day.

Each student writes a short essay to support the policies of one party. The teachers use the essays to select a candidate for each party in each class. All students choose roles in the campaign. The roles reflect their own abilities and interests: campaign worker, debater, poster designer, maker of radio commercials, pollster, returning officer, etc. The class discusses how to conduct a fair, ethically responsible campaign. The teachers encourage the students to foster care and concern for other candidates. That leads the students to conduct a campaign without slander or personal attacks. Supporters of one party even help others with posters and speeches. The students also compare their campaign with the nation-wide election taking place at the same time. They pray for God's guidance and for personal integrity in both campaigns. They also investigate how they can be a constructive influence in the political process.

»The 75 primary students sit facing each other on mats arranged in a large square in the multipurpose room, each grade level on one side of the square. A grade 1 student begins the assembly with prayer and the grade 1s then teach an action song, "I love Jesus," to all students and teachers. The kindergartners tell and show some things they have learned about fall, and teach the other children a song about shaking the apple tree. The grade 1s use a life-size cut-out of a person to share their knowledge of organs and other body parts, emphasizing that God made each person special. The grade 2s have the others guess what they have been learning about ("it hides in dark places," "it has eight legs"), and do a choral recitation on spiders. The grade 3s share what they learned about water and rain. The grade 3 teacher explains the four-house system for intramural games, which, to emphasize community fun, awards points only for participation. At the end, the children learn a new song, "I am the light of the world." They clap along and a teacher commends them for "good singing." About a dozen parents also participate in the assembly.

»Teacher Wayne Lennea teaches grade 10 consumer education. His textbook holds that consumers must make rational decisions based on their favored style and quality of life. Students, it suggests, must choose their own values based on their experiences, and remain flexible to explore and modify their values. They can exercise their voice in the marketplace by comparing the quality and price of various brands. They also increase their self-esteem by how and what they buy (Woods 1982, 1-13).

Wayne disagrees with this approach. He first discusses with his class what the Bible says about wealth and financial freedom. He shares his own definition of wealth: wealth is not what you accumulate but how your life has made a difference. Wealth, in other words, consists of the positive effects your life has had on others. Similarly, he asks students to react to his view that financial freedom is not the ability to purchase all kinds of things, but to be able to meet your basic needs in thankfulness to God. He discusses, for instance, how in North America today we squander resources by buying homes much larger than needed for comfortable living. The students explore what it means to use credit cards and make loans in a responsible way. They discuss whether prosperity is a blessing of God or the result of an unjust system where some go without basic needs. Only afterward do students read and react to the textbook and its themes.

In a 1891 speech republished in 1991, the Dutch theologian and statesman Abraham Kuyper called for Christian action based on repentance and renewal based on God's ordinances of love, mercy, justice, and compassion (Skillen in the introduction to Kuyper 1991, 22). Kuyper said that Jesus never preached revolution. Instead, He "placed the truth over against error and broke the power of sin by shedding his blood and pouring out his Spirit in his own" (Kuyper 1991, 37). In this way Jesus called back both rich and poor to their Father. He instructed his followers to scorn the lust for money and capital that leads to harshness and uncaring greed. Jesus personally demonstrated material self-denial and abundant compassion.

Kuyper then showed how the church, in response to Jesus' teachings, organized a ministry of charity so that no believer would go without the basic material needs. It was the influence of Christianity that, for all its shortcomings, snapped slavery at its root, showed concern for the poor and orphans, and held the accumulation of too much capital in check by forbidding usury. Today, Kuyper continued, the Christian faith should take the lead in opposing self-seeking materialism and in promoting human dignity and compassion.

To do so, Kuyper argued, we should be a God-willed community that alleviates suffering. We ought to ensure that workers are dealt with fairly so they can live as persons created in God's image. Vigorous deeds of love are indispensable; the poor cannot wait a just social structure. Yet the material help of the state should be minimal since the long-term welfare of people and nations lies in individual initiative. This makes it all the more important that Christians strive for economic justice. Faith in God leads not only to eternal life but also to restored human dignity that otherwise dissipates in sin.

Kuyper went on to found a Christian university, become editor of a Christian daily newspaper, and serve as prime minister of the Netherlands. He introduced some of the most progressive labor legislation of his time, basing it on the Biblical values described above. Kuyper's worldview also influenced the Dutch Christian school movement of the early twentieth century. The schools nurtured a humble attitude to life by which pupils would find their worth in Christ and be empowered to find and respond with forgiveness, mercy, and joy (Buytendijk 1922). The curricula emphasized that a Christian life is a total life-style promoting love and compassion for family members and others in society. Christians were to use God's creation and technology to bring about truth, justice, and wholesome conditions throughout society. The textbooks pointed out the results of neglecting such values. One reader, for instance, decried the health hazards of cocoa production and chocolate manufacture (Van Brummelen 1986, 123).

Values are desirable ends, things for which we ought to strive. They are important since they set direction in our lives. As Kuyper realized, values are not to be pursued just for our own betterment or self-interest. Rather, we seek and follow the values that God as creation's Lawgiver has established. Without them, His creation and creatures cannot function in the way that He intended. Kuyper's significance was that his worldview and its values shaped a generation of Dutch society. This generation sensed the need for applying personal faith in family life, politics and the justice system, business and commerce, the media, and the schools.

In schools today, Christians may attempt no less. Our starting point is a personal God as the source of values. Values are not self-imposed, nor subject to pragmatic revision. As Arthur Holmes put it, "What integrates life and gives rise to other values is the supreme end of glorifying, enjoying, and serving [God] in all our creaturely activities" (Holmes 1983, 158). The Bible as God's revelation is the ultimate source of values for Christians. That does not take away from humans the responsibility to define and explore the implications of those guidelines for our present-day society. The two most inclusive values of Scripture that characterize God himself are justice and love. For the Old Testament prophets justice meant granting people what they deserved as images of God—especially care for the underprivileged. In the New Testament Jesus used the word love in a similar way. We need to pursue and apply justice and love, therefore, for all areas of human concern (Holmes 1983, 160).

To present a detailed theory of values is beyond the scope of this book. I will just indicate some Biblically-based values that, I believe, ought to govern life and therefore also permeate life in classrooms, and contrast those with values often held in our society. I will first describe the general Biblical notion of *shalom* and then discuss specific values in various dimensions of life. I also will give some initial suggestions about the implications for curriculum.

Schools ought to seek *shalom*, the biblical peace and justice that heals and restores broken relations with God, with other humans, with self, with other creatures, and with nature. Shalom gives joy to life since it points to the redemptive power of Christ that restores our relationship with God. To experience shalom, schools seek to replace oppression, including abuse, racism, and sexism, with love and justice. They allow teachers and students to exercise their roles in gratitude and obedience and see all tasks, no matter how humble, as God's vocation for them. They honor all for their gifts and roles. They replace selfishness and faith in the autonomy of the individual with self-sacrifice, humility, and servant-hood.

Schools need structures that promote such *shalom*. For instance, teachers can introduce a consistent program of conflict resolution, starting at the kindergarten level. They can use collaborative learning where students learn to share each other's joys and bear each other's burdens. They can involve students in service projects at each grade level, giving them the opportunity to reach out to others within and outside the school. They can choose unit themes and literature selections that encourage students to deal with *shalom*-related issues. They can provide opportunities to celebrate the presence of shalom in the school and community, and to deplore its absence. Teachers can make decisions about curriculum topics, teaching strategies and class activities based on their potential for students to understand and experience *shalom*.

While schools foster the love and justice undergirding *shalom*, they should provide room, nevertheless, for students to explore and develop their own value base and implications. Trying to impose values unilaterally on students is counterproductive and leads to hypocrisy. Students, at the same time, may not undermine the type of community the school tries to establish, even when they disagree with the school's vision.

SPIRITUAL VALUES

Biblical values are all-encompassing. As such, all of life and all of the curriculum is religious in nature. All that God has given us is to be consecrated to His service. Secularization is the attempt to push religious faith out of the public and into the private domain. Where successful, a non-religious faith commitment replaces faith in the God of the Bible. Non-religious idols of our times include faith in individual rationality, faith in economic growth and material prosperity, faith in the power of technology to bring about a better world, and faith in security guaranteed by the government (Goudzwaard 1984). Such idols are the driving force of our society today. They distort the true meaning and purpose of life. Because of their pervasive influence, grasping the importance of Biblical commitment and faith for all of life is impossible without parents, churches, and schools nurturing Biblical values.

Schools, also Christian ones, are academic institutions. As such, their worship focus differs from that of the church. Like the church, Christian schools acknowledge their dependence on God through devotions, praise, and prayer. Teachers also model the importance of godliness and piety in their own lives, praying regularly for and with the students as needs arise. But the academic work of the school day is itself also a form of worship and a channel through which students come to know the Lord. By studying God's creation they consider the praiseworthy deeds of the Lord, and learn to praise Him and put their trust in Him (Psalm 78:4-7). The academic work of the school can also provide an atmosphere that nurtures spiritual commitment and maturity.

A case can be made that all schools ought to promote or at least deal with the worth of life-affirming faith and commitment. The spiritual provides a sense of personal meaning and purpose, something sorely lacking in today's generation. Moreover, evidence shows that a positive correlation exists between church attendance and positive social characteristics among adolescents. Also, at least some Christians bring qualities such as mercy and humility to our political system (Holmes 1992, 103-04).

Such factors suggest that curricula should at least show how people's faith commitments affect their personal lives, their communities, and all of culture. How did the Protestant Reformation shape Western culture for several centuries? Why did the Catholic underpinnings of Quebec lead to the most stable community life in North America during the first half of the eighteenth century? How did a Christian ethos undergird life in nineteenth century America and Canada? How did Biblical faith provide a necessary base for Mother Theresa's work in the slums of Calcutta? How has Hinduism affected Indian culture? What is the role of Islam in countries like Saudi Arabia and Nigeria? More negatively, why are many world political conflicts rooted in religious strife? Such curriculum content will demonstrate the crucial role of religious faith in people's lives.

ETHICAL VALUES

During the last generation, many schools have been reluctant to deal directly not only with the spiritual but also with the ethical dimension of life. This is partly the result of society believing that moral guidelines are nothing more than individual expressions of taste, with no need for communal acceptance (Lasch 1984, 255). Faith in the moral autonomy of individuals has resulted in a society that has lost its moral moorings.

Schools should do their part, therefore, to help students see and experience the importance of the ethical foundations of life: love and compassion for others, honesty and integrity, righteousness and forgiveness, respect for covenant in marriage and family life, and respect for others' property. Such morality, of course, is not for Christians only. Nor does upholding these moral laws make a person a Christian. But it is what God expects. Support for moral laws allows society to function in a human, humane way. That is why an organization such as the Association for Supervision and Curriculum Development can publish a set of "universal" moral guidelines for schools, guidelines that bear a striking resemblance to some (though not all) Biblical moral principles (ASCD Panel 1988). A good guide of moral values for teachers and high school students is Lewis Smedes' *Mere Morality* (1983).

There have been two major approaches to moral values education since the 1970s. These are Sidney Simon's values clarification (1972) and Lawrence Kohlberg's moral reasoning approach (1971). The shortcomings of these approaches to moral education have been extensively documented (Gow 1980; Kilpatrick 1992; Wolterstorff 1980). Let me review the major objections to each.

Values clarification encourages students to consider moral dilemmas and choose values with which they feel comfortable. The difficulty is that values clarification introduces students to complex moral dilemmas when they are not yet equipped with basic values such as respect for truth and respect for others. Students tend to exchange superficial information with their peers. Often they are unable to recognize the far-reaching consequences of their moral decisions. To use one of Simon's own examples, they are left with the belief that the choice of being or not being honest is one that they can make themselves. Many students therefore embrace ethical relativism: the choice to be honest depends on whether you can get away with it. Moreover, values clarification is far from neutral. Sex education programs based on values clarification tell students that they should decide themselves what to do with their sexuality. In other words, no binding rules exist. As Kilpatrick asks, "Why not rape if that's what you want to do? From a relativist standpoint, a question like this can't be answered very satisfactorily" (1992, 64).

Lawrence Kohlberg took a different approach. He believed that all people progress through six stages of moral development (although few reach the sixth stage). By discussing moral dilemmas and helping students reason at one stage above their own, teachers could help students progress from one stage to the next. Subsequent research has shown, however, that the stages are neither as clear nor as sequential as Kohlberg believed, and that the speed-up, in any case, is very slight (Wolterstorff 1980, 90; Leming 1993, 64-65). Moreover, Kohlberg used only boys in his sample, raising the obvious objection that girls may respond and develop very differently.

More seriously, Kohlberg has an unreasoned faith in rationality. There is little evidence that the ability to reason will lead to action based on such reasoning. The apostle Paul already said that what he did was not the good he wanted to do (Romans 7). Also, reasoning always takes place on the basis of certain worldview presuppositions. Kohlberg's own is the (male) western liberal faith in the ability of the autonomous individual to reason out and apply universal, ultimate standards of justice. Kohlberg's scheme has little room for compassion, commitment, or imagination. Moreover, Kohlberg thinks that cultural, family, and religious beliefs frequently hinder moral progress.

Both values clarification and Kohlberg's moral reasoning thus fall short of the mark. Teachers who effectively foster responsible moral action and commitment act as caregivers and models and help students care about each other—something Simon and Kohlberg ignore. They use discipline and conflict resolution techniques to habituate students to respect others and their property, and to obey legitimate authority. For moral tendencies to be internalized, such teachers accompany modeling and discipline by offering reasons, especially those that reveal how others would feel about the consequences of an attitude or act (Wolterstorff 1980, 67). Such teachers also encourage moral reflection "through reading, writing, discussion, decision-making exercises, and debate" (Lickona 1991, 70). They elicit and develop children's internalized moral standards, helping them apply them to the ethical situation presented. All these points are ones missed by Simon and Kohlberg.

Some may object that children in kindergarten or grade 1 as yet have little moral knowledge and commitment. Piaget and Kohlberg's stage theories have nurtured that notion. Those theories, however, focus on abstract, out-of-context reasoning. But children can react to and deal with moral values if presented in story or narrative form. Children benefit, for instance, from Bible stories and other carefully chosen books; they identify with the moral questions presented. Good stories are memorable because all details contribute to the dramatic tension that usually centers on clearly defined moral opposites such as love and hate or fairness and unfairness. Kieran Egan makes a case for structuring all curriculum units at the primary level around what he calls "binary opposites" (see chapter 7). The main point here is that moral narrative can be effective in raising ethical questions and helping children consider what human life ought to be. Children can build a deep and adequate vision of life from a fund of aesthetically rich and powerful literary selections (Kilpatrick 1992, 169).

POLITICAL/LEGAL AND ECONOMIC VALUES

If there is one sin that God condemns through His Old Testament prophets it is that of injustice and oppression: "Administer true justice; show mercy and compassion to one another. Do not oppress the widow or the fatherless, the alien or the poor" (Zechariah 7:9-10). When people refused to pay attention, God's anger left their land—their lifeblood—desolate. God promised restoration, but only when the people again loved truth and peace, rendered true and sound judgments in the courts, and no longer plotted evil against neighbors (Zechariah 8:16-19). While justice and love are values that transcend all aspects of reality, the command to be just has particular relevance for institutions related to the state. Here (public) justice means that treatment of all persons, communities, and institutions in society is even-handed, equitable, and well-balanced (Clouser 1991, 270). Governments and its related institutions have legitimate authority, but God grants such authority so that they enable people and institutions to function in a just, well-balanced way, not to wield power out of self-interest.

God also demands just economic and social structures. Not everyone has equal economic resources or social power. But God wants governments, the courts, and those who control the levers of economic power to treat everyone fairly. Indeed, God does not recognize absolute property rights. God provided land in trust to provide a livelihood. It could be sold and bought, but every fifty years land was to be returned to its original owner. In the same year economic liberty was to be proclaimed for all, with masters setting their servants free. Always, the poor should be able to buy food at cost and borrow money without interest. In short, the principle God established is that society should care for its disadvantaged. "Let justice roll on like a river, righteousness like a never-failing stream!" (Amos 5:24).

Bong-Ho Son argues that Biblical economic justice requires that societies distribute social goods in such a way that they provide all persons with basic needs such as the necessary amount of food, clothes, health care, and education simply because they are human beings, while luxuries be awarded according to one's contributions and achievements. The justice of Amos would thus mean that we protect and uphold everyone's basic rights and needs. Since injustice needs to be corrected, Christians are called to be agents of justice. That means Christians may have to make sacrifices themselves as well as to act responsively wherever we see injustice (Bong-Ho Son 1993, 97-107). E. Calvin Beisner also shows that the Bible demands that where the needy suffer because of injustice, they need justice, and, if not attainable, charity. Even where they suffer because of their own actions, they still need our compassion and mercy (Beisner 1993, 21).

What are the implications for schooling? First, schools and classrooms themselves should model justice and fairness. They set and administer rules fairly. They foster just communities where everyone has an equitable role. They evaluate students justly. All these actions affect how students experience the school curriculum. There may be no favoritism or prejudice in schools.

Curriculum content needs to address how justice is a prerequisite for *shalom*, in our personal lives and in society. Schools themselves cannot correct society's economic and social injustices. The problems we face are so complex that even economists admit they have few answers. Yet our school curricula can foster sensitivity to and a sense of responsibility for social justice. All persons and communities have the right to full participation in society, with access to basic services. Being unemployed prevents persons from exercising their task of contributing to society's well-being, for instance. In high school, students need to examine government taxation and investment policies that favor capital-intensive projects and look at alternate worker-intensive ones. Curricula also need to address justice issues for disadvantaged groups in society such as aboriginal people, the physically or intellectually or socially handicapped, and those who have been abused. Our students should consider structures and policies that encourage all people to contribute positively to life in society.

Schools can only begin to raise questions and explore initial answers as they make students aware of the importance of righteousness and justice. Students should be given opportunities to bring about healing in specific situations, and to reach out with grace where they cannot restore justice. Many schools today do so, particularly at the secondary level. A grade 12 class organizes biweekly recreation activities for jailed young offenders. A grade 11 class regularly helps a youth emergency shelter with maintenance work. A grade 10 class volunteers in a youth drop-in center. A school annually visits an aboriginal settlement, forming a long-term relationship that fosters mutual appreciation of each other's culture. A school reschedules its grade 11 program so that students spend four or five months working in a Third World setting while continuing their own courses by correspondence. All of these are important because students experience situations resulting, in part, from injustice. They also become able to distance themselves from their own community and culture and analyze its injustices.

The economic sphere of life today dominates all others. Society assumes progress means economic progress. At the institutional level, economic progress is in turn defined in terms of increase in the gross domestic product. Business generally strives for profitability and efficiency at all costs. At the personal level, this has meant that corporations use the media to glorify materialism and self-gratification. The underlying value is that economic growth is an autonomous and ultimate good. Yet we see a gross unevenness of capital distribution in the world, often caused by oppression. Even in western nations there is a widening gap between rich and poor. Citizens in Western nations clamor for governments to provide welfare to meet their wants, welfare that politicians cannot provide at a time of little economic growth except through ever-increasing deficits (Goudzwaard 1984, 56).

Wolterstorff argues that the "fundamental worth in our modern world-system . . . [is] increased mastery of nature and society so as to satisfy our desires" (1983, 65). Increased mastery can be beneficial, as advances in medicine show. But when the main aim of mastery is self-satisfaction, it becomes social idolatry. What drives cultural formation today is technological, efficient, rational action leading to modernization. The resulting characteristics of society are impersonality and standardization. This is considered progress as long as it makes available more consumer goods. But we lose values that matter a great deal: personal craftsmanship and skill, a reflective life-style, acting with justice and concern, living with joy and hope without needing all modern technological gadgets and toys. Society mostly views work as a means to satisfy material needs rather than as a way to fulfil one's calling.

Again, schools ought to show a different way from what characterizes the fabric of our culture. Taking care of God's garden means being stewards who hold economic resources in trust so that we can distribute benefits and liabilities equitably. Students should investigate how we can use resources to sustain an economy that provides a living for all. The curriculum upholds the value of individual responsibility, a simple and thankful life-style, fair wages and working conditions, an attitude of caring and sharing for each other.

Teacher Elaine Brouwer does so at the grade 5 level by having her students establish and operate a book publishing company. The students learn about and experience what it means to provide a worthwhile service or product, to raise and use capital responsibly, to decide on a fair level of profit, to ensure that everyone fulfils a responsible role. The students reflect on Scripture passages such as the story of Boaz and Ruth that give some insight into important attitudes in running a business. Students experience the joy of using their own talents to do a job well. They learn to bear each other's burdens as they help each other with difficult tasks. They exercise stewardship in how they use their time and resources, as well as in deciding how to use the profits. They begin to realize what it means to love your customer as yourself in the marketplace. Other schools have set up school stores so that students can learn about economic stewardship as they make and implement decision. In such simple ways students explore Biblical values for cultural formation and economic stewardship.

VALUES RELATING TO
SOCIAL INTERACTION AND PERSONHOOD

We live in a society where individualism and freedom of self-direction has led to self-centeredness, often expressed through competition and aggression as well as prejudice and intolerance. For instance, children no longer play games by themselves in parks. One reason is that parents cannot trust adolescents and adults; they may harm younger children. Another is that our society often takes away from younger children the responsibility to do things themselves. Adults organize official leagues, using adult rules and adult referees. Both reasons underscore the importance of schools fostering positive social and personal values.

Schools, first of all, should teach students to value kindness, loyalty, trust, and unselfish relations with others. They also help students develop values affecting their psychological make-up: emotional balance and self-control, realistic recognition of one's own gifts, sensitivity to others, perseverance and prudential risk-taking, a willingness to take on responsibilities. Teachers develop many of these through carefully structured classroom learning. Schools may also plan specific programs to nurture values such as respect throughout the school.

The content of the curriculum can also address these issues more specifically. Many kindergarten and grade 1 teachers plan units on *God Made Me Special.* At higher levels, units may focus on friendship, family life, personal development, and courtship and marriage. Units on multiculturalism can explore what it means to live in a pluralist society where, on the one hand, the right of minority groups to live by their ideals is celebrated, and, on the other, common social and other values are recognized as necessary for a community to function. Carefully chosen literary selections and works of art also may encourage students to consider what it means to live in families and communities that promote social and psychological *shalom.* In physical education students may learn to invent and carry out group games.

VALUES IN COMMUNICATION AND AESTHETICS

A society driven by a faith in economic growth distorts values in the communication and aesthetic aspects of life. The media, especially through its advertising, have legitimized deception to serve the end of profitability. Average citizens no longer trust the daily print and visual bombardment, whether the source is the media itself, politicians or so-called experts. Meanwhile, they feel voiceless. Canadians expressed this forcefully at the ballot box in 1992 when they rejected a constitution proposal backed by all major interest groups in society.

The school curriculum should help to restore effectiveness, meaningfulness, authenticity and integrity to communication. Theodore Sizer adds that this includes honoring those hearing or seeing and respecting the ideas being communicated by, for instance, listening well (Sizer 1992, 73). This requires an emphasis on oral and written communication skills throughout the curriculum, with teachers modeling honest and forthright communication.

The technical-economic basis of our culture has sidelined aesthetic values. Few of us consider aesthetics central to a meaningful life. Few take the time to create, playfully probe and pursue, understand, appreciate, and find joy in the suggestion-rich beauty, concord, and coherence of aesthetic works. Yet the Bible values beauty and harmony, both as created by God, and by artists and artisans. God enjoins us to take delight in the radiant wonder of His handiwork that shines through all of His creation (Psalms 19 and 104). The fact that God values expressiveness, imagination, and originality is reflected in the way Scripture itself is written. It is also shown in that God delights in our worship of Him through music, poetry, and dance in surroundings aesthetically designed for that purpose (Psalm 149).

Part of our cultural task as images of God is to use our creativity to display and unfold His creation. God calls us to respond aesthetically: in poetry, music and song, as did Miriam and David in the Old Testament; in sculpture and painting, as did Bezalel and Oholiab when commissioned by God and filled with His Spirit for that purpose in Exodus 31. This applies first of all to music, dance, art, literature and drama. But it also concerns how we approach our leisure, our family life, or our work in areas such as mathematics and science. The aesthetic feel of our homes affects the quality of our lives. Without imagination and creative insight into the design of the universe, Einstein would not have developed his theory of relativity. Similarly, students never fail to be surprised and intrigued by the aesthetic wonders of the Fibonacci sequence in mathematics. As a result, at least some will try to apply their creativity in posing and solving mathematical phenomena and problems.

ANALYTIC VALUES

Rationality itself is not the highest human aptitude or value. It is not the essence of selfhood, and it does not answer the most basic questions of the purpose and meaning of life. Yet all intellectual work in schools should foster a respect for truth and the ability to develop coherent, lucid, and convincing arguments. Students should be encouraged to exercise intellectual curiosity, and respond to what they experience and learn with wonder and awe. In the Bible, knowledge, wisdom, and discernment are all closely linked. Critical thinking abilities exercised within a framework of overarching values contribute to developing discernment and wisdom.

Teachers can use case studies rooted in familiar experiences to promote such critical thinking. For young children a story format serves best. Teachers first describe the situation as accurately and completely as possible. They solicit different possible courses of action from the students. They then help students establish the basic value principles that have a bearing on the case, and ask students to reconsider the options in terms of these basic values. The students may immediately rule out some possibilities, and perhaps add others. They decide how the values lead them to favor certain options, and try to predict the consequences of their choices.

Sometimes, of course, several basic values may conflict (e.g., the need to protect the environment and the need to provide work in mining). Then the students have to decide which value(s) ought to receive priority, or whether there is another solution where all values can be upheld. This approach generalizes from moral dilemmas to more general value questions the strategy that Wolterstorff calls casuistry (Wolterstorff 1980, 104-105). The key differences between this approach and values clarification are (1) the reasoning is based on universal Biblical values, not on students choosing their own; and (2) teachers model the values themselves and encourage students to commit themselves to such values.

BIOLOGICAL, PHYSICAL, AND MATHEMATICAL VALUES

The Bible rejects two conflicting views of nature. First, it does not value nature for its own sake, or seek divinity in nature, as New Age thinking often does. The physical creation exists so that creatures can honor God by fulfilling their God-given calling. On the other hand, Scripture also opposes mastery of nature just to satisfy human desires. Such a view leads to unacceptable exploitation. The curriculum, therefore, should emphasize nature's splendor, abundance, and potential to provide for all our needs. Concurrently, it also should foster the need for the preservation and responsible stewardship of the resources God has given to sustain and enrich life. Respect for plant and animal life complements the respect we should show for our own physical lives: health, fitness, and sexual purity. Further, in mathematics we value accuracy and responsible use of numbers and space.

CHRISTIAN AS BEARERS OF HOPE

The French Christian philosopher Jacques Ellul generally presents a bleak picture of the current state of our culture. Technology has become our new god, he says. The impact of Christianity has been reduced to the salvation of individual souls. Our technical-industrial culture has suppressed both meaning and the role of the individual as subject.

Yet, Ellul adds, there is hope. Christians can become iconoclasts who destroy the religious image of technology and see technology for what it is, as nothing but objects that can be useful. They can then become the bearers of freedom and hope in society since they reject the deterministic conditioning of technology (and, I would add, of economic growth), and rest in the affirming love of God. In Him and in Him alone the future is possible and positive (Ellul 1981, 108-110). Justice and love and shalom will not prevail until Christ returns. Meanwhile, however, God calls schools to help students become committed to values that, like points of light, penetrate our cultural darkness.

Can schools do so? Look again at the examples earlier in their chapter. Hildebrandt and Smith's election simulation emphasized fairness, respect and care for others, the importance of stewardship of physical resources, the importance of using and developing God-given gifts to benefit the community, and personal piety. The primary assembly reinforced the beauty and harmony of various aspects of reality, and the satisfaction of using creative abilities in music and choral reading to reflect such beauty. It also helped students develop effective communication skills. Moreover, both the assembly itself and the intramural games invitation reiterated the fun and joy of sharing in the life of the community. Wayne Lennea's consumer education introduction explored the importance of thankfulness when God meets basic needs, and of using our resources to affect positively others and our communities. Through its critical analysis of the textbook, it also fostered respect for truth.

Each example covers only a few of the values I described. The election simulation did little to foster a concept of justice. The assembly did not directly emphasize human care of creation. The consumer education unit dealt only with a few social values. But that is not the point of these examples. Rather, it is that the teachers used them to nurture certain Biblical values, values that point to a more joyful and hopeful life.

Teachers can be bearers of hope when they thoughtfully plan to foster commitment to values such as those described in this chapter. Schools can also ensure that its curriculum at each level fosters values from each category described in this chapter. And, when timely, schools can plan special ways to foster a value such as respect or integrity-- including ones for the halls, playground, office, library, school buses, and, yes, students' homes.

■ Rick Binder together with five other grade 5 and 6 teachers recognize the natural rhythm of the school year, and therefore plan a unit for the last five weeks of the school year that is different and appealing for their students, and yet not too difficult to teach once they design it. They are concerned about some of the racist attitudes that students display, especially toward the large number of Indo-Canadians in their community. The theme of the unit becomes that loving your neighbor as yourself means celebrating cultural differences and building bridges.

The teachers begin the unit with two activities. First, they ask students to complete a survey of their attitudes (e.g., I think Punjabi clothing is beautiful). Then they act out a skit that included all the racial remarks, slurs, and jokes that the teachers had heard over the last year or two. The teachers regroup the five grade 5 and 6 classes into five groups that rotate among the five rooms, three days a week from 10:30 to 12:00. The students all study five "strands": the history of Indo-Canadians in their community, the Sikh religion, contemporary issues facing Indo-Canadian families, food and clothing, and language and music. The strands emphasize concrete experiences: Indo-Canadian speakers, visits to a Sikh temple and the local Sikh market, preparing and eating Sikh food, music performances, and so on. Each student makes a personal scrapbook, and also gives a detailed evaluation of the whole unit. The final culminating activity consists of the teachers acting out the skit again, but now reacting to comments on the basis of what happened during the previous five weeks.

What were the results of the unit? First, the students addressed an issue affecting the whole community. They had very positive experiences with a different culture group. When they completed the attitudinal survey again at the end of the unit, the results were startlingly more positive. The next school year the teachers found that almost all comments about East Indian culture among the students were positive ones. The unit also stimulated parents to talk and think about their own attitudes. Most responded positively and said they had gained some knowledge and understanding. The school plans to teach a similar unit each year, with the focus on different culture groups.

What are some of the primary values nurtured in this unit? How can teachers use the unit to be bearers of hope?

THE IMPLICIT CURRICULUM

■ Jesus addressed many issues of faith and morality explicitly. To do so, he used talks like the Sermon on the Mount, parables, and personal dialogues. He also taught many things implicitly through the example He set in His life. He did not value comfort or wealth. Driving the money changers and merchants from the temple showed the importance he placed on prayer and worship of God the Father. His interactions with women showed that, unlike the Jewish establishment, He believed they were persons of worth. His first miracle of changing water into wine spoke volumes about His view that people should enjoy and celebrate God's blessings.

Besides His explicit and implicit teachings, Jesus also taught us through what He did not do. By not discussing ways and means to overthrow the Romans, He indicated to His followers that political action is not the primary way to spread His teachings. By seldom giving detailed rules He indicated that He wanted people themselves to take responsibility for applying general value norms and principles to their own lives.

A parallel exists in schools. We teach a great deal about values deliberately and explicitly. Our school and classroom ethos and structure teaches values implicitly as well. Moreover, what we leave out, either deliberately or through tradition or neglect, also affects our students' values. Consider, for instance, the physical education and sports programs of a school, and the student evaluation, grading and reporting system used in a school. For each, list the values the school teaches (a) explicitly, (b) implicitly, and (c) by exclusion of certain possible elements.

Schools have an explicit, formal curriculum. That curriculum changes dynamically as teachers implement it in the classroom. Nevertheless, it remains the planned curriculum. Many things happen in the classroom, however, that teachers do not formally plan. Usually they are transmitted through the normal, everyday goings-on in the school. Teachers have certain expectations with respect to behavior, and most students tend to provide teachers with what they expect. The values and ideals of teachers as well as how they view their roles and those of their students and the authority relationship between them will affect students' values. Some researchers have claimed that this implicit or hidden curriculum affects students more than the explicit curriculum. They say that the school's main latent function is to socialize students into what society generally holds to be socially acceptable behavior.

The ethos of a school and of a classroom sets the stage for the implicit curriculum. Some features of such an ethos are positive. Students learn to treat each other with respect. They learn to be punctual and work hard to accomplish both short- and long-term goals. They may learn to solve conflicts with fellow students in a peaceful way. They may learn work habits that will stand them in good stead throughout their lives.

However, the implicit curriculum can also have negative consequences. Academic competition may be stressed to the point where weaker students are labelled or give up trying. The grading system may just be used to rank students, rather than also helping them improve. On the other hand, the opportunity under a mastery learning program to rewrite tests until the students attains 80% may teach students not to take their studies all that seriously since if they fail, they can do it over again. They may learn to manipulate the system to their own advantage. The timetable that includes art during the last hour Friday afternoon leaves the impression that art is unimportant relative to mathematics and language arts. School rules may be so arbitrary that students learn to see authority as a power game which they try to undermine. A driver training program may influence students to want to buy a late model car.

Beane, Toepfer, and Alessi (1986, 192) give another example of the effect of the implicit curriculum. They point out that while almost all teachers would favor peace over war as a way to resolve conflict, a school's implicit curriculum carries a different message. They claim that history lessons often glorify heroes of war rather than peacemakers. Where students or parents have a conflict with the school, the school's institutional power usually prevails, rather than a rational or caring approach. Sports programs emphasize winning at all costs and even humiliating opponents.

Whether or not you agree with Beane et al., the implicit curriculum does influence students' values and commitments both positively and negatively. Teachers need to reflect on the effect of their work and the school environment on students. Such reflection may well lead to changes in structures and approaches. Further, it may mean that teachers in their curriculum planning begin to consider explicitly some aspects of school and learning structures that they traditionally accepted without much thought. This is one of the reasons why this book on curriculum contains a chapter on how pedagogy relates to the curriculum.

- For the four situations below discuss the values nurtured by the implicit curriculum.

»*Setting the tone*: In a kindergarten class, children choose their own learning center during activity time. They themselves regulate that no more than four persons are at a center at a time. For the more popular centers, students operate a timer so that others will get a chance, too. The teacher monitors which children visit various learning centers. If a child always plays with blocks, she may suggest another activity, sit at another center and invite the child to help her, or close the block center for a day or two. The only general rule is that all children must visit the writing center at least once a month.

»*Tracking students*: A high school provides three tracks of mathematics classes. Mathematics specialists teach the advanced classes. They emphasize collaborative learning and special projects, and frequently include computer applications. Teachers with little mathematical background teach the lowest stream. They avoid group work because of the students' negative attitudes in class. Instead, the students daily complete and hand in drill worksheets.

»*Using computers*: Most software in an elementary school computer lab is for drill and practice or tutorials. The programs help students learn and reinforce certain skills. They reward students for right answers. When the lab coordinator is asked about the lack of higher level thinking and the paucity of human interaction, he replies that these programs work like flight simulators that effectively train pilots to fly a complex jet (M. Streibel in Beyer and Apple 1988, 259-288).

»*Arranging special occasions*: Two schools plan for Halloween. (Whether schools should celebrate this festival at all is a question often not even asked.) In the first school the main activity in the primary grades is to color handouts of pumpkins and witches. The teachers display the differently-colored but otherwise identical pictures on the bulletin boards and windows, and read some Halloween stories. In the second school the main activity consists of small groups of students designing costumes and planning and putting on short Halloween skits.

I want to conclude this section by considering the null curriculum. The null curriculum in one sense is infinite. It includes everything that students do not have an opportunity to learn in school. Schools cannot teach everything. Society therefore decides that some things are best left to other agencies or not taught at all. In my community, learning how to swim, play piano, drive a car, or play hockey are parental rather than school responsibilities. Society also considers some things too esoteric or technical or insignificant to be taught in school. Schools do not teach the details of Gödel's proof that mathematical systems cannot be both consistent and complete, nor how to cut the lawn.

Yet for the sake of planning the explicit curriculum we do need to question the commonly accepted null curriculum. Why do very few students study economics when it is the driving force of western society? Why, for instance, does a unit such as Elaine Brouwer's on establishing and operating a book company remain part of the null curriculum even in schools that are aware of the unit and agree that it would be valuable and exciting? Why do most schools fail to acquaint students with civil and criminal law? Why does art become part of the null curriculum for most students in high school when mathematics is compulsory for all? Why, in my province, was health not taught either as a subject or as part of interdisciplinary units for fifteen years? Why do some readers exclude selections with wholesome family situations? Why do most North American textbooks make religious motifs part of the null curriculum? The inclusion or exclusion of each of these topics will affect what students believe to be important in life, and therefore their values.

For both the explicit and the null curricula, a key question is, "On what grounds do we include or exclude certain curriculum content and approaches?" We need to justify our choices on the basis of our worldview and the values we hold to be important. (This is a point I will develop further in chapters 4 and 8.) Simultaneously, once we have justified our choices, we also need to ask whether our implicit curriculum contributes to or detracts from our curriculum intents. Without serious attention to these questions, the general thrust of a school's program will soon promote the technical-economic direction of our secular culture.

SUMMARY

Whether intentionally or not, schools and teachers teach values. Textbooks, course outlines, unit plans, and classroom approaches all embody a blend of the predominant values of our culture and of the educators involved. Teachers should therefore choose carefully the values they nurture. They should ensure, at the same time, that their teaching does not become manipulative indoctrination that prevents normal rational growth and independence.

Values fostered by educators reflect their worldview and their curriculum orientation. Chapter 1 described how academic traditionalists such as the perennialists believe that the highest human attribute is rationality. They also value respect for authority and believe that knowledge consists of universal truths. Those favoring the technical orientation cherish efficiency and objectivity. The deliberative orientation values searching for what is right, and therefore fosters deliberation and reflection. Many in this orientation emphasize the importance of the aesthetic dimension of life. Finally, constructivists prize, above all, personal meaning making and persons being able to choose their own values.

Biblical values do not include moral values only, but also ones relating to the various aspects of reality (see chapter 5). The Biblical notion of *shalom* is a concept of well-being that encompasses basic Biblical values such as peace, love, justice, and truth-values that God intended to frame all of human life and culture. Important, more specific values related to each aspect of reality include:

Aspects of reality	Some key values
Spiritual/confessional	godliness, devotion
Ethical/moral	integrity, fidelity
Political/legal	justice, lawfulness, peace
Economic	responsible stewardship, compassion for the poor
Social	respect, kindness, humility, trustworthiness
Language/communication	authenticity, meaningfulness, clarity
Analytical/logical	validity, discernment
Aesthetic	creativity, expressiveness, beauty
Psychic/emotional	self-control, sensitivity
Physical health	physical wellness, vitality, coordination
Scientific/technological	thankfulness and respect for life and resources
Mathematical	accuracy, responsible use of numbers and space

Christian teachers ought to model the foregoing values, use discipline to uphold them, give reasons for them, and introduce stories and cases that lead students to consider how such universal values apply in particular circumstances.

Schools teach values both through the explicit and implicit curricula. Further, schools also foster (or fail to foster) certain attitudes, values, and commitments through the null curriculum, that is, through what they do not teach. To encourage tendencies and commitments in line with Biblical values, schools and teachers ought to consider, therefore, in what ways their total educational program affects students. Finally, Christian educators can remain bearers of hope as they implement and students experience a curriculum that calls for replacing, in God's strength, the prevailing values of our technical-industrial society with Biblical *shalom*.

REFLECTING

1. Thomas Lickona suggests a list of things teachers can do in their curriculum to encourage and enhance value reflection. One suggestion is to take time to deal with real-life issues involving values from the life of the classroom and the school. Another is to draw out students' own value dilemmas. A third to use role play to foster perspective-taking (Lickona 1991, 266). Make a list of other possibilities. Then design some specific classroom activities for the items on your list.

2. Give some examples of what you consider illegitimate value indoctrination of students. Are there ways to nurture the values in a fair and open way that contributes to students' normal growth in rationality and independence?

3. Choose a fairly general curriculum topic at a suitable grade level (e.g., your local community, trees and forests, weather, the history of your state or province, government, rock music, etc.). Choose some values that you would want to promote in teaching the unit. Then suggest learning activities that would foster the value or cluster of values that you chose. Consider how the implicit curriculum might affect the values you want to foster.

PART II:
Knowledge and Curriculum

Charles Colson (1993) has described the results of what he calls four myths that typify our times. First, the myth of the goodness of people has deluded many into thinking they are always victims. As a result, they shirk personal responsibility. Second, the myth that governments can resolve all problems has led to false hope—and to disillusionment. Third, the myth of the relativity of values has caused many people to abandon transcendent values. Fourth, the myth of radical individualism has idolized individual rights and pleasure at the expense of soundly-functioning groups and communities.

These four myths, Colson continues, are undermining the humanizing influence of the Judeo-Christian heritage: its standards of justice, its treatment of humans with dignity and respect, its belief that responsibility matches freedom, and its ethic of work, mercy, service, and personal virtue (Colson 1993). The myths have also contributed to the lack of trust that characterizes modern western societies.

School programs also perpetuate these four myths. Most educators subscribe to the basic goodness of humans and the government's duty and ability to solve society's ills. Constructivists with their view that knowledge is personally constructed contribute, directly and indirectly, to individualism and the relativity of values. But the view of many curriculum traditionalists and technicists that knowledge is no more than an objective body of information and skills has also resulted in many students fending for themselves when making choices about the purpose and meaning of their lives. The result is a generation with little sense of direction, one that lacks trust in themselves, in their leaders, and in the future course of society.

Often sustaining Colson's four myths are the views of knowledge that underlie the main curriculum orientations. Chapter 4 discusses how these views affect the curriculum. It then shows how an alternate, Biblical view of knowledge listens to God's revelation and demands personal response based on Biblical values. It also looks at the various modes of knowing, and the criteria used to make responsible curriculum decisions. Chapter 5 considers the organization of knowledge in the curriculum. Finally, Chapter 6 shows how a Biblical view of knowledge affects teaching and learning in the various aspects of reality.

Even with a curriculum based on a Biblical view of knowledge, students may still reject Christian faith and its implications for their own lives—and accept what Colson calls the great myths of our time. Teachers may not and cannot force commitment. Yet as they teach with commitment they also teach for commitment. And their Christian point of departure will at least open their students' eyes to the possibility of a life with purpose and direction, one that points to the sources of society's lack of trust and to the Source of an alternate way.

Chapter 4
Views of Knowledge and
Modes of Knowing

- Grade 11 English teacher Alisa Ketchum teaches an eight-week drama unit in which small groups of students write, act, direct, and produce a one-act play. She asks her students to choose a problem in their lives, their community, or society that is real for them as well as for members of prospective audiences of the play. Students are to deal with the problem in the light of the Gospel without being pedantic or assuming that easy answers can be found. In other words, the play that students write and produce has to identify and analyze a real life conflict or issue without sermonizing. The class examines the nature of dramatic conflict. Alisa uses examples of well-known plays to illustrate how a character changes as a result of conflict resolution.

  The unit teaches students much about writing and producing effective plays. How do you use dialogue to develop character? What about the use of sound and lighting effects? Do the theme and the plot weld together into a believable unit? What about blocking, sets and props, quality of the acting? Alisa supplies lists of criteria to ensure frequent self-evaluation. One day actors visit the school to confer about the plays-in-progress. They make comments like, "I really like your story but give the characters a past and make them more interesting." Throughout the unit, questions such as "Does this play cause you to question your life or look at things differently?" force students to consider the point and effectiveness of their play.

  The fact that students produce the plays for other students and parents gives the unit immediacy and purpose. The unit is effective for at least two other reasons. First, the plays looks at a slice of life in a fresh and focused way. Principal Stuart Williams, who first designed the unit, emphasizes to the students, "Make the play strong; pursue substance. You are only 16 or 17 once. Now is the time to make your statement about life as you see it from your current perspective. Question, affirm, poke fun at aspects of our society, our system, our school, prominent issues. Comment on what teens believe about themselves, about adults, about their faith. Penetrate problems in reconciling faith and reality. Propose your ideas on how things should be changed." Corra Lee, a visiting actor, comments, "It's great to dramatize aspects of life. Not just conversions [to Christianity]. There's so much more to the Christian walk."

  Second, to be successful the students have to exercise and experience servant leadership. They work through many frustrations, taking

88 STEPPINGSTONES TO CURRICULUM

risks, supporting each other. Eventually they carry out a team consensus. Students reflect in their journals after each group meeting. They answer questions such as "What practical area in the way your group functions can you improve?" and "How does your group work best?" They assess other group members on specific criteria relating to servant leadership. They also evaluate and adjudicate all other plays at a dress rehearsal. They write a detailed critique of one play. Before producing their play for the parent audience, they revise it on the basis of feedback from fellow students.

Alisa does not think explicitly about her view of knowledge as she implements the unit. However, it fits her intuitive view. She likes what the unit does for students and for her classroom as a community. The unit teaches students that certain standards exist for good drama. Students draw from a well of prior knowledge about play writing and production. But the learning becomes meaningful because it pertains to their own life experience, and encourages personal response. Meaningful knowledge is much more than a static bank of information. It involves students interacting with and acting on what they learn. Also, they often learn best in situations where small groups work together toward common goals. One student in his reflection wrote that the "one-dimensionality of other students was stripped away" as they learned to work together and support each other despite initial misgivings.

Teachers sometimes object to a unit such as this by saying that it is too time consuming. They can't "cover the course." Is this criticism legitimate? Why or why not? Teachers who object probably base their argument on a different conception of knowledge. Suggest in what ways their view may differ from Alisa's (implicit) view.

The predominant Western view of knowledge in the 1900s has been that knowledge is an objective body of facts, skills, concepts, and theories. The more knowledge individuals acquire, the better chance they have to do well in life. Already four hundred years ago Francis Bacon said, "Knowledge itself is power." By knowledge, he meant collections of facts. For Bacon, values were speculation and personal prejudice. In the 19th century Herbert Spencer also reflected such a static conception of knowledge when he said that "science is organized knowledge." His contemporary, poet Arthur Clough, like Bacon, separated faith from knowledge when he wrote that "grace is given by God, but knowledge is bought in the market."

Persons holding a Biblical view of knowledge do not identify knowledge with an objective body of information. The Bible teaches not only that the fear of the Lord is the beginning of knowledge, but also that true knowledge involves committed action. In other words, for Christians the basic point of departure in gaining and applying knowledge is reverential trust in God and an acknowledgment of and submission to His laws. True knowledge includes an active response to God and neighbor. Truth must be done to be known (I John 1:6). Human knowledge is not neutral since people's discovery, development, interpretation, and response is part of knowledge. All knowledge exists within a framework of beliefs. Faith itself is not only knowledge but the basis of all knowledge.

While constructivists share the position that knowledge is not neutral, they go one step further. They hold that all knowledge is personally constructed, provisional, and open-ended. Knowledge is therefore subjective, based solely on people's own values and cultural context, with no finite or unitary truths (Luke and Gore 1992, 7). They therefore cannot accept the Biblical starting point that God's laws for the physical world and for human interaction are the basis for human knowledge.

In this chapter I consider diverse views of knowledge and their effect on curriculum. I posit a Biblical view of knowledge and truth with its curriculum implications. I then describe the different modes or ways of knowing and how the curriculum needs to take these into account. Finally, I discuss how educators justify curriculum choices.

VIEWS OF KNOWLEDGE IN THE CURRICULUM ORIENTATIONS

In chapter 1 I considered four common curriculum orientations: the academic traditionalist, technical, deliberative, and constructivist ones. Certain beliefs about life, values, and education form the basis for each orientation. Each also embodies a certain view of knowledge, as I describe below.

The academic traditionalist orientation

Academic traditionalists look at knowledge as a highly organized and catalogued collection of facts, concepts, ideas, and theories. Schools exist to transmit this static body of knowledge. Teachers decide only the sequence, procedures, and pace of learning. Today, few academic traditionalists would fully support Plato's view that real knowledge consists solely of ideas in the mind that exist independent of experience. Yet most would agree that experience is an occasion for rather than the basis of knowledge. In other words, rational thought is central in generating and validating knowledge.

For the traditionalist, therefore, learning is often abstract. Students store knowledge and use it as a fund for rational thought. But they have few guidelines for action or experiences in applying their learning to real-life situations. Learning how humans have classified plants in biology is more important than observing how plants grow. This view allows for little personal quest for meaning. As such, its view of knowledge is a limiting one.

The technical orientation

For persons in the technical orientation, knowledge is also objective, value-free, impersonal, and independent of time and place. But more so than for the traditionalist, experience now is the basis for knowledge. The empiricist of the technical orientation gains certainty of knowledge primarily from sensory observations. Statements are meaningful only if they are logically self-evident or can be validated from experience. That means that religious statements and beliefs are not knowledge. They are neither logically self-evident nor verifiable by empirical data. The key to education is carefully structured inquiry based on observations. For example, a detailed set of questions guides students to observe the characteristics of plants. Using their observations, they learn to classify plants according to the standard classification system.

There are several problems with this position. First, sensory experience is incomplete and misleading. Even scientists usually interpret their data to fit preconceived theories. Those theories are not unbiased; they are based on certain assumptions. When scientists make striking or groundbreaking new discoveries, they typically call into question some long-held belief or theory. That happened when Einstein discovered the theory of relativity, for instance. Also, the theory that knowledge certainty results only from sense perception cannot be validated by sense perception itself: it is a faith assumption. Yet positivist curricula instill the impression that sensory-based knowledge is more valid and therefore more important than any other kind. As Wolterstorff writes, ''The logical positivist pledged his troth to science.'' He adds that, curiously, many contemporary Christians do the same (Wolterstorff 1976, 19).

The deliberative orientation

Curriculum thinkers in the deliberative orientation recognize that knowledge cannot be separated from the knower. They recognize that there are bodies and public traditions of knowledge and that to some extent knowledge is independent of individuals. They see there are limits to the degree to which learners can redefine knowledge and reconstruct meanings. Yet they also understand that humans interpret thought and action in its historical and social contexts. Human traditions and the fabric of their social life shape impressions and their use of knowledge. Observations are value-laden and open to dispute. Descriptions and interpretations vary because of perspectives and biases. Nevertheless, we cannot function in society without maintaining mutual understanding related to the fields of knowledge that we have discovered and developed. For deliberators, therefore, curriculum is not simply a linear and cumulative affair. They sometimes use structured approaches to the disciplines. They also study multidisciplinary problems that may lead to new and different worlds opening up. They provide a rhythm of types of learning experiences: concrete experience, reflective observation, abstract conceptualization, and active experimentation (Harris 1987, 43). They balance formal presentations with dialogue, critical interpretation, and creative activities. For example, small groups of students may develop their own way of classifying plants based on their observations. Then they may compare this with standard classification schema and analyze the strengths and weaknesses of each.

For deliberators, religion is an appropriate field of study since it is expressive of a way of life. Yet, as we saw in the last chapter, for most deliberators, truth ultimately also resides in human creative energy and abilities.

The constructivist orientation

Persons philosophically committed to constructivism believe that humans constantly construct, sustain, and change their world. As people make sense of the world they invent different knowledge systems. Students also reconstruct meaning and invent interpretations that give meaning to their environment and their actions. We must respect the pupils' own construction of reality. Therefore, neither so-called school subjects nor historical knowledge traditions are very important. Personal meaning is what counts. Frank Smith argues throughout his book *To Think* (1990) that pupils do not just interpret reality, but that they construct their own reality from the sensory data they gather. For example, based on a discussion of possible criteria and their observations, students would formulate their own way of classifying plants.

The radical constructivist view of knowledge leads to two conclusions. First, teachers and students reconstruct reality in their own way, with each being equally good. This, of course, potentially leads to persons constructing their own private world, thus contributing to the individualism of our age. Second, with everyone constructing and interpreting knowledge in their own way, teaching content is useful mainly to provide examples of how others have constructed knowledge. More important than presenting knowledge is helping children learn how to learn. That explains why, for the intellectual domain, one constructivist curriculum document lists twenty-eight process objectives (uses effective strategies, locates, organizes, applies, communicates, demonstrates, etc.), but only one content one (acquires information through reading, listening, and observing) (British Columbia Ministry of Education 1990a, 135).

Neither of these two constructivist conclusions is tenable, however. Frank Smith contradicts his own position by referring several times in his book to "objective reality." You cannot deny the existence of dog bites, photosynthesis, or immorality. Also, beliefs and theories are an integral part of our culture. Schools of necessity introduce students to socially shared knowledge, knowledge based on investigations of reality. Humans conceptualize, interpret, critique, validate, and sometimes reject knowledge, but knowledge does not consist solely of personal constructions. Indeed, the radical constructivist view that all knowledge is relative leads to a logical problem since the statement itself must therefore be relative and not always true.

One final note. Christians cannot agree with the basic presuppositions about knowledge made by rationalists, empiricists, or constructivists. Deliberators are in some ways close to a Biblical view, but not in holding that human deliberation in itself can lead to truth. Nevertheless, persons holding any of these views of knowledge can give us worthwhile insights, also with respect to curriculum theory and practice. Indeed, some calling themselves constructivists may do so more because they believe that students must be actively engaged in their own learning than because they agree with the philosophical tenets of constructivism. Christians always need to consider, however, which educational insights of these various orientations can be used within a framework of Biblical beliefs about the nature of knowledge, of the person, and of the God-given injunctions.

- In the last paragraph I claim that we can gain serviceable insights from proponents of each curriculum orientation. List some curriculum approaches that might be favored by each orientation and that you would implement if you taught Alisa Ketchum's drama unit. After you have read the next section, check whether the items in your list would fit the description given for a Biblical view of knowledge.

A BIBLICAL VIEW OF KNOWLEDGE

- In his book, *To Know as We Are Known: A Spirituality of Education*, Parker Palmer claims that the emphasis on fact and reason in education has perhaps made the world seem predictable and safe, but has also made it cold and mechanical. We rely on the eye of the mind but have forsaken the eye of our heart. Yet we need both. The heart's vision can include the mind. Knowing "draws not only on our senses and our reason, but on our intuitions, our beliefs, our actions, our relationships, and on our bodies themselves" (1983, xii).

Despite the benefits modern knowing gives us, we have sought knowledge to master and control. As Palmer puts it, we seek to "coerce the world into meeting our needs--no matter how much violence we must do" (23). Rather than curiosity or control, love as the primary motive for knowledge "will wrap the knower and the known in compassion, in a bond of awesome responsibility as well as transforming joy" (9). Education based on knowledge that originates in prayerful love can prepare us to see beyond facts into truth, beyond self-interest into compassion, beyond manipulation and despair into co-creation (12-14).

Education must convey more than facts, theories, and objective realities. Instead, the message must be "truth." To know in truth is "to enter into the life of that which we know and to allow it to enter into ours" (31). The knower becomes interdependent with the known, a "co-participant in a community of faithful relationships with other persons and creatures and things" (32). In other words, education creates "a space in which obedience to truth is practiced" (69).

Discuss the meaning of Palmer's view of knowledge. What are some of the implications for curriculum? Does his view correspond with the four mandates discussed in chapter 2? with the Biblical values in chapter 3? Why or why not?

It is beyond the scope of this book to develop a detailed theory of knowledge based on Biblical givens. But, while Scripture is neither a philosophical treatise nor a curriculum textbook, Christians believe that it contains norms and general guidelines that apply to life. As such, our understanding of the way Scripture views knowledge and truth affects our approach to education and curriculum design.

A Biblical view of knowledge is, in the first place, God related. We are able to gain knowledge through God revealing Himself in creation, in His Word, in Jesus Christ, and through His Spirit. That makes knowledge relational and personal, not just objective and factual. The Bible also makes clear that knowledge is faith based. All knowledge is based on religious faith in the true God or on faith in an idol such as that of the autonomy of human beings. A Biblical perspective also makes clear that knowledge is motivational, not just informational. It involves personal response. As such, it is active, not passive. Knowing means doing the truth. And truth must be done to be known (Al Greene, personal correspondence, Jan. 21, 1994). In this section I develop this Biblical view.

Christians recognize that God established all of creation and its inherent meaning. God is not only ultimate source of truth, but God in Jesus Christ *is* truth (John 14:6). He is the creator and sustainer of reality. The world, His creation, is real and orderly. All laws, beings, events, and ideas find their meaning in God. He reveals His greatness and purposes in both His natural revelation in the universe and in His written Word, the

Bible. God calls humans to be co-workers, but as His creatures we nevertheless must work within His law structures. In science, for instance, we make clear that we explore the laws God created. Einstein said that inner freedom and security come from contemplating the eternal riddle of a world that exists independently of humans (Schlipp 1970, 781). Human theories reflect God's laws imperfectly. Yet because of God's faithfulness we can use them to exercise His calling to unfold and develop our culture, encouraging and helping it to function as a loving and just society.

The Old Testament word for knowing, *yada*, always refers to active and intentional engagement in lived experience (Groome 1980, 141). You do not possess knowledge unless you immerse yourself in experience *and* until you exercise it by living your commitment in every aspect of life. Knowledge involves the heart, not just the mind. Knowing, being, and acting are all tied together in a Biblical view of knowledge. Moses did not know God until God had taught him God's ways (Exodus 33:13). God Himself says that to know Him means to do what is right and just and to defend the cause of the poor and needy (Jeremiah 22:15-16). Conversely, to lack knowledge means to ignore the law of God (Hosea 4:1,6). Rejecting true knowledge means breaking our relationship with God.

School knowledge may therefore never be just "head knowledge." We design units and learning situations so that resulting acts of knowing accomplish purposes in time and space. School knowledge should involve the opportunity and ability of students to respond personally to their learning. The end of knowledge does not have to be something that society considers "practical," however. It may be just taking delight in God's marvelous reality or grieving brokenness caused by sin. Knowledge rooted in an acknowledgment of and response to God and His creation helps students develop Biblical attitudes and values. It also leads them to act on deepened or new commitments, and exercise Biblical injunctions in the classroom and other real life settings.

The Bible considers knowledge to be relational. Knowledge originates with our relating to God with awe and wonder (Proverbs 1:7). Conversely, a lack of knowledge involves having broken a loving and faithful relationship (Hosea 4:1,6). When Adam knew Eve (Genesis 4:1, KJV) it meant that they had formed a sexual covenant of troth with each other. When Israelites knew God, they covenanted to walk a life of obedience and trust with Him. Even knowledge of the physical world involves listening to the daily outpouring of God's creation-speech (Psalm 19:1-2). Significantly, God presents Job with many facts about reality to help him gain true knowledge (Job 38-42). True knowledge of the physical world cannot be separated from knowing the Creator.

By New Testament times, Greek culture used its word for knowledge in a much narrower intellectual sense. Yet the New Testament also presents knowledge to be relational and interactive. Jesus accuses the Pharisees, despite their thorough intellectual knowledge, of not knowing God. Their rigidity and hypocrisy prevented a truthful and trothful relation with God (John 8:19). A knowledge of Christ is not just a factual knowledge, but it is knowledge based on a living, experiential relationship that transforms you as a person (Philippians 3:8-10). You become convinced that knowledge is valid "because you know those from whom you learned it" (2 Timothy 3:14).

Moreover, knowledge is rooted in faith and love. It can thus lead to loving, obedient service (1 John 2:3-5). Job did not have true knowledge of God until his eyes of faith put his intellectual knowledge into perspective (Job 42:3-5). It is in Christ that all treasures of wisdom and knowledge are hidden (Colossians 2:2-3). Paul says that knowledge without love is empty (1 Corinthians 8:1). His best-known chapter about love, 1 Corinthians 13, places all knowledge and all gifts under *agape*, the all-encompassing Biblical love. Growing in knowledge means growing in wisdom and understanding and doing good (Colossians 1:9-10). If you know the Spirit of Truth, He lives in you, and you obey Christ's commands (John 14:15-17).

It follows that in the classroom, relationships reflecting God's love for us form the basis for opening up and learning meaningful knowledge. Our relationship with God affects how we interpret and use knowledge. Relationships between teachers and students and among students themselves affect the willingness to accept and develop knowledge and the way we use it. Students experience and apply knowledge as they develop relationships within their community of learning, as well as in service opportunities outside the classroom. Science promotes an awareness of God, who acts in His creation, and His call to respond obediently to Him with our knowledge. Social studies helps students see and experience how social and cultural relationships can be used to strengthen—or weaken—our relationship with the Lord of Life.

In the Bible, knowledge is never objective and "out there." Knowledge, discernment, and wisdom form a unified triad. The discerning heart seeks knowledge and knowledge comes to the discerning (Pr. 15:14, 14:6). Knowledge and good judgment form a team (Ps. 119:66). Prudence, knowledge, and discretion accompany wisdom. All these lead to righteousness and justice (Pr. 8:12,20). Biblical wisdom does not depend on Greek intellectual knowledge or rationality. Wisdom ultimately rests in our relationship with Jesus Christ, in having the mind of Christ (1 Cor. 1 and 2). Biblical wisdom embodies a love for the author of wisdom and for what He enables us to know, and therefore applies knowledge with compassion and justice. In school, students must have opportunities to transcend intellectual knowledge by applying it in what for them are new situations. If done on the basis of Biblical values and mandates, they will be helped to gain wisdom and discernment.

Of course, sin taints all of life, including how we gain and apply knowledge. Our society uses knowledge to control our physical world, plant and animal life, and human life. We display much arrogance about the little we do know. We often cannot see beyond our own lives, communities, or nations. Misapplied knowledge, also when wielded by Christians, leads to illegitimate power. This occurs in family life, business, politics, schools, and church life. When the need to dominate drives knowledge, an ethical base for its use and the desire to do what is right are missing (Palmer 1983, 8).

A Biblical approach to knowledge keeps us humble. The Bible reminds us that "we see but a poor reflection [of knowledge] as in a mirror [of polished metal]" (1 Corinthians 13:12). In our teaching we therefore guard against arrogance about our "expertise." We admit our tendencies to fall short, misread situations, and make mistakes. We also show how humans often use technical knowledge for short-term profit but long-term catastrophe or anguish. We show how both our scientific and economic knowledge is often much more limited than "experts" are willing to admit, and that our lack of insight into the consequences of decisions often comes back to haunt us.

■ The predominant view of knowledge in our culture influences us so much that we find it difficult to accept that knowledge is not an objective body of information to be used to control our world. Think back to your own schooling. What view of knowledge was implicit in most of what you learned? Can you suggest what attitudes to life you learned in subjects like social studies? science? mathematics? art? Could the school have taken a different approach? A better one? Students sometimes claim that in a subject like mathematics they learn no values. Are they right? Why or why not?

THE BIBLICAL BASIS FOR TRUTH

A Biblical view of knowledge relates closely to our conception of truth. For the rationalist, truth is a coherent and reliable system of thought. For the empiricist, truth consists of verifiable facts that correspond with our observation of reality. For the constructivist, truth is subjective, relative to the individual. In all three cases, truth is rooted in ourselves, either through our rationality or through our senses. The Bible does not talk about truth in terms of rationally or empirically correct statements or intellectual information. The Biblical view of truth is closely related to the Biblical view of knowledge.

Believing the truth of Scripture means not so much *believing that* as it does *believing in*. Jesus said, "I am the way, the truth, and the life"

(John 14:6). That is more than just a theological statement. Truth came in Jesus Christ. He *is* the meaning of the world. Every created thing points beyond itself to Christ who holds the world together (Col. 1:17; Heb. 1:3; Greene 1990, 66). Jesus testifies to the truth and thus gives us understanding (John 1:17; 18:37; 1 John 5:20). If you hold to Christ's teaching, you will know the truth, and the truth will set you free (John 8:31-32). Whoever lives by the truth that is Christ comes into the light (John 3:21). Such truth leads to love with actions (1 John 3:18). God's love demands that we walk in His truth; truth and love may never be separated (Psalm 26:3; 40:10-11). When truth "has stumbled in the streets," so have justice, righteousness, and honesty (Isaiah 59:14-15). Truth, in other words, is not just a correct statement but a right deed.

Thomas Groome describes three dimensions of Christian faith: a belief conviction, a trusting relationship, and a lived life of *agape* (Groome 1980, 57). Recognizing the truth that is Christ leads people to respond with responsibility and compassion. Faith is in the doing. Truth is in the doing. Knowledge is in the doing. Lived Christian faith, truth, and knowledge arise from and lead to obedient response to God's intentions for the world (Groome 1980, 65). We seldom live up to God's intentions. That is precisely why our relationship with Christ is so crucial. Only if we live in the Truth that is Christ can we live with our failure and yet continue to receive the power to follow His mandates within a Biblical framework of values.

Considering truth either in terms of objective statements or in terms of individual subjective meaning prevents the possibility of meaningful community. As Parker Palmer says (1983, 46-68), only the concept of truth as troth will suffice. We know truth in personal relationships, not just in objective statements that tell the world what it is, or in subjective meaning-making that listens to no one except the individual self. That does not mean, Palmer continues, that Christ-followers just focus narrowly on leading persons to Jesus for conversion. Education in the truth treats humans as subjects, images of God, who participate fully and responsibly in unfolding reality. As we discover Jesus, we discover a whole universe, since through Christ all things were made (John 1:3).

Truth is a call to rigorous and demanding love in communion with God, other humans, animals, plants, and the physical world. A thinker like Einstein allowed the physical world to speak to him in exceptional depth while also relating to a scientific community. Education involves listening and submitting oneself to truth in community. In school, relations between teachers and students are crucial. Even the best curriculum will not lead to truth unless teachers themselves walk in the truth and allow students to search out truth and experience it personally and communally.

■ The last two sections may seem somewhat abstract. Our western minds seldom think along these lines. Before reading on, it may help you to consider what these views of knowledge and truth mean for your teaching.

Suppose you teach the concept of gravity. You hold a marble between two fingers. You ask your students what would happen if you opened your fingers. They predict that the marble would fall, and it does. You do it a second, a third, a fourth, a fifth time. Each time you have the same result. You ask, "Why?" "Gravity," says one of your students. But what is gravity? Why does it always work? You draw out that we can describe it as a force and predict its effects, also mathematically. But we don't really know what it is or why it works. You discuss the law structure of the universe established by the Law Giver. You then have your students experiment to discover some results (e.g., a large and small marble will accelerate equally because of the pull of gravity). Your students are actively involved. They respond by seeing how faith in created, unfailing laws makes science possible, but that what they discover is but a pale reflection of those laws. They learn how science results, even if tentative and approximate, help us to fulfil God's creation mandate if we apply them responsively and responsibly.

Now suppose that you teach a unit on food and nutrition. Think of specific ways in which you can base learning on the Biblical view of knowledge and truth described above.

A BIBLICAL APPROACH TO KNOWLEDGE AND TRUTH IN THE CLASSROOM

■ Teacher Derk Van Eerden admits openly that his attempts to lead students into the truth in grade 12 biology do not always seem to have long-term effects. He wonders, in fact, whether schooling by itself can change lifestyles. He says that "planting seeds" is perhaps the most he can do. He realizes that a key to meaningful learning is having good personal relationships.

Derk uses the first month of his course to set the stage for the remainder of the school year. The month has two complementary components. He has his class plan a four day biology field trip and retreat during the third week in September. He uses this to draw the class into a community. The students and teachers involved get to know each other in different settings. They need to work together on chores like preparing their meals, and in doing tasks in small groups on ecology and geology hikes. This trip affects students' relationships in the classroom for several months. It strengthens group and collaborative learning, with far more students willing to interact and do their share of the work. The students also sing and pray together. They get to know each other as persons.

The other component is an introductory unit that looks at human relations with nature. Students analyze modern scientific, aboriginal and

Christian views of such relationships. They view and discuss films and articles on wildlife and forest management issues. They consider Biblical passages to analyze Scripture's views of humans' relationship with God, each other, and with nature. They react to articles by aboriginal people that regard the earth as our mother and describe people conversing with animals. Are their insights closer to Biblical views than western technological ones? They discuss a satire about it being too late to save our planet. Derk concludes the unit by convincing students that we all act on the basis of beliefs. He then shows that often we say one thing but do another, also in how we relate to and use the physical world, and discusses why this is so. He then invites students to act on their convictions and commitments.

Derk's biology students will not know what it means to love God and neighbor as stewards of the earth unless they experience positive relationships with each other and the physical world. He also knows that the more abstract learning they will do as they prepare for government examinations the rest of the year will have little long-term meaning, unless he can present the topics within the framework of basic values that his class develops during the first unit.

Discuss in what ways Derk has implemented a Biblical view of knowledge and truth. He is concerned himself that he is not influencing students as much as he would like. Is the role of the school a limited one? If so, how? Or may the home and school consider this only one of many legs in an ongoing journey, some of which will be more successful than others? Can you suggest any improvements in his start to the course? Derk spends a month on a topic that will not be tested on the year-end government examinations. Assuming that this might affect students' final grade and even the possibility of entering a specific university, do you think this is warranted? Why or why not?

Derk Van Eerden makes education an affair of the heart as well as the mind. He actively and intentionally engages his students in discussions about real issues. He also takes them to a wilderness area where they concretely experience the relationships discussed in class, with God, each other, animals, plants, and physical things. Their new insights, he holds before students, are intended to nurture such relationships rather than to give control for personal or communal self-interest. We deepen our knowledge so that we are better able to serve.

Derk's students learn to appreciate each other for who they are, rather than just for their intellectual strengths. The field trip helps them recognize that intellectual gifts are only one type God gives us. Others are just as necessary for a community to function well. They learn a great deal about responsible stewardship of time and resources, loving your neighbor, living as a supportive community. During the unit they also consider the importance of values such as economic, social, and biological justice, and respect for the views of other cultures. In short, Derk gives his students a great deal of space to experience and practice truth. The possibility of providing such space is enhanced by recognizing the importance of the implicit curriculum, and of making aspects of the implicit curriculum explicit. Classroom structures that nurture warm, caring, and supportive relationships while Derk set high but realistic expectations help students to take on roles as servant leaders. They may then develop and use their specific gifts to contribute to the whole learning community. Derk uses collaborative learning to foster a sense of community. I will say more about this in chapter 7.

> ■ A grade I I student was writing about the Song of Songs just after living through her parents' divorce (her father had an affair). "From personal experiences I can tell you what I think is the biggest problem with the world right now. It's not the ozone layer or that we are running out of trees . . . but the biggest one I see is how lightly people take their wedding vows. Nowadays people take sex for granted. In the Song of Songs it says, 'do not arouse or awaken love before its time,' but how many people do you know who actually follow this verse?" In what ways has her learning fostered a Biblical view of knowledge and truth? If you were the teacher, how would you follow up this assignment?

EXPERIENCE AND THE RHYTHM OF LEARNING

Students learn best when their own experience serves as a lead-in to more abstract knowledge. Their concrete experience strengthens active and intentional engagement in knowing. Sometimes that can be done by referring to students' own background and experience (Did you ever. . .? What do you know about . . . ?). At other times a real life situation should be used to give students the opportunity to experience and informally explore a phenomenon. Teachers may pose a problem or ask students to formulate problems themselves about familiar situations. They then encourage students to stand back and look at the situation in a fresh way as they find solutions to the problems posed. Material learned outside a meaningful experience context, especially when presented without any motivating challenges, all too often becomes a body of abstract concepts to be regurgitated on a test and then forgotten.

Unlike what extreme constructivists believe, a core of knowledge exists that all students should learn. Students are part of a community and culture to which God calls them to contribute. They can do so only if they can understand and participate in the shared knowledge that our culture has uncovered, expanded, and refined. We may disagree about the precise content of such a core. Students, however, can function and interact in society only with some common content base. As I discuss in the next chapter, such a knowledge core is much more than a memorized body of facts.

Teachers use students' experiences as a base for considering phenomena in a more focused way. They help them take distance from everyday experience so that they deepen their understanding and insight. Such learning is sometimes playful and pleasant, but may also be difficult and at times even onerous, particularly when it is cumulative or requires deeper analysis. What makes it worthwhile for students is that they can see that the knowledge they learn is grounded in and useful for everyday situations. Once they have gained a deeper understanding, we give them the opportunity to respond to new situations in a personal way.

There is a natural rhythm as students grow in knowledge. First, teachers set the stage in real life experience. Then they disclose by considering and analyzing a situation or problem in a more formal way. They allow students to reformulate and practice. Finally, in a transcendence phase students apply their learning in new, creative, and divergent ways and make personal choices and commitments. Each phase of learning lends itself to active involvement and response. The last one I call transcendence because here students go beyond what they have learned more formally in earlier phases. This phase is particularly effective for students solving more complex problems. Here they use their imagination and creativity, and develop discernment and wisdom. Kieran Egan suggests giving units a narrative structure that leads to a climax and denouement. Such a structure would lend itself very naturally to units that include the four phases of learning described here. Note, however, that the different phases may also occur in individual lessons or groups of lessons. I discuss this further in chapter 7.

STRATEGIES FOR INTENTIONAL KNOWING

If knowledge involves active engagement and response, students also benefit from a second order of knowing called *metacognition*. That is, they ask themselves how they learn, how they manage progress, and how they cope with problems and frustrations and doubts. To encourage such reflection, we teach them to set their own objectives and evaluate their own understanding and progress. We also spur them to judge what is important, and to identify their strengths and weaknesses. Teachers may have to avoid their natural tendency to do this for the students instead of providing ways for students to do this regularly themselves.

Students may do well in assignments and yet at the end know little. What is needed in addition is that the learning is intentional. That is, students set out to achieve objectives using purposeful strategies rather than just getting the right answer or completing the task (Carl Bereiter and Marlene Scardamalia in Jackson 1992, 525-26). Teachers can suggest specific strategies for self-regulation in most learning. If teachers and students together develop lists of criteria, students can assess their progress in integrated units as well as in reading, writing, and mathematics problem solving skills. In writing, for instance, many teachers help students develop strategies and criteria for planning, actual writing, and reviewing and revising.

Effective problem solving calls for students to use certain strategies. Students who analyze what is happening and deliberately use problem solving strategies show superior learning. High achievers do not just try to find an efficient path to a solution. Instead, they find out whatever they can from what is given, consider the implications, and then look for general applicable laws. Note that problem solving abilities do not seem to transfer from one subject area to another, however. Carl Bereiter and Marlene Scardamalia conclude from recent research that "teaching problem solving skills may be an illusion, like teaching babies to talk" (Bereiter and Scardamalia in Jackson 1992, 528). Courses intending to teach general problem solving and higher order skills cultivate such abilities only in very limited ways.

Therefore, giving students opportunities to pose and solve problems in specific subjects may be more successful in developing their metacognitive strategies. We can structure problems to encourage students to pay attention to general strategies, not just to find one specific answer. In mathematics and science, researcher John Sweller achieved better learning when he changed the standard answer-focused problems to ones where teachers ask students to use the given information to find out everything they can (Sweller 1988). Teachers can model and coach problem solving skills. What seems more important, however, is that teachers develop in students the ability and tendency to set goals themselves, ask thought-provoking questions, and evaluate their own approaches and understanding (Bereiter and Scardamalia in Jackson 1992, 533). The disposition for such reflection is the best preparation for successful learning, particularly in the transcendence phase.

Let me give an example that high school teacher Janet Hitchcock related to me. She had seen a teacher explain how to find the area of the figure shown. The teacher divided the figure into two rectangles (see broken line), and then worked out the area as follows:

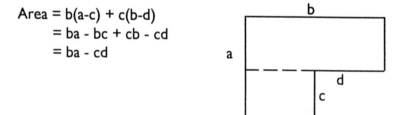

$$\text{Area} = b(a\text{-}c) + c(b\text{-}d)$$
$$= ba - bc + cb - cd$$
$$= ba - cd$$

The teacher had shown how to get the correct answer. A more productive approach, said Janet, would be to ask the students to discover as many different ways of finding the solution. At least the teacher should have asked the class to consider why the answer turned out to be an unexpectedly simple one. What is the explanation? Could we have found the answer in a different way? How can you apply what you have learned? Solving knowledge problems becomes more meaningful when students learn to ask questions that go beyond finding a mechanical procedure that quickly yields the answer.

In short, knowledge is active and motivational. Students need to process phenomena actively. They must (1) be aware of their goals, (2) summarize and paraphrase information, (3) identify and review possible strategies for working toward their goals, (4) regularly ask themselves questions to monitor comprehension and success of the strategies they use, (5) learn from falling short, and (6) self-reinforce success (Good and Brophy 1994, 245-47). During all this, students are active and actively engaged with a situation, also relating with the originators of the situation, their teacher, or fellow students.

EXHIBITING LEARNING

If students do not use their knowledge, it is inert. Theodore Sizer suggests that students should therefore regularly exhibit the products of their learning. He suggests that students prepare presentations for highly personal yet universal issues that often cut across traditional subject lines. Such exhibitions give students an incentive. They allow students to use their learning to convince others. They provide a focus for the school's program. They help students develop habits of thoughtfulness and responsibility. They also serve as affirmations for students and the school community that the learning has paid off (Sizer 1992, 24-27).

Exhibitions may involve portfolio or poster displays with written or oral explanations, demonstrations, performances. Audiences may include classmates, other classes, parents. At the elementary level, exhibitions would usually be less extensive than at the high school level. The point here is that student exhibits of their learning are crucial if their knowledge is to be more than objective information on the one hand or subjective personal meaning on the other.

■ Consider the following situations:
  »a city has to decide where to put a new garbage dump
  »a family has to decide whether to buy a larger home if that means that leisure spending and charitable donations are cut back
  »a government has to decide whether to spend $2 million on advanced equipment in a hospital that will save twenty lives per year, or using the

funds to launch a preventive health program that in the long run will save tens of millions of dollars

»a friendship flounders because of petty jealousies

»a musician has to decide whether to earn a living from music by playing in bars and at dances, or to get an office job and use his music talent mainly as a volunteer in church

»a school has to decide whether to put all its athletic resources into selected teams that will compete in a league, or into an extensive intramural program in which most students participate

Discuss whether each situation is one that would be worthwhile for inclusion in the curriculum. If so, where would it fit? If not, why not? For one of the situations, discuss some problems the students could pose and explore. How would you actively engage the students in their learning? What means would you include to encourage students to use metacognitive strategies? Can you suggest some learning activities for setting the stage? disclosure? reformulation? transcendence? What are some ways in which students could display the results of their learning?

MODES OF KNOWING

■ Students in Paul Smith's grade 4 Biblical studies class learn about the forty-year desert trek of the Israelites. Paul's theme for the unit is that God provides for His people, and that therefore we can trust God and accept His blessings, especially salvation in Jesus Christ. Paul recognizes that knowing, to be meaningful, must involve personal response. He also realizes that students prefer different modes of knowing, that is, different ways to consider and deepen their knowledge.

Paul therefore provides opportunities for learning and responding that involve diverse modes of knowing. Students work in groups to review parts of the story by dramatizing it. Some make or construct models of the tabernacle or of an Israelite encampment. Some write and perform music that the Israelites might have sung. Others create poems. Small groups make a booklet about the forty-year journey. All write personal responses to issues that arise, and make a personal dictionary for the new words they learn.

Note that Paul is aware of different ways students deepen their knowledge: communication (oral and written), aesthetic (dramatic, visual, and musical), and interpersonal. There are other modes of knowing as well. You may encourage some students to use and expand their spiritual mode of knowing by putting together a meaningful worship experience. Others may use and foster their logical mode of knowing by developing a detailed time line and map of the journey. Can you suggest other modes of learning that are important for a unit such as this or in other school learning?

There are different realms or forms of knowledge, as shown by the different subject disciplines that exist. There are also different *modes* or *ways* of knowing. Howard Gardner refers to these as *multiple intelligences* (Gardner 1993). Whatever we call them, clearly all human beings possess and have the potential to develop each mode of knowing to some degree. All have a unique constellation of potentials for the various modes of knowing. Also, our ability in one mode of knowing is largely independent of our ability in other modes. Schools have, by and large, emphasized the numerical, logical, scientific, and verbal modes of knowing. Regrettably, that means they have often neglected other modes such as the interpersonal and aesthetic ones.

Classifications of aspects of reality (or knowledge disciplines) and modes of knowledge are similar, and also parallel the types of values discussed in chapter 3. This reflects the fact that God's creation forms a unity. Still, the aspects affect curriculum differently, and I will leave the discussion of aspects of knowledge to chapter 5. Mathematics, most people will agree, is an aspect of reality that forms a discipline of knowledge. Yet doing mathematics involves various modes of knowing. The most obvious are numerical and logical knowing, and spatial knowing in geometry and topology. But mathematicians also use scientific, intuitive, and aesthetic knowing (Nel Noddings in Eisner 1985, 117). Mathematicians often arrive at new conclusions intuitively or by looking at aesthetic patterns, using deductive reasoning only afterward to prove their results.

Why is it important to be aware of the different modes of knowing to plan school curriculum? Any curriculum that we implement embodies various modes of knowing. If students are to internalize knowledge and respond in personal ways, they benefit from the opportunity to learn and react using modes of learning to which they are naturally inclined. They should also use other modes of knowing so that they learn to appreciate and become somewhat comfortable with them. While not everyone can excel in all modes, the development of modes such as interpersonal and aesthetic knowing are important for all. Sensitivity to the diverse modes of knowing helps us design curriculum and pedagogy (Connelly and Clandinin in Eisner 1985, 181).

Without giving a detailed analysis, let me list some of the modes of knowing. We do not know precisely how many different modes exist. Howard Gardner lists seven multiple intelligences. Yet when he makes the musical one of the seven while subsuming visual art under visual/spatial intelligence, he is less than convincing. Here I will discuss the following modes of knowing: numerical, spatial, physical, scientific, intuitive, aesthetic (musical, visual, and dramatic), logical, verbal/linguistic, and interpersonal/social.

Numerical, spatial, physical, and scientific knowing

Some students are strong in *numerical* knowing. They quickly sense relationships and patterns among numbers. They have a knack for calculating and estimating with numbers. Other students shine in the spatial mode of knowing. They easily recognize relationships of objects in space, can form mental images and make graphic representations. Significantly, students who are strong in numerical and spatial knowing may not be disposed to become mathematicians because they are not strong in logical or intuitive knowing.

The *physical* or *kinesthetic* is also a separate mode of knowing. Persons as diverse as athletes, surgeons, jugglers, and wood carvers can solve problems involving space and movement or make products using physical coordination. Such coordination depends on mind-body connection that allows one to make and carry out successfully almost instantaneous decisions.

Plato downplayed the *scientific* mode of knowing because he felt that the changing world of sense experience was inferior to the eternal abstract ideas that the mind could envision and analyze. However, until very recently, the dominant view was that of logical positivism. Logical positivists believe that knowledge is scientific knowing. It involves rationally generating concepts and theories from observation and sensory evidence. For them, even the word "science" is equated with "knowledge" (D.C. Phillips in Eisner 1985, 38-39). Yet the scientific mode of knowing has been difficult to teach, as the failure of the observation-based programs of the 1960s and 1970s showed. When viewed as one among many ways of knowing, the scientific mode of generalizing from investigations of physical phenomenon is a useful one to foster in students. When seen as the main or only mode, scientific knowing becomes stifling.

Intuitive knowing

I do not know of an adequate description of the *intuitive* mode of knowing, or even whether we can help students cultivate this mode. Yet the intuitive mode of knowing exists. It is the ability to perceive directly or apprehend immediately the dynamics of a situation or the solution of a problem--without applying formal reasoning power. Intuitive knowledge has to do with feeling and perception, sizing up the *gestalt* of a situation. It can include having an accurate perception of oneself and how one fits into a new social situation (thinking, for instance, "I'll have to be careful here" even before any words are spoken). It may also be quickly sensing the undesirability or immorality of a situation ("There's something not kosher here."). It may be reacting instantaneously and successfully to an unexpected traffic situation when driving, without any awareness of intervening mental processes.

Henri Poincaré, one of the world's foremost mathematicians around 1900, could not add simple numbers. His spatial mode of knowing was equally abysmal: he got a zero for drawing on his university entrance exam and his geometric diagrams were indecipherable. What modes of knowing, then, allowed him to be a great mathematician? First, his analytical prowess was astounding. But he also had what he himself and others have called intuitive power, the ability to perceive at a glance the situation as a whole. Poincaré has described how he often found solutions to difficult problems suddenly and with immediate certainty. He had, as he put it, sudden inspirations or revelations, often unexpectedly after putting the problem aside following several days of fruitless work on it. After such an intuitive grasp of the situation, he would use logical reasoning to verify his earlier conclusion. Poincaré added that the feeling of absolute certainty usually proved valid. Sometimes, however, his intuition deceived him without being any less vivid (Poincaré 1956).

Rudolf Arnheim argues that both the intuitive and rational share in every cognitive act. The intuitive mode of knowledge allows us to grasp the structure and function of a situation and its components. We need reasoning, however, to validate initial conclusions and draw conclusions. Thus intuition and reasoning complement each other, with each having a legitimate place in classroom learning. Not knowing how to improve students' abilities in the intuitive mode of knowing should not prevent us from recognizing it as legitimate and valuable in learning.

Aesthetic knowing

The *aesthetic* mode of knowing allows us to create and experience products that imaginatively capture a slice of life. To know aesthetically means to portray or understand a "work" that has an allusive or referential meaning. Such a meaning could not be captured in the same way by words or cognitive analysis. Aesthetic modes of knowing point to certain aspects of life and help us experience them in imaginative and often playful ways. Aesthetic knowing allows persons to make new mental connections, providing them with insights and understandings not available through other modes (Shapiro 1993, 27).

Aesthetic knowing comes to the fore particularly in the visual arts, music, dance, poetry, and drama. However, social and physical scientists also work imaginatively, for instance, with metaphors. The most effective theories often are aesthetically attractive ones (Eisner 1985, 26-28). The visual arts require more than the spatial mode of knowing. They also require the aesthetic mode that alludes to or symbolizes while imaginatively capturing an aspect of life. Music requires sensitivity to sounds and its structure, and the ability to use the creation of music to set a mood or impression (its referential function).

Logical and linguistic/verbal knowing

Schools have long stressed both *logical* and *linguistic* knowing. For the logical mode this began with the ancient Greeks. For Plato, a sign of a good education was the ability to manipulate abstract concepts. That is why for many centuries Euclidean geometry, consisting of logical proofs of geometrical propositions, was a required study for any educated person. Today, Piaget's followers continue to assume that the logical is the foremost mode of knowing (e.g., Kohlberg's emphasis on moral *reasoning*). The logical mode of knowledge enables persons to discern relationships, connections, and patterns, and to reason both inductively and deductively.

Enough has been said about students with verbal facility and learning through writing and narration that I do not have to convince anyone of the importance of this mode of knowing. Students who do well in the logical and linguistic modes of learning are also the ones who do well on so-called IQ tests. Yet the other ways of knowing could just as much be called types of intelligence (Gardner 1993, 8).

Interpersonal/social knowing

Howard Gardner shows that the *interpersonal* or *social* mode of knowing is independent of the linguistic one (Gardner 1993, 22-23). Until teachers began to use collaborative learning, they often neglected the interpersonal mode of knowing inside the classroom. Students have graduated from high school knowing little about interacting positively with others. Yet this mode of knowing is a crucial one for the welfare of persons and for society. I know an executive of one large corporation whose main task is to develop interpersonal sensitivity and competence among his staff so that they promote each other's well-being. His success in creating supportive relationships has made solving the technical, logistical, and economic problems "a piece of cake." Another large corporation reported that its *primary* reason for firing workers was their inability to get along with superiors or co-workers (E. Berscheid in Eisner 1985, 64). These factors underscore the fact that students will benefit from classroom structures that regularly encourage students to nurture positive interpersonal interaction. We help students work cooperatively in groups, be sensitive to each other's moods and feelings, discern underlying motives and perspectives, and learn to interpret non-verbal communication.

Other modes of knowing

The foregoing are, I believe, nine separate ways of knowing that schools need to incorporate in their curriculum. A social studies teacher dealing with the structure of government can, for instance, make use of the numerical, spatial, intuitive, logical, verbal, and interpersonal modes of knowing. For a topic such as communities of plants and animals a teacher could help students use and develop their numerical, spatial, physical, scientific, aesthetic, logical, verbal, and social ways of knowing, especially if the unit involves a field trip and other project work.

We still have many unanswered questions about the modes of knowing. We speak, for instance, of persons having economic know-how, political "savvy," moral discrimination, and spiritual insight. Do these also reflect distinctive ways of knowing or do such abilities comprise combinations of other modes? Intuitively I suspect the former, but scientifically or rationally that has not yet been established. We still have difficulty defining the intuitive and aesthetic ways of knowing and recognizing how to nurture these modes of knowing in schools. Also, while we can show that all modes of knowledge are important in life, are some more important or more suited for school curriculum? Is certain curriculum content or structure particularly appropriate for teaching specific modes of knowledge? While answers to such questions may be unclear, we do know that in the past schools have focused too narrowly on numerical, logical, scientific, and verbal modes of knowledge. The curriculum needs to take into account the other modes as well.

■ In the next-to-last paragraph in this section, I list the various modes of knowledge that students could experience and develop for two topics: government and communities of plants and animals. Suggest classroom activities for each topic for each mode listed. Would you include any modes not listed? If so, which ones and how?

JUSTIFYING CURRICULUM CHOICES

■ In a well-known article, Israel Scheffler (1958) argues that schools must have clear and explicit grounds for their curriculum decisions. He shows that schools cannot justify choices without explicit principles and commitments. His own guiding principle is that the curriculum is to help learners attain maximum self-sufficiency as economically as possible. For Scheffler, "economically" means efficiently and with maximum transfer value to a wide range of situations. "Self-sufficiency" means that learners can make responsible personal and moral decisions, and have the technical skills and intellectual power to carry them out.

Scheffler is right that often we do not pay enough attention to our rationale for making curriculum decisions. Often we make decisions just to meet the expectations of departments of education. Yet Scheffler's own principle prompts some questions. Why does Scheffler speak of the need for commitments and yet say little about the values to which he is himself committed? Does his conception of maximum individual self-sufficiency not lead to self-centeredness? Does it not neglect that we are part of communities and a society whose interests we must take into account? Discuss the strengths and weaknesses of Scheffler's basis for justifying curriculum decisions.

If we do not justify curriculum decisions and choices explicitly, we allow others to make such decisions for us. We may, for instance, let a government curriculum outline or a textbook determine what we teach and how we teach it. Sometimes using such material may be legitimate. A curriculum guide may stipulate knowledge and skills that you agree to be necessary or desirable for students to function in society. A textbook may match the aims you have set for a course. You may disagree with a curriculum guide for a course, but still decide to teach it because an external examination based on it will affect your students' university entrance.

Using such materials, however, may also undermine your basic educational beliefs and aims. The likelihood of this happening decreases when you use some clear criteria for curriculum decisions, criteria that reflect your beliefs about education. And a person's basic view of knowledge affects how one makes and defends curriculum decisions. Let me give an example in each curriculum orientation.

The Council for Basic Education (1991) begins with the essentialist view that students need "a solid, academic foundation" in the basic subjects. It then defines "the knowledge and qualities we cherish as a society" in terms of intellectual development. A large chart of its recommended standards emphasizes the logical, scientific, and verbal modes of knowing. The Council does include the arts as one of the basic subjects. Yet even here it emphasizes analytic content and skills: know the history, critically appreciate, define, think about the meaning, possess a background, explain the function. Only one item asks students to create art. The implicit view is that the aesthetic, and, even more so, the physical, intuitive, and interpersonal modes of knowing are not the direct concern of the school. Knowledge and education consists mainly of information that students learn to process.

The technical orientation to curriculum in the English-speaking world hails back to 1854. It was then that Herbert Spencer asked and answered his famous curriculum question, "What knowledge is of most worth?" He began his justification for curriculum by stating what he considered the obvious and indisputable criterion for choosing content:

curriculum content must have intrinsic value, with true value being its applicability to some aspect of life. That means we must classify and rank the leading kinds of activity of human life. Spencer's activities were ones for self-preservation, for securing the necessities of life, for the rearing and discipline of offspring, for maintaining proper social and political relations, and for filling up the leisure part of life.

From this Spencer concluded that the most important content we could teach included (in order of priority) the truths of science (including mathematics and especially technologies such as mechanics), knowledge of our own language, and health and physiology. History as usually taught, on the other hand, had not the "remotest bearing" on any of our actions and is therefore of little value (Spencer 1911). Knowledge, for Spencer, consisted of directly useful information and skills, with the scientific and verbal modes of learning taking precedence.

Australia's Donald Vandenberg (1988) takes a more deliberative approach. His basic criterion for curriculum content is that it must enable students to understand and interpret things, to make sense out of the world. Therefore they must explore phenomena in the natural and social world. Since making things and play have great human significance for living meaningfully, curriculum content must emphasize the practical knowledge of the arts, crafts, trades, sports, and professions. Further, to make students aware of the lived world in sensitively articulated ways, a disciplined study of the humanities (including ethics and religion) will allow them to consider accumulated cultural knowledge. In short, we choose content to bring significance and order to students' feelings, fears, hopes, and aspirations (Vandenberg 1988).

For a constructivist justification I go to a feminist view of the curriculum (Jane Kenway and Helen Modra in Luke and Gore 1992, 140-43). For Kenway and Modra, "a useful starting point" is that "knowledge is produced, negotiated, transformed, and realized in the interaction between the teacher, the learner, and the knowledge itself" (140). Yet the knowledge hierarchies of the curriculum, they claim, favor the concerns and interests of males: "the school subjects which emphasize the rational and impersonal, autonomy, predictability, and control are much more highly valued than those associated with the artistic and emotional, the intersubjective and interpersonal" (141). That means that the curriculum neglects and denies the cultural experiences of girls and women and does not allow them to be fully involved in producing knowledge. Therefore the curriculum must, for instance, include new courses such as Women's Studies and Family and Work Studies, and redesign existing courses to allow for small group learning, cooperative problem solving, and girls' interests. Students themselves must be involved in negotiating the curriculum, since process is all important in students producing knowledge and acting upon the world.

■ What are the strengths and weaknesses of the criteria used to justify curriculum choices in each of these examples? Before going on, try to formulate a basic guideline that you might use yourself in making curriculum decisions, one that reflects your beliefs about education and about knowledge. Compare it with the list given in the next section.

A BIBLICAL BASIS FOR JUSTIFYING CURRICULUM DECISIONS

A Biblical view of knowledge holds that God has given us a created reality. We interact with that reality: the world challenges us and we challenge the world. We respond in personal and diverse ways as we encounter, understand, interpret, and develop knowledge. God calls us to do so within the contours of His Biblical mandates to be responsible stewards of the earth, to love God and neighbor, and to live according to the principles of Biblical *shalom*. This paragraph not only sums up the theme of this book up to this point but also provides the foundation of a Biblical approach to curriculum justification.

The guiding principle for justifying curriculum decisions in this book is whether the curriculum enhances the possibility of students becoming responsible, responsive disciples of Jesus Christ. Disciples are not blind followers, but persons who take the principles of the Teacher and make them operational in their own setting. Do students experience and become familiar with a Christian worldview? Do students explore their experiences with the world around them and analyze them in terms of Biblical guidelines? Do they create products and artifacts and procedures and theories that unfold God's reality and develop their gifts? Do they become aware of and critique the shared meanings of our culture? Do they respond and have the opportunity to choose and commit themselves to Biblical values? Do they develop their diverse talents? Does the curriculum encourage them to be and become servant leaders? While some modes of knowing may come to the fore more than others in particular instances, curriculum decisions should take into account the diverse ways of knowing that contribute to the richness of our lives.

Scheffler's guiding principle for justification was that the curriculum is to help learners attain maximum self-sufficiency as economically as possible. This book's principle, in contrast, is that the curriculum is to help learners become responsive disciples of Jesus Christ. To be useful, such principles need elaboration. A small group of teachers led by Paul Still used this basic principle to develop more specific criteria for making curriculum decisions. While written for the middle grades, the criteria apply to most grade levels:

1. How does the curriculum enhance understandings needed for exercising responsive discipleship?
   a. Does it contribute to an understanding of some aspect of a Christian worldview, especially the importance of Biblical *shalom*?
   b. Does it help students to consider Biblically-based values, and encourage them to form dispositions and commitments based on such values?
   c. Does it help familiarize students with our Christian as well as our Western cultural heritage?

2. How is the curriculum relevant for students?
   a. Does it connect with and expand students' previous backgrounds, experiences, and knowledge?
   b. Does it address meaningful and significant current issues in the world, and encourage response in personal ways?
   c. Does it foster students seeing and investigating interrelations with different subject disciplines where this contributes to understanding issues and their applications?

3. How does the curriculum meet students' pedagogical needs?
   a. Is it imaginative enough to maintain student interest?
   b. Does it provide for active response suitable for the learners' stage of development?
   c. Does it support diverse learning activities appropriate for diverse learning styles and other individual differences?
   d. Does it encourage the development of different modes of knowing?

■ Consider a curriculum topic such as "transportation" or "measurement." Choose a specific grade level. Indicate what you would have to do to teach the unit on the basis of the list of foregoing criteria. Is it possible to take any topic and teach it according to these criteria? Why or why not? Give some examples.

SUMMARY

Some educators look at knowledge as an objective, organized body of information, with either reasoning or observation or a combination of both providing such knowledge. For others, knowledge is personally constructed and therefore subjective. A Biblical view is that God has created the world, and humans are able to uncover layer upon layer as we gain deeper understanding. Knowledge involves unfolding *and* shaping reality, but we do so based on our own faith presuppositions and interpretations. Therefore knowing also involves personal and communal response and commitment.

Since we learn through diverse modes of knowing, we should plan the curriculum to include modes such as the interpersonal and aesthetic besides the scientific, verbal, and logical ones. Basic principles guide and justify curriculum choices. Such principles and ensuing criteria, when made explicit, can provide a clear framework for curriculum planning. This book's guiding principle is that the curriculum nurtures students to be and become responsive disciples of Jesus Christ.

REFLECTING

1. This chapter presented views of knowledge prominent in four curriculum orientations. Think back to your own schooling. Probably all four views came to the fore at different times. Possibly a teacher may even have promoted two or three different views on different occasions in one course. Which view or views dominated your schooling? What effect did that have on your education? on your life? Would the implementation of a Biblical view of knowledge have made a difference? Why or why not?

2. The section on knowledge and truth in the classroom suggests that the curriculum includes a core of knowledge. In view of Paul Still's list of criteria to justify curriculum content, what should such a core include?

3. This chapter claims that knowledge, to be meaningful, involves active engagement and response. Some suggestions made are relating learning to students' own experiences, having students pose and solve problems, emphasizing metacognitive strategies, providing opportunities for "transcendence," and having students exhibit the results of their learning. Give some examples of each of these at the level at which you teach or plan to teach. Can you suggest other ways of encouraging vibrant involvement and response?

Chapter 5
Organizing
Curriculum Content

■ For one-third of the school day, Rita Bot and Kathy Huizing each teach two grade 8 classes. They use the long block to teach humanities, formerly taught in the three separate subjects of Biblical studies, English, and social studies. They also have a daily time slot for planning their program together. The first unit of the year is *Self in Community*. The unit includes a wide variety of fast-paced learning activities, with aspects of all three subject areas integrated to form a unified whole.

One student activity includes a journal response to John Donne's quote that no man is an island. A series of individual, small group, and whole class activities begins with students looking at the images that our culture cultivates. They then complete an eight-category chart on the elements of culture. They use it to contrast how they fit into the dominant culture with the way a film portrays life in an Amish-type Hutterite colony. Personal accounts of Canadian racial discrimination against Ukrainian and Japanese immigrants provide a backdrop for considering prejudice, tolerance, and acceptance within a Biblical framework.

Toward the end, the unit shifts once more to how students see themselves and their peers. The students discuss how the media and society idolize physical appearance. They study the story of David to see how God uses very different criteria to judge the worth of a person. They then use this as background for making a silhouette/collage about themselves. One of their three final responses to the unit is answering the question, "Think about your role within the communities to which you belong: learner at school, believer (or skeptic) at church, athlete in sports, child/sibling in family, etc. What have you learned about your role and responsibility within the body of Christ? Be specific and give examples."

Why do both teachers and students react positively to this unit? Kathy and Rita identify a number of factors. The unit deals with issues that are real for the students. It frequently includes current magazine and newspaper articles relevant for thirteen- and fourteen-year-olds. The students have many opportunities to react and respond personally to issues ranging from self-image to social intolerance. Students fill the walls quickly with exhibits of their work.

Also, the students react well to the long blocks of time spent on one topic. Kathy and Rita plan carefully to ensure frequent change of pace and choice of activities. They use the long blocks of time to forge the class into a community where students care for each other and become accountable for their tasks. Student self-reflection and close contact with their peers and teacher leads to an open, positive class atmosphere. The teaching is in-depth, with students often working in pairs or small groups. Kathy and Rita deal with big issues and come back to them in a spiral fashion, deepening students' insights each time. They find that their joint planning takes more time but helps them clarify expectations and keeps them on track. The new structure has revitalized their teaching; their teaching methods and assignments have become more creative.

In the grade 8 timetable, teacher Clarence Janzen also combines mathematics and science into one integrated subject. A typical unit is the one on mass, volume, and matter. It first deals with integers and graphing and then reinforces the mathematical ideas as students apply graphing techniques to the science topics. For instance, they graph a person's weight from birth at one-year intervals. The students like this since they sense the usefulness of their mathematical knowledge. Clarence also paces his classes carefully. He plans a lab every other day, often one that shows and analyzes an unexpected result (in a portable classroom without water or gas hookups!). He finds, too, that the double block helps him to get to know the students and develop a better class atmosphere.

Rita, Kathy, and Clarence all enjoy their new curriculum organization. They switched from a system in which six or seven different teachers taught individual subjects to each grade 8 class. But are there any drawbacks? Is there a danger that a subject "loses out," as is sometimes claimed? List what you see as the strengths and weaknesses of this curriculum organization. Would this kind of organization work well at the grade 6 level? in grade 10? Why or why not?

In this example, the curriculum includes blocks intended for an integrated approach to education. Yet Kathy, Rita, and Clarence keep the humanities separate from mathematics/science. Moreover, they do not integrate fully. For example, Kathy and Rita teach a unit on the gospel of Mark separately but at the same time as a social studies/English unit on China. Clarence has non-integrated units like earth science in science and algebra in mathematics. Further, their grade 8s take French, physical education, and various subject electives in separate time slots.

This example underscores that usually schools organize their curriculum in terms of a fairly standard set of subjects. Most often, language arts and mathematics form the nucleus. Subjects like art and health wane and wax in importance in cyclical fashion. At the primary level many teachers use interdisciplinary thematic units. Some schools plan theme weeks for certain grade levels. Nevertheless, usually most work is organized in separate subject disciplines. Such subjects may deal with one particular aspect of reality (e.g., chemistry), or a combination of several aspects (e.g., social studies may include geography, history, economics, sociology, political science, and anthropology). Schools base their organization on their view of knowledge, their aims for education, and society's expectations.

This chapter considers how schools organize their curricula. Are there characteristics that can lead us to identify the different aspects of reality? If so, should subject disciplines correspond to these aspects? If schools develop a "core," what should it include? When and to what extent is subject integration desirable? After a brief section that stipulates a definition of integral units, the chapter concludes with a discussion of practical concerns that affect curriculum organization.

■ "In many accounts of schooling, the written curriculum . . . has often been treated as a neutral given, embedded in an otherwise meaningful and complex situation. Yet in anyone's own schooling, it is known very well that while some subjects, topics, or lessons were loved, others were hated. Some were learned easily and willingly, others were rejected wholeheartedly. Sometimes the variable was the teacher, or the time, or the room, or the people, but often it was the form or content of the curriculum itself." (Ivor Goodson in Lewy 1991, 58-59)

Goodson goes on to say that the school curriculum even in its organization is far from neutral. There are reasons why, for instance, some schools teach history and geography separately while others teach social studies. Some make consumer education compulsory while others do not deem it a worthy subject. In the United States many students graduate without taking any foreign languages; in Europe, students may have to take as many as four. Teachers often delete geometry and statistics from mathematics courses, yet elsewhere these are separate, required subjects. Art and music are often compulsory only in lower grades, but mathematics must often be taken up to grade 11. Can you suggest reasons for such arrangements? Can you give other examples to show that curriculum organization reflects certain beliefs about the purpose of education?

One question that arises here is the extent to which certain subjects should be compulsory. We are all stronger in some modes of knowing than in others. For instance, to do well in high school physics, you need to have some aptitude for numerical, spatial, scientific, and logical knowing. But since physics is an important aspect of life in a technological society, should not all students take at least some physics, even those whose strengths are not in these modes of knowing? If so, should it be part of a practical science course where we diminish the level of numerical and logical aptitude required and teach it so that persons with strengths in verbal and interpersonal knowing can also benefit? Or should we make aspects of physics compulsory only as part of some interdisciplinary units on technology in society, with students choosing the types of activities in line with their strengths? What do you think?

Before reading the rest of this chapter, list the subject disciplines that you believe should be compulsory ones in the school curriculum, if any. Suggest the grade levels at which you think they ought to be required. Give reasons for your choices.

CATEGORIZING THE ASPECTS OF REALITY

The Bible does not provide a formula for organizing the curriculum. Such organization changes as culture unfolds. The Bible does convey, however, that all education must be used to nurture obedient living. Curriculum organization, therefore, must allow students to examine God's call for the place and task of humans in the world. That means that schools should acquaint students with the diversity of God's created reality and also prepare them to participate in modern society. Students should become conversant with the range of aspects of reality from the numerical to the ethical and spiritual as well as with, for instance, using modern modes of communication and computers. This section discusses how the various aspects of reality may be categorized and what that means for curriculum organization.

For many centuries philosophers have debated how to categorize knowledge. We experience reality wholistically. At the same time, we recognize that we deal with facets of phenomena in what often seem natural categories. For instance, when you spend a day on the beach, you use *arithmetic* to buy an ice cream cone. Marking off a volleyball court in the sand requires *geometry*. Someone who explains why it will get foggy before nightfall uses her *science* knowledge. A mother uses *psychology* to discipline her child. The book you enjoy is an example of *literature*. You may, however, be bothered by the loud *music* that blasts from a nearby car. You (gently) discuss with the perpetrators the *law* against noise and the *ethics* of inflicting such music on those on the beach. Later, around a campfire, you use *theology* to explain what you believe about God's providence. *Economics* is factor in deciding whether to make the long drive home in the fog or to stay overnight in the local motel.

Usually we do not think in subject categories as we experience and use geometry or economics real life. But these and other aspects are embedded in all situations. To gain deeper insight we focus on particular aspects in a more formal way. For instance, you may want to analyze how the mother disciplined her child and review alternate ways based on psychological theories. Or you may study with your book discussion club the literary merits of the book you enjoyed. Psychology and literature and the other subjects mentioned are different realms of knowledge related to diverse aspects of reality.

Philip Phenix, for one, showed that human beings experience meanings in different realms of knowledge. He identified six distinct realms on the basis of three characteristics: (1) their leading ideas, (2) their distinctive structures, and (3) their typical methods of inquiry. Phenix identified these six fundamental (though interrelated and complementary) realms of meaning: symbolics (language and mathematics), empirics (science and health), aesthetics (music, visual art, and literature), synnoetics (personal knowledge), ethics, and synoptics (history, religion, and philosophy). According to Phenix, these realms give us the basic ingredients of all of life, including logical thinking, feeling, expression, and conscience. Therefore, he concluded, the realms should also form the components for organizing the curriculum (Phenix 1964, 6-9).

Paul Hirst used somewhat different criteria in arriving at his categorization of what he called forms of knowledge. Hirst believed that Phenix' last criterion, the characteristic methods of inquiry, does not add much to Phenix' two others (Hirst 1974, 86-87). Methods of inquiry indicate how knowledge is pursued in the disciplines. This is certainly important. As we saw, there are different modes of knowing or different ''intelligences.'' Phenix, however, did not distinguish between modes of knowing and knowledge disciplines. You may use the logical way of knowing to arrive at a result in number theory, for instance, but that does not mean that arithmetic and logic are the same discipline. Perhaps the most we can say is that in working in different realms of knowledge or aspects of reality the degree to which we use certain methods of inquiry differs.

Paul Hirst replaced Phenix' method of inquiry criterion with one for validity of claims. Thus his three criteria for identifying a form of knowledge are (1) the uniqueness of its key concepts, (2) the logical structure relating the key concepts, and (3) the criteria for truth used to assess claims. On this basis he identifies mathematics, the physical sciences, knowledge of persons, literature and the fine arts, morals, religion, and philosophy. History and social science, Hirst believes, are too complex to be separate forms of knowledge. He feels they fall partly under the physical sciences and partly under interpersonal knowledge.

A problem Hirst cannot resolve, however, is that his criteria for truth only admit those within his parameters of rationality. For Hirst, rationality is the ultimate justification for any claim to truth. He fails to see that reason always operates within the bounds of belief presuppositions. And since even in the foundations of mathematics we must necessarily make certain faith-based assumptions, Hirst's last criterion does not help us much.

Both Phenix and Hirst assume that the disciplines reflect our experience of reality. While human observations and interpretations are tentative and subject to revision, they nonetheless hold that knowledge exists independently of people. Constructivists disagree with this view. They admit that humans have constructed distinguishable subject categories. They argue, however, that these are not very important for curriculum purposes since in other contexts humans would create other categories.

Roy Clouser takes issue with the constructivists and begins with a step that precedes the criteria of Phenix and Hirst. He begins with the principle that everything except God Himself is God's creation, and that nothing in creation, about creation, or true of creation is self-existent. He then uses the work of Dutch Christian philosopher Herman Dooyeweerd to propose a list of fifteen aspects of reality, each of which has unique and irreducible meanings, concepts, and laws (i.e., created orderly structures). Clouser does not claim his to be definitive since further reflection may lead to revisions. He adds that all aspects function together in human situations but we may focus on one or two to gain deeper understanding. The aspects form a unity that coheres in Christ: each aspect is the work of the Word of God. Clouser therefore warns against regarding any aspect of creation as the only genuine aspect or as making the existence of any other possible (Clouser 1991, 202-215).

Below I show a revised version of Clouser's list of aspects with their irreducible key meanings and related subject disciplines. My revisions are based in part on Stuart Fowler's conclusions (Fowler 1991, 210-225). From the bottom to the top of the list, the aspects show increasing complexity. The laws unique to each of the last five aspects (psychic/emotional to quantitative) govern the way things are in a pre-determined way. Humans cannot change the law of gravity, for instance. But the laws in the first eight aspects are normative. Humans can decide whether or not to live according to God's laws for those aspects. One of God's laws for social life is that we love our neighbor as ourselves. Obeying the law leads to *shalom*; defying the law, to hurt and brokenness. Each day again, we choose whether or not to follow such laws. In school, students experience, consider, and apply both types of laws. What is important is that they see both types as God's laws for creation, and that we help them explore the implications of accepting or rejecting God's norms in the first eight aspects, both personally and as a society.

Human thinking about aspects of reality corresponds to subject discipline content, that is, to distinct organizations of knowledge in one or more aspects. I have indicated examples of such disciplines in the second column. Knowledge in the disciplines results from the work of specialists. Schools plan their curriculum so that their students become familiar with the key meanings, concepts, laws, and methods of inquiry in each category. What needs to be remembered is that the knowledge of specialists is also affected by their beliefs about reality, about humans, and about the purpose of life. Therefore Christian educators should discern the spirit behind the knowledge offered in terms of Biblical norms and directives (Steensma and Van Brummelen 1977, 17-18).

Aspect of reality	Key meaning	Related subject disciplines
Confessional	Allegiance	Theology, religious studies
Ethical	Integrity	Ethics
Political/legal	Justice	Law, political science
Economic	Stewardship	Economics
Social	Personal interaction	Sociology
Lingual	Symbolic meaning	Language
Analytical/logical	Rational analysis	Logic, computer science
Aesthetic	Creative allusiveness	Visual art, music, dance
Psych./emotional	Perception and feeling	Psychology
Biotic	Life	Biology, physiology
Physical	Energy	Chemistry, physics
Spatial	Space	Geometry, topology
Quantitative	Number	Arithmetic, number theory
Cultural formation (Great Mandate)	Faith, love and justness (God's great injunctions)	History, interdisciplinary studies

My list may not be logically defensible in all its details. Clouser himself splits the physical into two, adding a kinematic aspect with motion as the key meaning. Where do subjects like geography or physical education fit? Philosophy is missing; Clouser argues that it is an overarching discipline that relates to and interprets all aspects of reality (for example, we speak of the philosophy of science). I have also removed "cultural formation" from Clouser's list. It seems to me that it also overarches the other aspects: you have cultural formation in each aspect and in the totality of aspects.

Two conclusions follow despite these uncertainties in the categorization. First, philosophers using their own criteria have arrived at hierarchical categorizations of knowledge that have striking similarities. This suggests that humans can analyze and deepen their insight into reality by considering inherent, identifiable forms of knowledge. Second, a curriculum must cover a wide scope of forms of knowledge for learners to know about all aspects of human life.

CURRICULUM SUBJECTS AND THE ASPECTS OF REALITY

Suppose we agree with the categorization of a list such as the one given above. The question then still remains whether we should plan to organize our curriculum on the basis of the subject fields shown. We can argue that when they graduate, pupils should have some knowledge of each aspect of reality, especially since each has its own key meaning, concepts, and laws. If we teach each aspect explicitly at some point in the curriculum, and explore how to use them in modern society, pupils would receive a balanced view of reality and be able to function well in our multi-faceted world. The difficulty with this argument is that it is not clear that the key meanings and laws of the aspects are best taught in thirteen or more separate subjects. Indeed, five factors militate against this position.

First, situations in real life never fall neatly into one or another category. We can learn all about the physics of a television set in science, but television exists in and affects social situations. To study only the physical-electronic aspects of a television set would deny students the opportunity to consider its impact on language, aesthetics, economics, ethics, and faith. A more meaningful unit about television might be one that integrates the study of all these aspects, allowing students to experience and respond to the pervasive effect television has on our daily lives.

Second, the separation of academic disciplines into independent pigeonholes contributes to the fragmentation of knowledge. It overlooks the fact that many interrelations exist among the disciplines. You cannot get very far in physics without knowing some mathematics, nor in biology without knowing some chemistry. Some knowledge of the history of science and the economic impact of scientific and technological inventions places science in a more meaningful context. The difficult decisions that have to be made today with respect to reproductive technologies and ecological questions demand that the study of ethics be an integral part of genetics and ecology units in biology.

Third, some school subjects combine or cut across several aspects of reality. New subjects arise as we use our cultural power to unfold God's creation. For instance, we usually combine the quantitative and spatial aspects of reality in mathematics. Social studies embraces cultural formation in at least the confessional, ethical, political/legal, economic, and social aspects. Literature and drama involves cultural formation as it comes to expression in the lingual and aesthetic dimensions. Subjects with a practical emphasis such as physical education, home economics, business management, and industrial education do not fit in any one category. Yet they have a legitimate place in the curriculum.

Fourth, some modes of knowing and some aspects of reality can be learned well in the context of subjects focusing on other aspects. For instance, ethics for young children is best taught through literature. Visual arts and writing skills are best practiced in the context of units with relevant, cross-disciplinary themes (although we should teach specific skills in each area). Logical reasoning is best taught as a part of all other subjects, especially since the concepts and methods taught in logic as a subject seldom transfer to other situations.

Finally, students' own developmental levels affect how we organize the curriculum. As people unfolded reality during the course of history, they gradually developed more specialized disciplines. Psychology became a separate discipline only late in the 19th century; computer science, only in the middle of the twentieth century. There is a parallel with students' intellectual development through the years. When children enter school, they have experienced reality wholistically. Integrated thematic approaches allow them to build on and relate to those experiences. As children grow older, they gradually can specialize and take more interest in specific aspects of reality.

For example, younger pupils learn about the psychic aspect of reality in school, but not in the subject of psychology. They study units such as "I Am Special" and "Friendship." Sensitive teachers consciously and continually address their pupils' emotional growth in a community setting. But psychology as a subject is not taught until the senior high school or college level. The same is true for sociology, economics, law, and ethics. In North America, most schools teach social studies in the lower grade levels. Gradually at higher levels they begin to teach geography, history, and economics separately, with sociology, anthropology, and criminology providing further specialization at the college level.

In short, identifying the aspects of reality or the forms of knowledge still does not give us easy answers for the organization of the curriculum. But there are several guidelines we can follow. First, does the curriculum include all aspects of reality and deal with their key meanings? Is that true even when the curriculum does not include the particular disciplines corresponding to some aspects of reality? Second, does the curriculum organization take into account students' developmental levels? Does the organization allow content to be rooted in students' own experience and pose problems that are relevant for students at their level of understanding? Third, does the unity and interrelatedness of knowledge become clear to the students? Is there sufficient opportunity to experience how the aspects of reality are interconnected? Fourth, does the organization enable students to live faithfully according to God's will? Will the organization lend itself to students reconciling what is harmed by sin and understanding and proclaiming love and justice?

One implication of these guidelines is, I believe, that we teach a core curriculum--but one that differs substantially from the way core curricula are usually defined. Another implication is that students benefit from integrating some content. However, in-depth considerations of the key meanings, concepts, and laws of each aspect of reality are probably best done in subjects that highlight one or two particular aspects. There also are subjects, especially ones with more practical emphasis, that do not correspond to a particular aspect of reality and yet enable students to serve society and help reform it. We will consider each of these points in turn in the remainder of this chapter.

- Go back to the list of compulsory subjects that you made at the start of this section. Would you now make any revisions? Why or why not? Do you agree that a core curriculum is desirable? If so, what should it include?

PLANNING A CORE CURRICULUM

- *Living in Hope* is a series of eight modules for grades 11 and 12 high school students intended to help them understand themselves and their role in society within a Biblical framework. It focuses on what it means to be ambassadors for Christ and to bring about reconciliation and healing in different aspects of our society and culture (De Moor 1992, 5). Each module considers four questions:

    1. What does the Bible teach us about this aspect of society?
    2. How has history and tradition shaped people's ideas and the development of social institutions?
    3. What is the present state or condition of this social institution in Canadian society?
    4. What changes and alternatives can Christians propose and implement, at least in part, to honor more fully the task of handing on God's reconciliation to Canadian society and the world? (De Moor 1992, 6)

    The *Perspectives* module shows how beliefs influence what people do and say. The *Community* module focuses on the need for both individual and communal action to bring healing and hope, and deals specifically with the dangers of ethnocentrism and racism. In the *Self* unit students consider how their environment has shaped them and how they deal with issues such as rejection, feelings of inadequacy and self-acceptance, depression and suicide, and homosexuality. The *Troth* module deals with friendship, marriage, and family. The remaining modules are *Government and justice, Education in the Schools, Work and the Job,* and *Communication.*

    Each module has short descriptive sections interspersed with frequent and diverse student activities. What is unique is that the latter part (at least half) of each module consists of various "key materials" from a wide variety of sources. These are used in the student and class activities. The *Community* module, for instance, includes source articles about Canada's multicultural policy; Canada's aboriginal, Italian, Doukhobor, Irish, Chinese, and Hutterite communities; the role of religion in community, ranging from the Christian church and Islam faith to cults; and examples of discrimination such as racial intolerance and prejudice against a labor union, the Christian Labour Association of Canada. One article about the Hutterites taken from a magazine also reproduces the advertisements in order to show "the stark difference between the message of the article and North American affluence described in the advertisements" (De Moor 1992, 16).

When we think of a "core curriculum," we often think in terms of the "three Rs," that is, of basic reading, writing, and arithmetic skills. Sometimes we add some basic social studies and science concepts and skills that we believe students need in order to function in society. But we seldom think of a course such as *Living in Hope* as "core." Yet if "core" means innermost or most essential, the issues in *Living in Hope*, at least for high school students who have attained basic literacy and numeracy skills, are more likely essential for responsive discipleship than being able to pick out parts of speech or solve quadratic equations. Being able to live in an informed and responsible manner in our society requires a great deal of discussion and thought about the issues we face, particularly with the media giving students a skewed impression about life.

At the end of the last section, you considered what a core curriculum might include. Did your description include a course like *Living in Hope?* If not, should it? Some years ago philosopher Nick Wolterstorff suggested in a speech that the one "core" course every student should take is home economics. If taught properly, he argued, that course would prepare students for responsible family life, and that, in turn, would be the basis for a healthy society. Do you agree? Why or why not? What are the essentials that we should include in the required core curriculum?

It is instructive to look at some examples of core curricula. They have usually come about because of parental unhappiness with what they perceive to take place in the schools. What educators define as core depends, like other curriculum choices, on their basic aims for schooling and their matching curriculum orientation. Academic traditionalists, for example, influenced British Columbia's 1977 core curriculum. It included the "essential skills and knowledge" students should acquire in reading, writing, listening, speaking, arithmetic, geometry, science, social studies, health, and research and critical thinking skills (British Columbia Ministry of Education 1977). The Minister of Education introduced this core curriculum to certify that schools taught the "basics." For several years, the Ministry used the document to plan more detailed curriculum guides and to evaluate whether government-funded independent schools met curriculum criteria.

Parental unhappiness, however, waned only temporarily. A government task force and subsequent commission eventually led to British Columbia's *Year 2000* documents. Unlike the earlier core curriculum, they do not list information to be "covered." Instead, the documents reflect the influence of both the technical and constructivist orientations. Technicists tend to define the core curriculum in terms of specified behavioral student outcomes. They emphasize cognitive processes students should be able to do. Constructivists are usually reluctant to define any core curriculum, preferring to give only the broad contours of student developmental areas.

For example, the *Year 2000* primary curriculum guide based a 30-page section on the premise that all students have the right to receive a level of mathematics instruction appropriate to their needs and abilities. Technicists provided almost 250 specific, measurable learning outcomes (e.g., "Use the correct notation for date: 1991-09-25."). But, constructivists hold, such a list inhibits the exploratory nature of learning. It reduces knowledge to a list of narrow behaviors, determined beforehand, to be learned and demonstrated. The constructivists' influence shows up in two ways. First, each group of descriptors is prefaced with the statement *"Teachers provide opportunities for the child to."* Second, student achievement reporting will list only what students have accomplished, not what they cannot yet do nor where they stand in relation to their classmates (British Columbia Ministry of Education 1990b, 279-309).

On the one hand, the program thus includes descriptors of learning that are "more focused, more precise subsets of the widely-held expectations against which a child's growth and development are interpreted" (BCME 1990b, 361). On the other hand, "the Primary Program refers to the program that *you*, the teacher, envision, create, and, together with your students, call into being" (BCME 1990b, 356). Teachers could and did choose either path, or a mixture of both. The lack of a consistently implemented core curriculum resulting from this inner contradiction led to much parental unrest.

The Core Curriculum for Australian Schools, developed by the Curriculum Development Centre in Canberra (1980) had a very different approach to defining a core. It listed nine areas of knowledge and experience: arts and crafts (including literature, music, visual arts, drama, wood, metal, and plastic crafts); environmental studies; mathematics; social, cultural, and civic studies; health education; scientific and technological ways of knowing and their social applications; communication (verbal and non-verbal); moral reasoning and action, value and belief system; and work, leisure, and life-style.

What is significant is not only the wide range of issues considered worthy of the core, but also the deliberative approach to curriculum. The document admits that arts and crafts and health education need review and stronger rationales. Yet it includes them since arts and crafts are fundamental forms of human expression and self-help health education would support government health initiatives. The document also mentions that a lack of unanimity about the extent of foreign language courses in the core requires continued deliberation. It leaves open the question of whether teaching morality and values should be done in a separate course or be incorporated in other areas, although it emphasizes that it should not be neglected.

The Australian core curriculum document takes the social impact of learning to be important. Environmental studies is part of the core since it is essential to develop a disposition to sustain and protect the environment. Mathematics contributes to a view of the world. Social, cultural, and civic studies include consideration of the place and significance of belief and value systems in society. Students undertake practical action projects related to students' experiences and interests. Schools incorporate into the core an introduction to the work environment and household management. The document also readily admits, however, that the case for the extent of "education for life" is complex and unresolved. In short, a deliberative approach to core curriculum points to essential curriculum issues, but admits that there are no hard and fast answers.

Any core curriculum should be based on what is considered fundamental and indispensable, even when different contexts and social demands mean that a core is never static. What I consider fundamental is that educating for responsible and responsive discipleship requires the unfolding of a Christian vision of life. That includes understanding and being able to apply four Biblical injunctions: the Great Mandate, the Great Commission, the Great Commandment and the Great Community. Also, students cannot function as disciples unless they know the important ideologies, theories, concepts, and skills of our culture and respond with competence and creativity. They must be able to discern and critique the issues of our time. We design our core to nurture values, dispositions, and commitments in harmony with Biblical norms. The overriding values include love, compassion, peace, justice, righteousness, and truth.

The scope of a core curriculum based on these principles will be all of human culture. At the elementary level teachers will often include the core in integral units whose themes focus on language arts, social studies, and science. There they can bring out the importance of Biblical love and compassion in units on friendship and community, of peace and justice in units on civics and national history, of righteousness and truth in units on the environment and economics. But the core also includes the Biblical principles governing each aspect of reality. As such, much of what I describe in chapter 6 is part of the core, even when taught in separate subjects.

Basic skills are also part of what is essential. Often we can develop communication, research, and art skills as part of integrated units. The sequential nature of numeracy skills and the need for regular reinforcement means that we usually teach mathematics as a separate subject. The same is true of physical education and music, although we may use integral units to reinforce and extend skills and insights developed in these subjects.

In the middle and secondary schools, we continue to offer units that focus on cross-disciplinary situations that students face in their everyday life. This core provides a focus for the curriculum. If other curriculum content relates to this core, we help students grasp the unity of knowledge and their role in the whole of human experience. We can organize the core into one central course such as *Living in Hope*, or teach core units in the different strands of the curriculum.

At the middle school level, for instance, units on understanding ourselves, life in community, communication, work and leisure, and economics can be taught in the humanities strand. Units on technology and the environment could be incorporated in science; ones on the role of computers, architecture, and the church in society in mathematics, art, and Biblical studies respectively. Alternately, schools could design one core course offering such units over a two- or three-year period. At the senior high school level, some schools offer a core course in each of grades 11 and 12 that combines the *Living in Hope* modules with Biblical studies.

For students to receive and experience a balanced overview of key issues facing society, elements of all thirteen aspects of reality should be represented in the core curriculum. How does faith affect our stance in life? What does the Bible have to say about sexuality and marriage relationships? What is the government's and our personal role in promoting justice for our aboriginal peoples? Why is it important that we address the problem of poverty and how can we do so? What is the nature of a healthy community and what do we do to overcome prejudice and racism? How do we respond to communication through advertising? How does modern music affect our attitudes and values? Why does rational argumentation fail to sway people on how to vote? What is a Biblical view of self-esteem? How do Christians respond to issues in genetic engineering, ecology, and technology? What is the role of the scientific method in our lives? Are we using space in a stewardly way as we plan our suburbs? Is it right for governments to make decisions on the basis of statistical polls?

Many of these questions are complex ones. At the kindergarten and primary levels, we introduce the topics piecemeal, usually in the context of a story. A kindergarten unit on transportation may include the teacher reading a book on the pollution problems caused by cars and trucks, with a field trip allowing the children to experience public transit alternatives. A grade 4 unit on aboriginal people may show students some positive features of their culture, and the problems resulting from dependence on paternalistic governments. Only when older will students be able to analyze some problems in depth and speak with aboriginal leaders about possible solutions.

The core curriculum, in short, touches on all aspects of life, focusing on students' knowledge leading them to loving action. That does not mean that basic literacy and numeracy skills are not part of what is essential: without them, students cannot begin to understand the core issues nor can they function as responsive disciples in society. What we need to remember, however, is that for Christians the ultimate basics deal with how we respond to God's call to obedience in our everyday life. For that our students need skills. More importantly, however, they need the ability to identify, analyze, and respond to the issues of our time based on a Biblical framework of values.

■ Based on this section, make an outline of what you would include in a core curriculum. Suggest how you would structure the curriculum to include your core. Share your list with another person and discuss the pros and cons of each of your approaches. If you worked together in one school, could you reach a consensus? Why or why not?

INTEGRATING CURRICULUM CONTENT

Dictionaries define the term integration as combining different parts into a unified whole. In education, such combining is done in many different ways. For instance, we integrate racial minorities or children with handicaps in "regular" classrooms. We also speak of integration of faith and learning. Learning is always rooted in certain beliefs. As such, we do not combine faith and learning. Yet this is called integration since the harmony of faith-based learning results in an integral whole. Schools also integrate curriculum subjects. In this section, I consider the latter meaning, viz., the integration of curriculum content.

Note two points. Also with respect to curriculum content, the commonly-used term "integration" is sometimes a misnomer. Students experience real life situations integrally or wholistically. For the sake of in-depth understanding we often focus on separate aspects or subject disciplines. It is then possible once again to integrate two or three of those subjects. We can also, however, study the original situations as wholistic ones, without differentiating and reintegrating. If so, it would be more accurate to speak of an integral rather than an integrated curriculum. However, I will use the term integration since it the one commonly used, although later I will use the term "integral unit." My second point is already implied in the foregoing. The term integration when applied to curriculum content is not a unitary one but has several meanings.

■ Below are examples of four types of curriculum content integration. What are the strengths and weaknesses of each approach? Which kind do you think is most common in schools? Why?

»Berta Den Haan taught a grade 7 unit on ancient Egypt. The students first brainstormed all they knew about Egypt and categorized their knowledge. Students' resulting questions and areas of interest gave focus to the unit (this is sometimes called the K-W-L strategy: I know, I wonder, I learned). In language arts, Berta simultaneously discussed a novel about ancient Egypt, Bert Williams' *Sword of Egypt*. The novel deals with a boy asking Egyptian gods to help him get his father a proper burial and join his mother in the hereafter. Thus the novel showed the students how religion dominated the life of the ancient Egyptians. During the Bible period in the morning, Berta followed up students' responses to the novel by talking about their personal faith commitment and its implications.

»Glenda MacPhee is a gardening enthusiast. During May, she taught her grade 2-3 class a science unit on gardening. A widow next to the school allowed the class to use her backyard. The students planted two large gardening beds, one for flowers and one for produce. The students divided into small groups to take on specific tasks: rototilling, building frames for the beds from donated lumber, spreading top soil, and so on. They learned much about gardening: how mulching helps preservation of water, how composting helps us return nutrients to the soil, how gardening provides us with products that may be more or sometimes less desirable than those in the supermarket. The students also learned much science in an experiential setting: the parts of plants and how they all work together, the conditions needed for successful growth, the various types of flowers and vegetables.

   While this was a science unit, the children also did activities that related to other subjects. They practiced their mathematics as they calculated how much lumber they needed to build the beds. They discussed the ethics of respecting their neighbors' property. They drew pictures of their garden at different stages. They wrote thank you notes to all those who helped with supplies and advice. In the fall, together with their new classmates, they analyzed why some things worked and some didn't. They planned a closing chapel for the whole student body that became a time of praise for God's provision of food and the beauty of plants and flowers. Throughout the unit, children learned a great deal about cooperation, about being responsible, and about taking on leadership roles.

»Emma Johnstone taught an integrated unit about a small Scottish village, Chapel Hill, a five-minute walk away from her school. Throughout the study she allocated special times for fieldwork and class lessons, but she integrated most of the work into the daily program. She divided her seven- and eight-year-olds into groups of three, of mixed ability. She gave each child a kit with eight assignments: a look at the village, making rough plans and scale plans, the village in the past, the main street in detail, the bungalow, the general store, designing and building a house, the village within the surrounding area. Emma built specific skills into the assignments: observing, describing, using reference books, making models, making rough maps and updating older topographical maps, interpreting change from old newspapers and photographs, writing stories, displaying work, reporting orally to the class (each child gets turns), and so on. While Emma taught the unit as an integral whole, the students learned about many aspects of reality. For mathematics, they made plans and charts, read bus timetables, and priced items in the store. For science, they tested materials used in building and did some pollution experiments. For geography, they did map work. For history, they created a picture of what life was like in the village 50-100 years ago. For art, the children took some photographs of the village and used them to make paintings of village scenes. For language, they recorded written work from observation, conducted interviews, and wrote poems, stories, and letters. For religious education, they considered how religion and morality have changed over the last 50-100 years. Emma emphasized, however, that while she could identify these aspects "for convenience," her approach was an interdisciplinary one.

»Anna-May Taekema worked with a group of seven other primary teachers on a two-week unit on *The Jungle*. Its theme was that the jungle is part of God's intricate design. God calls humans to care for, develop, and enjoy the jungle. Mismanagement, however, continues to affect the world and we ourselves must help preserve its ecosystem. The teachers completed large charts with spokes from the center showing objectives and activities in six developmental areas: faith, intellectual, aesthetic, social and emotional, physical, and social responsibility. They then each chose one jungle topic (e.g., reptiles of the jungle, rafts, or going on a jungle hunt).

The teachers divided the eight classes into eight cross-grade groups, and these groups rotated from class to class from 10:30-12:00 each morning. Each teacher provided several centers. Small mixed-age groups worked at the centers, with the older children helping the younger ones. Activities included writing a short story about the adventures on a trip to the jungle, making rafts, creating indigenous jewelry, making reptiles from playdough, building an Amazon village, writing a three-day diary of tenting in the jungle, and painting pictures of themselves in the jungle. Classes did grade-specific activities at other times. The grade 3s, for instance, made posters on the "save the jungle" theme. All students shared initial and culminating activities.

The examples given illustrate four possible ways to integrate curriculum content. To use a food metaphor, these are, respectively, the steak dinner, the pizza, the casserole, and the potluck dinner approach. When teachers align curriculum content so that they deal with similar themes in different subject areas, the resulting parallel discipline approach can be thought of as a steak dinner. The plate contains a steak, a baked potato, two types of vegetables, all separately identifiable but together forming one meal. Berta Den Haan kept social studies and language arts in separate time slots but the content in each complemented the other. Another example is a grade 10 ecology unit. The biology teacher might provide scientific content. The mathematics teacher might teach a unit on statistics highlighting ecological data used later in science. The English teacher might teach a unit on writing a research paper, with students completing one on an ecological topic. Such concurrent teaching on similar topics is fairly easy to arrange, but students do not experience the topic as a unity.

The gardening unit is an example of what we might call the "pizza approach." There is a subject discipline "crust"; this unit focuses on science. But the teacher brings in different kinds of "toppings" from other subject areas that enrich the unit in two ways. First, the students experience and see the interrelatedness of knowledge. Second, the students reinforce and exercise skills from other areas in the curriculum. While the subject "crust" remains evident, the unit is a far more interesting and meaningful whole with the additions. As we saw, the gardening unit focuses on science but incorporates language arts, mathematics, and visual arts activities. It also includes social studies when students investigate the community people involved in gardening and garden marketing.

The "pizza" type of integration is probably most common in schools. Kindergarten and primary teachers frequently teach thematic units of this type. Teachers at higher grade levels often teach units with a social studies or science theme in which students also use their language arts and mathematics insights and skills. With clear goals and careful planning, such units often provide stimulating and comprehensive learning experiences. Teachers need to ensure that the topics chosen are meaningful ones and that balanced concept and skill development takes place.

Emma Johnstone's community study is the "casserole" approach. A casserole is a main course dish made from various ingredients, but even when we can identify some of the ingredients, what makes it special is the overall texture and taste of the mixture. We focus on the whole effect, not on individual ingredients. This approach uses large blocks of classroom time, possibly even a fully integrated day. If carefully planned, students can experience a real life phenomenon or issue very meaningfully. They can become very excited about their learning.

The "casserole" approach, though worthwhile, is used much less than the "pizza" one. To put together and effectively implement this type of unit is very time-consuming and takes sophisticated organizational management. Also, most teachers prefer to teach skill-oriented subjects such as reading, mathematics, and physical education in separate time slots. They find that otherwise they cannot teach and reinforce the necessary skills and keep track of each student's progress.

Finally, the "potluck dinner" approach is one that has recently become popular in some schools, mainly at the elementary level. Here a group of teachers puts together, perhaps once each year, a cross-grade thematic unit where groups of students move from classroom to classroom. Together the teachers design an overall plan to ensure that the whole unit has integrity and coherence. They then all contribute some personal "dishes" to the "potluck dinner." Teachers may plan some activities in a particular subject area, or interdisciplinary ones.

An example of a "potluck" unit is one where each homeroom class studies a particular country. As part of their study, they develop center-based activities to highlight the country for other classes. On successive days, the other classes rotate through each classroom to learn about the different countries. In this way, students get the chance to learn about several countries and also exhibit what they learned in their own in-depth study. Schools have used this type of integration effectively to study major current events such as the Olympic Games. While planning is time-consuming, schools find that an annual cross-grade unit of this type forges teachers and students into teams where they learn from and support each other.

Before asking what type and how much curriculum content integration should occur, I want to consider the advantages and disadvantages of the "pizza" and "casserole" types of integration more fully. For convenience, I will use the term "integration" in the rest of this section to refer to just these two types.

Integration allows students to consider and develop their experiences and interests as a unity. Students often cannot see the relevance of the narrowly-focused content of separate subjects. Integrated units can deal with issues, problems, and experiences that cut across disciplines, themes that relate to practical living, and responsible decision-making. Spiritual and moral questions are not set aside. The unity of knowledge can become clear if teachers show the links and connections between various aspects of reality. They can more easily include the diverse modes of knowing. The larger time blocks often used for integration mean that students don't have to switch as frequently from one subject to another. They help students to focus on investigations for sustained time periods. Particularly if several teachers plan units jointly, integration can lead to renewed enthusiasm for teaching. The more creative teaching approaches that often result also lead to increased student interest and motivation (Jacobs 1989, 51).

Integration also has disadvantages, however. A curriculum with much integration may pay little attention to overall structure. That may result in meager continuous conceptual development or a lack of balance. An integrated curriculum may also neglect sequential skill development. Further, teachers may oppose integration for personal reasons. Secondary teachers who have in-depth knowledge in one or two fields may feel uncomfortable with topics that go beyond their expertise. They may claim that they deal with important personal and social issues within their discipline, and that students need to understand the structure of their disciplines (A. Glatthorn and A. Foshay in Lewy 1991, 161). Planning integrated units with teacher teams also is time consuming. One grade-level planning team estimated that it took 164 hours of time to brainstorm, research the subject matter, develop and sequence activities, find resources and materials, set up speakers and field trips, plan each day, monitor student and teacher progress, and keep parents informed (Jacobs 1989, 51).

The most troubling potential shortcoming of integration is one that can be overcome. It is that units lack focus or significance. Teachers may choose topics because they think of interesting activities rather than because the issues are important. Topics may be vague, narrow, or trivial. Topics such as change, equilibrium, or evidence are too indefinite. The resulting units may lack unity, especially if teachers do not write a clear thematic focus statement. A topic more focused than "change," for instance, is how changes that occurred during the 1960s affected Western culture. A topic like the microscope is too limiting; this could be subsumed under a topic such as cells as the building blocks of life. Units on the circus, balloons, or dinosaurs may include a wealth of fascinating activities, but the topics are superficial or of secondary importance. While teachers can do valuable things for each, there are more socially meaningful topics to investigate. Communities of living things has more significance, for instance, than dinosaurs (although dinosaurs could be investigated as a historical community that died out within this broader unit).

What do we conclude from the advantages and disadvantages of curriculum content integration? First, no one plan is best for all situations. Schools and teachers may remain flexible, especially since research findings suggest that students learn to read, write, and compute about as well with strict subject organization as with more integrated approaches (A. Glatthorn and A. Foshay in Lewy 1991, 161). Second, students benefit from both integrated content and individual subject disciplines. Integration is particularly desirable for investigating cross-disciplinary experiences, issues, and problems relating to student interests and practical living concerns. Organizing curriculum content by subjects is especially useful when developing more abstract conceptual schemata or sequential skills.

The amount of integration in the curriculum usually decreases as students progress through the grades. At the kindergarten and grade 1 levels, the study of themes through class activity and learning centers may take 60% to 75% of the available time. Skill development becomes part of the integrated theme. Teachers may offer only Biblical studies, mathematics, and physical education in separate time slots. At the grade 4 and 5 levels, teachers may have 80 to 105 minute blocks before or after

lunch each day for integrated unit study. The theme may be interdisciplinary or focus on a science or social studies topic. Teachers include
activities that relate to many aspects of reality. Middle schools may
integrate on the basis of curriculum strands (e.g., humanities, math/
sciences). High schools may integrate a core block. They may also
encourage, for example, social studies and English teachers to work
together by scheduling their classes next to each other, at the same time.

Some integration can also take place within blocks set aside for
individual subjects. The thirteen aspects of reality are interrelated.
Physics makes use of mathematics; biology of chemistry; history of
geography, and so on. Further, issues that arise in one aspect of reality
affect and are affected by considerations of other aspects. Studying trees
or forestry in science in a responsible way will include a consideration of,
for instance, (1) economic stewardship, (2) the historical background to
the claims and needs of aboriginal peoples, (3) the biological, aesthetic,
and social concerns of clear-cutting, and (4) the ethical dilemma of
providing jobs or preserving a species of a particular bird. Thus the
"pizza" approach, while focusing on a particular subject, lends itself
well to content integration. For individual teachers, that means that even
with a timetable arranged strictly by subjects, they can still provide
integration if they plan what I call *integral units*.

CHARACTERISTICS OF INTEGRAL UNITS

■ Donna Ferguson taught a unit on trees and forests similar to that just
mentioned to her grade 4 pupils. The theme was particularly relevant since
her school community depends to a large extent on the forest industry.
Her theme was that, as stewards of God's earth, people must be
concerned about natural habitats and therefore develop a new approach
to forestry, one that replaces immediate greed with long-term care and
responsible harvesting of trees.

Donna planned all activities to relate to her theme. The class made
a "giving tree" showing all the things that God provides through trees. She
discussed God's righteous anger at ecological abuse. The students made
personal books about trees and forests that included much personal
response. Six fields trips (to a forest company logging operation, a wood
veneer plant, a tree sanctuary, a forest museum, an original growth forest,
and a forest tour organized by an environmental group) provided the basis
for structured activities and student response. Donna kept in mind her
general goal of discipleship not only in these learning activities, but also by
students planning and directing a fund-raising effort for tree planting in
Ethiopia. She emphasized that responsible stewardship can lead to hope
for the future. She designed the unit so that students learned much not
only about science but also about language arts, geography, and art.

Students can experience the advantages of both integration and subject-focused curriculum if teachers plan most of their units to be *integral* ones. I use the term *integral* rather than *integrated* deliberately. In the "casserole" approach to integration we bring together different aspects of reality. The integration of Donna's unit on trees and forests is somewhat more limited. It uses the "pizza" model, targeting science while frequently bringing in other subjects. Still other units may deal with themes almost totally within one subject. Yet they may do so in a wholistic way, bringing in other aspects of reality only occasionally when they naturally arise. An integral unit, in other words, can be fully integrated in the "casserole" sense of the term, or have very little content integration. I define an integral unit as one that has three characteristics: (1) internal unity, (2) external consistency, and (3) inclusion of pertinent and meaningful aspects of reality related to but going beyond the dominant focus of the unit.

First, an integral unit is *internally unified*. That is, it has a clear thematic focus or unifying theme toward which teachers direct all thought and activity. Such a theme focus is more than a natural phenomena or an event or an issue. It does not just list a topic such as world hunger or pioneers or light (all topics with good potential!). Rather, it contains the key idea(s), values, and dispositions that the unit theme intends to foster. Thus the thematic focus provides the framework for the unit's objectives, content, activities, and structure (for examples, see chapter 8). Themes often soar beyond the particular topic or subject discipline, contributing to the personal development of students and encouraging them to commit themselves to live by what they learn (Van Brummelen 1992, 117).

Secondly, an integral unit is *externally consistent*. That is, it explicitly intends to attain some of the overall aims of the school and, where applicable, the goals of subject discipline(s). Further, the unit is planned on the basis of a well-defined curriculum orientation, and it promotes some of the Biblical values set out in chapter 3. Two curricular consequences may result if teachers do not plan for external consistency. The unit may be internally unified but address issues or use approaches that the school considers insignificant or that detract from its basic aims. Also, the unit may have interesting content but not nurture values and commitments considered crucial for the well-being of students and society.

The third characteristic of an integral unit is that it *includes significant, natural interrelations that exist between its central concepts and aspects of reality that are not the unit's main focal point*. In this way students experience how the aspects of reality interrelate. They begin to understand the unity of knowledge and life that exists within the diversity of our experiences. Many unforced, meaningful relationships exist for almost any topic. A history unit on revolution may consider, for instance, how the arms industry technology affected the Iranian revolution, how art posters are used to maintain internal support for a revolution, how psychological feelings and economics play an important role in the cause of revolutions, whether armed revolution is ever ethically justifiable, and how religious beliefs affect events leading to revolution or to the peaceful resolution of a problem.

Good integral units have other features, of course. They have a carefully designed scope and sequence. They provide for students with diverse learning styles and different aptitudes, and do so with a spectrum of modes of knowing. They include activities that foster understanding, skill development, problem solving, and creativity. They use assessment and evaluation to promote their aims. Chapter 8 will outline how to plan integral units with such features. An integral unit with these characteristics could be a unit taught within a particular subject area. It could also be one, however, with the features of any of the four types of integration: the steak dinner, pizza, casserole, or potluck dinner approach. In other words, although much is to be said for some longer time blocks used for content integration, a teacher can plan worthwhile integral units whatever the total curriculum organization in a school.

How do we choose topics and themes for integral units at different grade levels? Topics and themes should help students experience and explore their place and task within the context of their heritage and community. The criteria at the end of chapter 4 provide a good starting point. The particular choice of units should be a collaborative effort by a school staff. Only school-wide decisions will ensure that the curriculum will deal with all aspects of reality without undue repetition.

■Analyze the unit outlined below. From the short description, can you speculate what the unit's theme would have been? Which type of integration does it illustrate? Suggest how you might structure this unit using the other types of integration.

»Glenda MacPhee taught a unit on *Garbage*. She began the unit by discussing the diversity of things in creation and how all things have a place in reality. Her students considered various naturally-occurring cycles, such as the food cycle, as well as cycles resulting from human activity. They then explored how human activity produces garbage. The students visited a garbage dump to experience how much our society throws away, and investigated how much of what is wasted could be recycled. In the classroom, they decided how they themselves could reduce consumption and reuse products. They implemented an appropriate plan of action. Meanwhile, the students read and discussed a book about an empty lot that its owner planned to sell for a gas station development. The owner discovered, however, that the lot is not just a place where people dump litter, but that its every nook and cranny contained much life. This story led the students to look for garbage and for life on an empty lot close to the school. The students also began composting their school room garbage, opening it up two months later to see what had happened (the students planted and later harvested some cherry tomato seeds that had sprouted). Throughout the unit, the students used their journals to react to issues as they arose.

FACTORS THAT AFFECT CURRICULUM ORGANIZATION

■ A grade 6-9 middle school appointed a joint committee of parents and teachers. This committee developed a list of topics considered of prime importance for that age group but currently not taught. The committee gave a detailed rationale for including ten topics: (1) different religions represented in the community; (2) moral values in the lives of students; (3) crime and justice in the local community; (4) war and peace in the world; (5) the operation of small business; (6) work and the job; (7) the influence of rock music on our culture; (8) teenage gender relations; (9) the impact of technology since the introduction of computers in the 1950s; and (10) how statistics is used and misused in society.

The teaching staff agreed that these topics were significant areas of study. They were divided, however, about the way the topics should be included in the curriculum. The school had a traditional timetable of six 50-minute subject blocks per day. Some teachers wanted to insert each topic in a current subject, without changing the timetable. Others argued that the timetable should be revised with long blocks assigned to humanities. If given somewhat more time than English, social studies, and religious studies were in the past, they argued, the humanities teacher could include many of the ten topics. Still others believed the topics were best taught as part of a "core" course, with English, social studies, religious studies, and science each losing one period per eight-day cycle to make room for the core. Several teachers felt that each year the school should dispense with the regular timetable for two weeks and tackle two topics in depth with the whole school. Topics clearly within a subject field could be taught in that subject (e.g., statistics in mathematics).

The debate was heated. The English teachers opposed giving up any periods, nor did they want a general humanities course to subsume English. The mathematics teachers favored the "core" course option, but did not want to teach it. The social studies teachers liked the idea of a new humanities block. They said they were willing to plan and implement the program jointly with the English and religious studies teachers. What are the strengths and weaknesses of each organizational approach? Which do you favor? Why? If as principal your board had instructed you to ensure that the topics were included next year's curriculum, how would you go about coming to a decision?

There is no one "right" way to organize the curriculum. A host of factors influence how schools and teachers decide how to arrange their curriculum structure. Moreover, teachers with a clear understanding of the school's aims, and the values they want to nurture, will be able to accomplish a great deal with any curriculum organization. Yet, as we saw in the example at the beginning of this chapter, certain timetable structures may promote (or hamper) desirable consequences.

Many components affect the way teachers and students experience the school day. Society has certain general expectations, and therefore parents do also. Such expectations include that (1) the curriculum enables all students to attend school until grade 12; (2) all students learn to read and write their first language; (3) all students take mathematics at least up to the grade 9 or 10 level; (4) schools use a grade-level curriculum structure; (5) students in grade 6 and up, if not earlier, receive grades that enable parents to compare their progress with "average" students; and (6) schools uphold if not teach the prevalent values held by the supporting community.

A few public and non-public schools maintained by unique parent communities may succeed in defying some of these accepted conventions. For instance, a Gitksan native Indian school in northern British Columbia uses cross-aged, clan-based schooling with great success. However, most schools or systems that counter such deeply-held convictions usually backtrack within a couple of years. This may result from parental pressure or from teachers, despite directives from the top, paying only lip service to the changes. Primary teachers forced into cross-aged or family grouping, for instance, may divide their classes into three groups, and teach each as they would otherwise teach grades 1, 2, and 3 respectively.

That is not to say that the curriculum and its organization cannot or does not change. National and regional commissions may be instrumental in adding courses or topics to the curriculum. Strong officials with government departments of education may be able to impose rigid time requirements for individual subjects if they are academic traditionalists, or encourage timetable flexibility if constructivists. The school experience of politicians responsible for departments of education may lead them to set policies that require all schools to implement a core curriculum that includes the three R's or a subject such as consumer education. Because of parental pressures for higher standards, school boards may insist that teachers plan separate time slots for spelling, reading, and writing at lower grades; and for grammar and composition at higher ones. What needs to be remembered is that while change does occur, the reality at the classroom level changes much less than public rhetoric implies.

There also are many school-level factors that affect curriculum organization. The school sets certain expectations, often adapted from state or school board level guidelines. Christian schools usually organize their curriculum within some broad parameters, although their curriculum topics and organization most often resemble those of other schools. School principals usually insist on teachers adhering to time and other guidelines for specific subject areas. Together with the staff they specify topics and themes at each level. Once the classroom door closes, teachers' own inclinations as well as their planning time, the availability of resources, student interest, and class dynamics also affect the actual curriculum organization.

At the K-5 levels, teachers typically teach one class for most of the day. As a result, they have much leeway in their curriculum organization. Longer blocks of time used for interdisciplinary themes or significant topics related to social studies and science enhance the possibility of meaningful investigation and experience of what it means to live as a Christian in society. Within such a learning context, students recognize the usefulness of the skills and can apply them better in various settings.

For these reasons, many elementary teachers, instead of planning separate social studies and science time slots, plan larger blocks of time each day for integral units. Such blocks may focus in turn on a science or social studies or interdisciplinary topic. Language arts and research skills are introduced or, at least, practiced during the units. A grade 4 teacher might plan a series of consecutive units on insects, the local state or province, trees and forests, aboriginal culture, and electricity and magnetism. The study of novels might be integrated into several of these units.

The attitudes of students in middle schools (grades 5 or 6 to 8 or 9) appear to benefit from having one teacher responsible for teaching them for a fairly lengthy time block each day. At this level more specialization occurs. The humanities teacher may not feel comfortable teaching science, and a specialist may need to teach a foreign language or music. Nevertheless, a rigid subject-centered timetable would hinder the implementation of units that are particularly relevant for such students (such as some of the ones in the example given earlier in this section).

Students at this level may not have yet reached what Piaget calls formal reasoning. Yet their interests broaden significantly. The grade 7 and 8 curriculum, however, often does little more than reinforce and extend topics already dealt with in earlier grades. At this level, teachers can maintain student interest in learning through interdisciplinary topics that have not yet been addressed in the curriculum, capitalizing on the increased awareness of what is happening in society as well as on the need to assume increased responsibilities. For similar reasons, the inclusion of a large variety of short, elective, exploratory courses and other minicourses is particularly effective at this level.

The secondary level curriculum becomes more discipline-centered. Teachers are specialists in one or two subjects. Colleges and universities or external examination agencies demand the completion of specific subject sequences, especially in grades 11 and 12. Students are at a developmental level where they appreciate investigating particular discipline-based issues with their causes and effects in more depth. With the complexity of providing a range of electives, the timetable is more rigid than at lower levels. Yet schools do well to provide time for a core such as described in this chapter and a willingness to allow organizational flexibility when teachers plan meaningful integrated experiences for their students.

Finally, schools at all levels should check whether their curriculum content and organization takes into account all the aspects of reality. Many schools today fail to do justice to the confessional, ethical, political/legal, and economic dimensions of reality. Yet students who become skilled mathematicians, scientists, musicians, or writers need to understand how their faith, their morals, and their political and economic values frame and direct how they use their abilities. Otherwise, they ultimately lead empty lives and, worse, lead others to lead empty lives. The separation of facts and skills from values has wreaked havoc with our civilization.

Schools can make a difference if they base all their curriculum on a clear vision of their aims, the values they want to foster, and the different aspects of reality that need to be investigated for a holistic life in society. A key question for schools is how their curriculum decisions contribute to what they believe what kind of persons their graduates should be.

SUMMARY

As a student progresses through the grades, the curriculum gradually becomes more specialized by subject disciplines. Roy Clouser, using the work of Herman Dooyeweerd, identifies fifteen different aspects of reality, beginning with the quantitative and ending with the confessional aspect. Subjects at higher grade levels often (but not always) focus on one or several aspects of reality. If they do, students can investigate the key meanings of the aspect(s) in some depth.

However, we experience everyday situations in integral ways, not as isolated aspects of reality. To make learning meaningful for students, therefore, schools should allow for the exploration of phenomena in their contexts. At a younger age this is often done through integral units with activities that involve many aspects of reality. What is important at all grade levels is to provide a core curriculum and other integrated approaches where students explore topics and issues crucial for being and becoming responsive disciples of Christ, including interdisciplinary ones.

More significant than specific curriculum organization is the insistence that all units promote the aims of the school. Units should have a clear focus relating to the values the school wants to promote. Also, they should draw natural content and skill connections with other aspects of reality. In this sense each curriculum unit can be an ''integral'' one.

REFLECTING

1. Neil Postman in his book *Technopoly* makes the point that a curriculum not only organizes but also serves as a mechanism for information control. What the curriculum includes and excludes, he continues, reflects a theory of the purpose and meaning of education. Schools teach astronomy but not astrology and evolutionism but not creationism. The curriculum thus gives expression to what is considered legitimate knowledge. He then goes on to decry that "cultural literacy" in the curriculum often means mastering thousands of names, places, dates, and aphorisms, but excludes learning that is more valuable for life. Postman concludes that "cultural literacy" is a case of calling the disease the cure (Postman 1993, 74-75). Respond to Postman's claims on the basis of what this chapter has said about the organization of the curriculum.

2. Choose a grade level at which you teach or want to teach. Design what you consider an "ideal" timetable for that grade level. Justify your choices. What factors might militate against you being able to implement your timetable?

3. In what ways and to what extent should parents and students have a voice in influencing the organization of the curriculum? Is curriculum organization solely a professional responsibility, with parents and students giving input with respect to content? Or, if organization affects the attainment of aims, should parents and students also be represented when a school considers major timetabling changes?

Chapter 6
Teaching and Learning
the Aspects of Reality

■ "A Christian worldview encompasses all my teaching," says high school English teacher Margaret Barlow. "Everything about my classroom must demonstrate that worldview. The physical environment is rich. Just look at the art prints and the poems around the room that say something about God's world. My classroom ambience stresses that it is better to give than to receive—just look at the photographs I've taken of the class and posted on the bulletin board. Unconditional love for all precedes calling students to account—I first welcome latecomers and deal only later with their responsibilities. I also constantly try to instill a sense of wonder and playfulness. After all the child in us is the best learner."

I ask, "What would that mean for teaching grammar?"

"Well," Margaret responds, "I start with spidergramming to see how much the students know. Everyone contributes. Usually they're excited about how much they already know. Then, to learn the parts of speech, they stand in a circle. As they throw a ball to someone else they call out a part of speech. That student then has to give an example, and repeats the process. This teaches them to listen. They're moving around a bit as they learn. That's important for adolescents. Later they imagine that they are a specific part of speech and write a short story that shows their function. Later they share each other's stories. Other ideas emerge from the classroom situation. For instance, I may ask them to write different types of sentences about my art reproductions, being as creative as possible."

Margaret realizes that her students should learn about grammar as an important tool in understanding language. Her classes focus on how we use language to communicate, both orally and in writing. She uses diverse modes of knowing, including psychomotor and aesthetic ones. Moreover, she draws as many natural connections as possible between her subject and others. As they learn grammar, the students also practice and develop their writing, and learn about the history of art. At other times, she may relate their story writing to science (e.g., "write a story about how our muscles interact"). Yet clearly she teaches one particular subject, English language and literature.

In the last chapter, we discussed a possible categorization of reality into thirteen aspects, each with its own leading ideas and structures. A balanced curriculum, I concluded, should take into account all aspects of reality. Often, however, we have good reasons not to organize learning into subjects that correspond to a particular aspect. First, new learning is most effective when based on students' own experiences. Such experiences often are complex, multifaceted ones. Second, many important issues cut across several aspects of reality. Third, closely related aspects can often be taught well as a combined subject. Fourth, many worthwhile school subjects (especially ones with application emphases) do not relate directly to just one or two aspects of reality.

Nevertheless, most common school subjects relate closely to specific aspects of reality. In this chapter I consider basic goals for common subject fields, relating them to the aspects of reality and to what a Biblical worldview means for teaching the subject. I also touch on some important issues in each field. One chapter can do no more than give a basic framework for thinking about a subject. The general guidelines, however, provide one more steppingstone for planning a classroom program.

I have sequenced my discussion to correspond roughly with the thirteen aspects of reality, including also cultural formation. I discuss the following subjects in a generally increasing order of complexity: mathematics, science, physical and health education, the fine arts, language studies, ethics, religious studies, and social studies. I then also deal with subjects that usually have more of an application emphasis than the foregoing, and that may involve several aspects of reality. Many subject goals have changed little since Geraldine Steensma and I co-edited *Shaping School Curriculum: A Biblical View* (1977), and often I reflect its thinking. However, this chapter makes clear that knowledge about the subjects and about learning does not stand still. As the example of Margaret Barlow's class points out, for instance, today we are more aware of different modes of knowing, and of the need to teach basic skills in meaningful contexts even if that involves situations and phenomena that cut across traditional subject divisions.

MATHEMATICS

- At the primary level, mathematics learning recently has stressed exploration of mathematical meaning and results using a variety of manipulatives. Teachers report that children have a better understanding of basic concepts. They also develop creativity as they design problems and find alternative solutions. A criticism of this approach is that students do not learn basic math facts and skills well enough. Is it possible to combine an exploratory approach with reinforcement and drill? Or does that defeat the purpose of a manipulative approach? In an age of calculators, how important is a thorough knowledge of addition and multiplication facts?

Mathematics is more than a construction of the mind. It does not consist of just a series of pure formalisms that we manipulate using rules of logic. Mathematics originated from human experience and activity with two aspects of God's created reality: the quantitative and the spatial. Once people discovered mathematical results through observation and informal reasoning, they developed symbols to represent their conclusions. Only after using the results for many years or even centuries did they prove the results logically using "self-evident" assumptions.

Today we know that it takes faith in the continuing validity of mathematical laws to do and use math. The "self-evident" assumptions do not always hold. Rejecting such an axiom led, for instance, to non-Euclidean geometry. More significantly, in 1931 the German mathematician Gödel proved that it is impossible to design a mathematical system that is both complete and consistent. That means that mathematicians must live with certain inexplicable paradoxes. They can do so because they have faith in the basic order and law structure of the universe.

The first key meaning in mathematics is discrete quantity, i.e., natural numbers. Numbers function according to certain laws that we discover from experience. People have named numbers and gradually improved their designation. Our present system is probably too firmly established to make further advancements (e.g., some believe that changing from a base 10 to a base 12 system would make our mathematical lives easier). Basic mathematical laws stay constant, however, even when human descriptions of the underlying structures change.

The second key meaning in mathematics is continuous space. This cannot be reduced to or explained in terms of discrete numbers. We have no way to designate all numbers on the number line as fractions or terminating or repeating decimals. Yet we need numbers to describe space and figures in space: a plane has two dimensions; a quadrilateral, four sides. In other words, we use numbers to think about geometry, but numbers or numerical descriptions will never do full justice to geometry. Mathematics may, however, develop understanding of the numerical and spatial aspects concurrently, as in graphing and coordinate geometry.

Mathematics plays an essential but limited role in other knowledge. It points beyond itself to the other aspects of reality. Mathematical models are useful tools in physics, psychology, and economics, for instance, but never describe fully the meaning of a situation. Physicists, psychologists, and politicians must consider more aspects of reality than the mathematical ones to analyze situations and make responsible decisions. Mathematics cannot be equated with logic. Clear, logical thinking is important in all subjects. The content of mathematics involves the two simplest aspects of reality. Therefore we can prove mathematical propositions with deductive logic more easily and convincingly than theses in other areas of knowledge.

Our first concern in mathematics is to deepen students' understanding of God's creation and of how math helps them fulfill their calling. Students can abstract the mathematical aspects of real life situations, analyze them, and use the results of their learning in applications. They can explore how we use math in science (e.g., leaf surface area and water loss, pendulum swings and functions). However, applications go beyond science. Mathematics is part and parcel of human culture.

Three main goals for learning mathematics follow. First, students should gain an understanding of the concepts of number and space and their interrelationships. Second, students should deepen their awareness of mathematics as a functional tool in solving everyday problems in diverse settings. Third, students must realize that math is a developing science. It is not a fixed body of knowledge but one that is fallible and growing. For instance, the Babylonians for years used an incorrect formula for the area of quadrilateral fields, using the results to levy taxes.

We should therefore base classroom mathematics on everyday situations. We should give students time to explore situations, pursue hunches, and draw conclusions from their observations. Such situations may involve experiences from students' lives outside school or classroom explorations with manipulatives, science lab experiments, mapping skills, or human geography. Students then also need more formal instruction and practice to ensure a clear grasp of math concepts and the ability to apply them. Such instruction originates from situations where students pose and try to solve problems using a variety of strategies. With the use of calculators, the scope and nature of practice has changed, but students still need dexterity with basic number skills and estimation. Mental mathematics has a place in the grades 2 through 6 curriculum. Students still need to be able to do simple calculations quickly—and it can add an element of accomplishment, fun, and joy to learning.

Students should experience the use of mathematics in various relevant contexts. They should apply math results from one situation in a variety of settings. The broad scope of mathematical applications lends itself to much meaningful problem solving. Students can, for instance, explore functions by looking at relationships and patterns in real situations, developing their own notations and strategies. Mathematics is not an isolated, self-sufficient body of knowledge, but an indispensable tool in most areas of life.

Note two points. First, most sets of problems in textbooks have students apply only one algorithm at a time. As such, they promote convergent thinking. Students look for one pattern and apply it mechanically. Real problem solving ability depends on critical and creative thinking. It requires more active involvement: transforming and simplifying given problems, writing different versions, modifying problems to yield different solutions, and constructing original problems (J. Kilpatrick in Lewy 1991, 848). Students need this type of experience with everyday graphical, statistical, and financial data, using calculators and computers when appropriate.

Second, society often bases decisions mainly on the numerical aspects of a situation. Politicians use polls, while businessmen look solely at the short-term balance sheet. Students should learn that we cannot reduce complex situations to mathematical ones only, even when quantitative aspects provide useful insights. A decision to buy skis should involve deeper questions than their price. What should be our financial priorities? Why? If we neglect those aspects in math class, students get a skewed view of life's priorities.

The history of mathematics should also be part of the curriculum. Students should see how mathematicians unfold new concepts and techniques, often in informal, intuitive, and creative ways. They learn that mathematics is an important but limited part of culture, and that intuition and value judgments affect its development (A.M. White in Lewy 1991, 892). Historical approaches can make clear how mathematical problem posing and solving has contributed to cultural development. One small book that does this at the junior high level is *The Story of Numbers and Numerals* (Hamming *et al.* 1984).

Teaching and learning mathematics is not a neutral activity. Textbook examples and problems often promote an individualistic, materialistic way of life. According to Paul Ernest, current mathematics learning values individual, reproductive, and formal approaches rather than cooperative, creative, exploratory, and applied work. He shows how this as well as streaming usually discriminates against females and minority groups. To overcome this, he suggests using approaches such as cooperative projects and problem discussions, studying the origins of number systems and geometry, pursuing mathematical investigations not preplanned by the teacher, and exploring value-rich issues such as misleading uses of statistics and real data on military spending (Ernest 1991, 265-273). In short, to support their aims, teachers may need to design alternate examples and learning strategies.

■ The math books available to teachers often lack diverse, open-ended problem situations in meaningful contexts, ones that benefit from the use of varied learning strategies. That means that teachers may gradually have to develop a resource bank of suitable problem situations. Curt Gesch mentions, for instance, his neighbor who pours concrete for a living. The neighbor asked him how to figure out what the exact length of the diagonal should be so he can determine whether his angles are right ones, and how much concrete in cubic feet comes through a six-inch pipe per foot. At the kindergarten or grade 1 level, you might set up a supermarket with play money as a learning center. At the grade 5 level, students might draw as many conclusions as possible from statistical data about countries in the world, and present them in graphical ways. At the grade 9 level, students might investigate how architects and engineers use geometry. Can you think of other learning activities where students learn and apply mathematics in meaningful contexts?

THE PHYSICAL AND BIOLOGICAL SCIENCES

■ Scientists genetically engineer human genes into goats who produce scarce human proteins with their milk. They engineer tomatoes that will not rot and salmon that grow ten times faster than normal. They also apply such research to genetic cures for diseases. But this technology gives rise to troublesome questions. Is it right for human genes to be inserted into animals? Can virus genes stitched into plants to increase disease resistance lead to the creation of "superviruses"? What would happen if genetically engineered salmon escape and breed with normal ones? Should parents be able to pay to have genetically superior babies? Should animals, or humans, be cloned? How should governments regulate genetic engineering and its products? Nobel prize winner Michael Smith says he does not have enough expertise to make ethical judgments about this research. Other scientists claim, however, that unwillingness to face the implications means that the commercialization of genetic research is already out of control (*Vancouver Sun*, December 4, 1993, pp. B1-B3).

This describes, in brief, a science development with vast consequences. Should you deal with this issue in your science classroom? If so, at what age levels? Can you think of creative approaches that would help students explore the underlying issues? To what extent should school science deal with the consequences of technology rather than just with scientific concepts and theories?

The key meaning in physical science is energy; in biology, life. The physical sciences (physics, astronomy, geology, physical geography, and chemistry) make much use of numbers and space. Mathematical descriptions and models, however, do not exhaust the meaning nor fully describe physical concepts such as motion or gravity. Similarly, a full understanding of biology requires some knowledge of chemistry. But life cannot be explained in terms of physical or chemical attributes. Rather, something that is alive has been created with life or vital functions that allow, for instance, for growth and reproduction.

Scientists examine the physical and biological aspects of phenomena with the intent of hypothesizing, formulating, and checking the likelihood of results. Scientists try to replicate evidence for theories and laws. However, repeating an experiment several hundred times, even if the results are consistent, still does not prove a conclusion. On the other hand, two or three instances with conflicting results may disprove a theory (although proponents of firmly-believed theories usually find ways to account for contradictory data). Advertising notwithstanding, results cannot be "scientifically proven."

Assumptions and commitments color scientists' findings. In 1850 French physicist Jean Foucault "proved" the wave theory of light on the basis of an experiment with mirrors. The scientific world accepted this conclusion until a 1927 experiment endorsed an alternate theory based on Einstein's thinking. What scientists expect to see affects what they see and how they interpret what they see (M. Poole in Francis and Thatcher 1990, 373-74). School science programs should show scientists at work, struggling with uncertainties and the effects of their presuppositions.

Scientific knowledge is much more tentative than school science implies, and scientific theorizing is not neutral. Thomas Kuhn (1970) described how scientists work within certain paradigms based on cultural beliefs and values. Such models influence what scientists investigate, how they go about their investigation, and what kinds of results they reject. This, in turn, affects curriculum. A deeply held value of scientists today, for instance, is that quantitative predictions are preferable to qualitative ones (Kuhn 1970, 185). This colors both research and high school science curricula.

Another example that science is not neutral is that the basic faith and interpretative framework for most biologists is evolutionism. They hold that organisms emerged from adaptation to the environment through natural selection operating through chance. The acceptance of this belief raises an unanswered question. For adaptation to occur, it must do so on the basis of underlying structural laws. A fish "develops" gills to be able to take in oxygen from its water environment. But what caused the fish to "know" that to live it needed oxygen? The fish itself cannot have developed the structural laws for its existence as it developed. In other words, the evolutionistic concept of adaptation fails to consider the origin and nature of the structural laws of reality (Zylstra in Steensma and Van Brummelen 1977, 125-26).

As is true for proponents of evolutionism, my basic interpretive framework for biology rests on faith assumptions. My starting point is that biology is possible only because God created and sustains a law order. Biologists, like physical scientists, discover God's creation order. The first chapters of Genesis make clear that God is the origin of all reality, including its structural laws. Thus God created fish with gills to enable them to live in a water environment, taking into account His laws for the physical and biological aspects of reality. God created each living being with a particular fitness for a specific niche where He put it. Evolutionists have no choice but to find the meaning of life in non-living matter. Christian scientists, on the other hand, find it in God's faithfulness in creating and upholding reality and calling humans to be stewards of the earth. A helpful publication in this regard is *Teaching Science in a Climate of Controversy* (Price et al. 1986).

Curricula often implicitly promote a dogmatic reliance on science. Yet such reliance "leads to elitism, to an excessively technocratic philosophy, to authoritarianism and antidemocratic behavior, attributes that in turn provoke indifference and even disenchantment" (Nadeau and Desautels 1984, 56). Science textbooks promote that science is objective and that its methods can provide solutions to all problems facing society. They also often lead students to accept unquestioningly that all pure scientific research leads to truth and progress. Yet science continually raises philosophical questions that go beyond science (Price et al. 1986, 23).

Scientific laws, theories, and conclusions reflect current understandings of scientific phenomena. They are not "truth," however. They are compelling but incomplete explanations. Each new discovery brings about more questions and reveals a complexity we did not know about. Scientific theories and laws are useful approximations of God's laws structures. Newton's laws of motion are apt representations but break down at high speeds. Einstein's theory of relativity gives more insight about what happens at high velocities and about the relation between energy and motion. But even Einstein's theory fails to account for some phenomena. As scientists go about their work, they are often surprised!

The scientific mode of knowing involves drawing reasoned conclusions from experimental data. Most textbooks, however, overplay the role of "the" scientific method. The method seldom results in new discoveries in science. Scientists more often use mathematical analysis, deductive and inductive logical reasoning, creative hunches, intuition, and accidental discoveries (e.g., penicillin). Scientists may use the five steps of the scientific method to strengthen or weaken support for a conclusion. Even then, however, scientists' observations are necessarily informed and guided by some theoretical presuppositions (M. Degenhardt in Francis and Thatcher 1990, 238). The scientific method, in other words, is not the final arbiter of truth. We therefore need a more reflective and critical approach in science education. Incorporating topics from the history of science may dispel the mystique of the "scientific method."

That is not to say that "hands-on" activities are not important in science. Students benefit from reconsidering everyday phenomena through experimentation with simple science materials and equipment. They learn a great deal, for instance, from growing plants or investigating rates of fermentation with yeast and sugar. Direct experiences enhance the meaning of the more formal instruction that follows. But, especially at younger ages, science education should be more of a workshop than a series of laboratory experiments. Each step of such workshop activities should require exploration, action, and explanation. Perhaps then we can overcome the problem that even the best science students can often do little with science information and skills except repeat them for tests (NASSP 1993, 1).

Too often curricula treat science in isolated fashion with little reference to the rest of life. Nearly 85% of high school graduates enrolling as physics and engineering majors in the U.S.A. cannot relate science concepts and processes to real situations (NASSP 1993, 1). David Layton gives examples of why this happens. The usual theoretical account of the bonding of hydrogen and oxygen atoms in water deals only with "objective," abstract information. A very different approach would be to teach it in the context of removing impurities from the water supply of a poor Third World community. Introductory chemistry courses describe the electrolysis of brine without any mention of mercury losses on ecosystems. Similarly, textbooks seldom make explicit the moral dimensions of scientific statistical data such as risk from nuclear waste. In such ways, chemistry promotes technical efficiency and excludes concern for the environmental or social impact (Layton in Tomlinson and Quinton 1986, 161-63).

Physical phenomena and living things exist in environments that affect human life and culture. God gave us physical things to support life. He created plants not just for themselves, but with animals and humans in mind. We may apply science-related technologies only after we have tried to understand their implications on our environment and on human life. New reproductive technologies, for instance, have serious ethical and social implications. Similarly, the automobile is not just a technical means of transportation. The number sold has become a barometer of our economic health. Cars affect our social interaction, our environment, the way we lay out our cities, how we shop, and how much money we can spend on longer-lasting things. Science curricula should deal with such implications of science and technology for our culture.

Recent middle and high school course materials put more emphasis on science and technology issues. In part this stems from the paradox that most authors—and students—see science and technology as a cause of problems, but also as a solution of those same problems. It also stems from concerns in society. Indiscriminate use of technology has led to health risks. Research findings may be used for harmful ends. And science imposes on us an incontestable way of looking at life (e.g., progress without limits, technology without cost).

Science and technology courses benefit from a problem-based approach. Examples might include problems in copper mining, the effects of fertilizers in farming, the dangers of X-rays, or chemicals in food. Such problems often involve more than the purely scientific aspect. Suppose someone must decide to buy bread baked with either natural or bioengineered wheat. Science and technology provide information about the alteration of wheat leaf cells and potential health hazards. But students should also consider the economic aspect (how much does each cost? should I support a new business venture?), the social-political aspect (what are the social disruptions caused by the new technology?), and the ethical aspect (should I support a product that calls for manipulating gene pools with unknown long-term implications?) (Aikenhead 1980, 40). Whenever possible, a problem-based approach should begin with situations well known to students. They should investigate both the science and technology involved in the issue and its social relevance. This type of approach leads to different content choices than teaching standard science units and adding some applications.

I will sum up by describing two basic goals of science. First, students should investigate physical and living things as part of God's plan. They examine scientific aspects of daily phenomena in experiential, hands-on ways. They also survey the fundamental concepts, structures, and theories of science. They investigate the complexity and unity of these physical and biological aspects with wonder and delight, as well as with perseverance and humility. Second, students should identify and experience God's unique calling for humans to develop science and technology as cultural activities that honor God and His creation. They learn to use science and its applications responsibly. They also recognize the important but limited place of science in society, and develop a critical understanding of issues related to science (Van Brummelen et al. 1985).

> ■ North American surveys show that most primary teachers teach little science. Also, the amount of "hands-on" activities in science has decreased since 1980 (N. Gehrke, M. Knapp, and K. Sirotnik in Grant 1992, 91-94). Choose a primary-level topic or situation related to science that you could teach. Can you think of some meaningful learning approaches and activities? What would keep teachers from implementing such activities? What needs to be done to make the teaching of science a higher priority?

PHYSICAL AND HEALTH EDUCATION

> ■ Before reading this section, think about some physical and health education issues that have been contentious. Should physical education be compulsory at all grade levels? If so, should it be taught every day? Should physical education accentuate or downplay competition? Should it emphasize team sports or individual skills? What is the role of creative movement and dance in physical education? Should we include emotional health in health education? How much should we teach children about sexual health? At what levels?

Physical health and fitness affect all of life, including emotional well-being and mental ability. Physical and health education are therefore important in schools. Physical education deals mainly with the kinematic, biotic, and aesthetic aspects of reality. It involves movement of the body to perform tasks, to maintain physical fitness, and in and through motion to express and communicate creatively. Health education is concerned mostly with the biotic and psychic aspects. It focuses on maintaining bodily and emotional health: care of the body, nutrition, substance use and abuse, disease prevention and care, and so on. Schools teach some of these topics in elementary science or in human physiology in high school biology.

Our physical bodies are an integral part of our humanity. The Bible indicates that we must glorify God with our bodies as well as with the rest of our being (I Corinthians 6:20). The physical care of our body is part of our service to God. Thus physical and health education are essential in the school curriculum, especially in an age when many students get little physical exercise. A responsible life-style includes participating in physical activities, spending leisure time productively, and eating a balanced diet. Physical fitness and health, at the same time, should not glorify personal prowess or beauty. Instead, students should learn to see good health and fitness as a way to enrich their service to God and those around them.

One curriculum guide lists three interrelated goals for physical and health education. First, it should develop a motor proficiency and health knowledge base. Students should become aware of their bodies and how to care for them, of functional and creative movement, and of the physical potential and limitations of their bodies. Second, physical and health education should encourage and enable students to achieve optimum health care and fitness. Programs should provide possibility for carry-over into students' present and future lives with respect to weight control and posture, strength and muscular endurance, and proper health habits. Third, students should practice health habits and motor skills in a variety of activities. The ultimate goal is students' commitment to maintaining suitable activities and making wise health decisions later in life (Boersma et al. 1982). Besides these goals, physical education can also develop desirable social values and attitudes.

The Bible says little about athletics. It does, however, promote cooperation and self-sacrifice rather than competition. I conclude from this that competition in sports and physical education is desirable only when students strive together to develop their physical potential, and when they try to better others as well as themselves as they participate. This we can promote by measuring success in terms of participation, effort, and improvement rather than just in terms of winning. Some schools have "houses" that gather points mainly for participation and improvement of individual skills. It also helps to have students compete with those with similar abilities. To build the type of Christian community of which Paul speaks in Ephesians 4, "participants should learn the joy of team membership and their responsibilities to each other, refine and excel in skills while becoming committed to an active life-style, and use sports as an avenue of self-expression" (Boersma *et al.* 1982, 5).

To encourage students to include physical activity in their life-styles, schools should offer various activities that can be done individually or with a partner: hiking, jogging, table tennis, bicycling, weight training, swimming, cross-country skiing, and so on. Through these we try to foster individual growth. Sometimes that is not easy. Teachers may be frustrated in falling short of their goals. Common reasons include student apathy toward participation, teachers' needs to maintain order, oversized classes, and lack of suitable facilities. As a result, the latent function of many physical education classes becomes keeping students busy and happy, rather than developing skills and attitudes (M. Steinhardt in Jackson 1992, 975 and 988).

To encourage participation some teachers allow students with poor coordination or low skill levels to practice in non-threatening settings, giving frequent encouraging (but honest) feedback. They help students not to feel totally defeated or intimidated by allowing them some choice, involving them in designing games to develop certain muscles or skills, and planning some units such as basketball around the theme of cooperation. Some of these students may be able to take some leadership in using their bodies in aesthetic expression in creative movement. Developing positive attitudes to physical activity is the most important single effect on adult physical activity patterns.

Health education deals with physical and emotional health. Often we do not teach it as a separate subject. Kindergarten and grade 1 teachers teach integral units on *God Made Me Special* or *Families*. Elementary teachers also teach units on friendship, nutrition, our bodies, and health and disease. At higher levels, core courses may include units on substance abuse, understanding oneself as an adolescent, or courtship and marriage. High schools may also include health-related units in their physical education and guidance programs, or teach a psychology course. The effectiveness of such programs in promoting positive values and behaviors usually depends on the extent of home support.

Schools should avoid two pitfalls. First, it is easy to neglect health topics, particularly when no formal health curriculum exists. Yet many parents spend little time with their children on health-related issues. Therefore schools often are the only place where students can receive guidance about the consequences of health-related decisions they make and the habits they establish. Schools should plan a year-by-year health education program, even if they do not teach health as a separate subject.

A second pitfall is that, to sidestep controversy, schools may teach only the biological aspects of health issues. One disturbing example is the tendency for schools to teach only the physical aspects of sex (e.g., how students can reduce their chances of contracting venereal diseases). Schools shirk their responsibility if they do not concurrently teach about the emotional, social, economic, and ethical consequences of sexual relationships. By dealing only with physical aspects, schools mislead students into believing that sex is a purely physical act. The curriculum should include a Biblical understanding of family life, friendship, and sexuality, including how God allows us to find joy and meaning in such relationships. Parents can be involved in planning the program, and encouraged to discuss topics with their children as they arise in school. For such a program, see DeMoor (1994).

■ North America values egocentric competition: "Winning isn't everything; it's the only thing." In sports, players see what they can get away with in order to win. Yet some cultures play games (and keep fit) without keeping score. Games, in a sense, are laboratories for value experiments, ranging from winning at all costs to emphasizing fair play to valuing cooperation (there is usually a mixture of all three). Design some games that develop fitness and skills while emphasizing cooperation and care for others, sensitivity to the feelings of classmates, and reflection on personal involvement.

■ Suppose a grade 8 physical education course distributes its time as follows: 20% for fitness activities; 15% for individual and dual activities; 15% for gymnastics; 10% for rhythmics and creative movement; 25% for team games; and 15% for outdoor pursuits. Is this a suitable distribution? Why or why not? How would you change the distribution for lower grades? for higher ones?

■ The topic of sexuality has been a controversial one, especially in public schools where parents have widely diverging views about the related values. What content about sexuality would you include in a school curriculum? How would you justify your position? In what ways would you involve parents? What precautions would you take so that your teaching would not lead to parental or student resistance?

THE FINE ARTS

■ John F. Alexander tells the story of going to the Rodin Museum in Philadelphia with his daughter's class. He thought the students would discuss beauty, how the sculptures made them feel, and which ones were the most beautiful. But the teacher dealt only with details of Rodin's life and the methods of bronze casting. Alexander concludes that the crucial things in life such as awe, beauty, and holiness have been replaced in the curriculum with things that fit on multiple choice tests. Schools, he says, leave out everything that might fill our hollowness and the emptiness of our culture (Alexander 1993, 28-29). Is Alexander right? Is this how the fine arts are generally taught in schools? What values do we foster? What values should we foster? How would you plan a trip to an art museum or a concert?

Aesthetics is an integral part of life, not something that happens only in museums and concert halls. Artistic gifts are gifts of God's Spirit, whether to Christians or non-Christians. God Himself wants to be glorified through artistic and musical expression. God's written Word includes poetry and song. God gave explicit instructions for the art work in His tabernacle and endowed the artisans with His Spirit. The Bible encourages people to dance to express their joy and thankfulness for God's blessings. God wants us to use the arts in responsive and creative ways. The arts enrich our daily lives. (In this section the "arts" is a general term that includes the visual arts, music, dance, film arts, and drama.)

But the arts are vulnerable in a technological, profit-driven society. Today, business interests often dictate art decisions. The first "contemporary Christian music" radio station in Canada in 1994 made clear that it made its decision to change to this format to make the station profitable, not because of the quality or message of such music. Politicians and business leaders feel that the arts fail to promote marketable skills or a healthy economy. As a result, they quickly suggest displacing them in the curriculum with more "practical" content.

Yet the arts are an important dimension of life. They affect our personal lives more directly than scientific formulas or economic theories. They enrich life through joy, delight, playfulness, and creativity. They enhance and change the way we see and understand ourselves, others, our society, and the purpose and meaning of life. They affect our perspectives by presenting a point of view in aesthetic, symbolic, and often striking ways. They stimulate us to investigate the perspectives and values of others. We discover some of life's possibilities through the arts. Further, the arts illustrate that sometimes in life there is no one right answer, and that uncertainty may lead to a surprise and wonder that enriches life.

The fine arts can be used to serve God and one's neighbor, but also one's idols. The dominant aesthetic images of our society become "a crystallized version of what is true, good, or proper—a representation of society, personal relationships, or political practices" (L. Beyer in Pinar 1988, 395). That means that schools should critique those prevailing images with their students. It also means that schools should help students explore how a Biblical vision of *shalom* that incorporates compassion, justice, and peace may provide the foundation for aesthetic activity. Christian artists serve God through their art. They may be agents of reconciliation as they manifest *shalom*. Their art may witness God's redemptive grace and love as well as the distortion and despair of sin. The work of Christian artists should not be superficial propaganda for the Christian faith, or reflect an innocuous view of life. Such bland, moralized presentations misrepresent the meaning of living as Christians in today's world. Instead, Christian art symbolizes real life, including experiences of fear, sin, guilt, and joy (Deborah Kellogg Kropp in Steensma and Van Brummelen 1977, 89).

What makes an aesthetic work "art"? Basically, its imagery and symbolism. In other words, it presents images of some aspect of life visually or audibly (or both) while alluding to other meanings. We can therefore experience and feel works of art in different ways and at different levels. Often the images "appropriately and surprisingly articulate those tensions and resolutions of feelings which we experience in reality" (Dengerink 1987, 27). Works of art evoke and refer.

In the curriculum, the arts have at least three goals. First, they make students critically aware of the role of aesthetics in society, both past and present. Second, they help students enjoy and appreciate aesthetic products through experience and performance. Third, they unfold students' aesthetic potential through composing works of art. These three goals are interrelated. For instance, performance and composition enhance critical awareness, and critical awareness can give new insights for the creation of works of art. What is clear is that a range of aesthetic experiences, experimentation and exploration, and thoughtful instruction are all necessary components of arts education.

Schools foster critical awareness through a wide range of aesthetic experiences. Such experiences should include various aesthetic forms in familiar and unknown cultural settings. Students should "unwrap" works of art to appreciate and understand them. Initial encounters should be open-ended: "What do you notice? How do you react? What surprises you? Why?" The students observe imagination, beauty, and striking symbolism. They share multiple perspectives and meanings. They give their interpretations of what the artist is communicating. They may perceive, for instance, how the values of an aboriginal culture affect its art, design, and music. Our intent is to help students see the world around them with new understanding based on fresh insights of visual and aural qualities.

Good artists balance aesthetic surface, symbolism, and worldview perspective to create works with an integrated unity. Students respond quickly to the aesthetic surface, to the form or composition of images or sounds. They may also respond to the artists' symbolism, to the imagery used to portray elements of life. Finally, while they usually cannot identify underlying worldviews from single works, teachers can help students recognize and react to the life perspective that forms the base of an artist's total body of work (Dengerink 1987, 30-31). An understanding of oft-implicit worldviews leads to fuller response. It also paves the way for students to be conscious of the suggestive qualities and driving forces behind their own compositions. This helps them consider how image and value interact, and how art can address value-laden issues such as cruelty, despair, and environmental devastation. They then become more aware that art products embody social, political, economic, ethical, and religious values and functions.

To give worshipful praise to God through the arts it is not enough to analyze and respond, however. Students should also perform music, dance, and drama, and create and compose works of visual and aural art. They explore, experiment, invent, shape, and share as they express their perceptions. They also learn in a more formal way about the principles of composition and style. They begin to perceive how form is part of a work's content and meaning. They evaluate their own work, learning from their successes and mistakes. Gradually they learn to base their work on their own sense of values. Schools support creativity in the arts by providing frequent opportunity for exhibitions and performances. Valuing the arts in this way encourages students to make the arts an integral part of their lives.

The visual arts include drawing, painting, sculpture, stained glass, photography, pottery, weaving, stitchery, and quilting. The latter do not involve as much allusiveness as the former, but most students use them more easily in gratifying vocational and leisure settings. Schools should give sequential instruction in visual arts without inhibiting self-expression. Students need free exploration with a variety of media as well as instruction in specific techniques.

Music begins with the exploration of sounds that people purposefully organize. It captures and presents stylized sounds and silences in a cultural and artistic way (Zuidervaart in Van Brummelen and Steensma 1977, 96). Today, music has become so pervasive that it not only expresses but shapes our culture. This pervasiveness spurs us to teach students what excellence and aesthetic richness mean in a diversity of styles, including rock, jazz, and electronic music. To do so effectively, students should express themselves personally through musical sounds: they manipulate, explore, create, and compose. They play simple percussion instruments, guitars, ukuleles, and recorders. In this way they learn to "sing to the Lord a new song" (Psalm 98:1).

Drama, literature, and filmmaking embrace both the communication and aesthetic aspects of reality. Works in these areas portray a vision of human existence. Here students interpret and assess life experience through involvement with situations that may be unpredictable or surprising, full of tension, challenging to accepted values. Performing and creating such works can sharpen students' imagination and deepen their insight into life-related issues and values. Alisa Ketchum's drama unit at the start of chapter 4 is a good example. Similar though simpler creative activities are possible in lower grades.

It is particularly at the middle and high school levels that students can begin to understand the place of aesthetics in culture. How aesthetics has interacted with culture becomes clear, in part, through the study of history. Such diverse activities as studying poetry and patterns in math may enhance aesthetic sensitivity. Yet to do justice to the goals of aesthetics education we also need separate courses in the arts for all students. Usually only high school level students, with particular studio talents, take such courses. If we believe that aesthetic knowing adds an important dimension to life, however, all students should choose and take some courses in the fine arts. Otherwise, too often, students do little more than "ape" popular culture in their aesthetic attitudes and behavior.

- John Zuidema's grade 7 spends three weeks on contemporary music. With his students, he explores standards for good music. They may suggest that it should be original, have unity as well as variety, be wholesome, have balanced instrumentation and voice, and be understandable. The students bring any recording they own to class, with a written transcription of the lyrics. John plays the music. "If you haven't heard it before," he asks, "did you like it? Why or why not? If you like it right away, does that necessarily mean it is *really* good? How would you evaluate the music in terms of our standards for *good* music that we discussed?"

  Would you teach this unit? Why or why not? Can you think of additional ways of meeting the three goals for aesthetic education in this unit?

- Hugo VanderHoek teaches a grade 6 unit on *Comics* that combines aesthetics, language, and media studies. He considers comics an important genre since they promote values and transcending qualities. His students analyze different types of comics. They consider the underlying values and how cartoonists portray them. His students develop their own comic strips using cultural, moral, and artistic standards that they have formulated. The class publishes a collection of these cartoons for the community. Are comics significant enough to warrant a lengthy integral unit? Why or why not? It is fairly easy to see how this unit would meet the three goals of aesthetic education. In what ways would it meet the overall goals of a Christian approach to schooling (in other words, how is the unit externally consistent?)

LANGUAGE STUDIES

■ Joan Konynenbelt believes that her workshop approach in her middle school language arts class is a Christian one. Usually she begins her language arts block with a brief lesson on a topic that needs attention (e.g., punctuation, formal essay writing). Then she asks her students about their progress. She arranges individual conferences where she gives them personal attention. Her students become responsible for their own work. Normally they themselves choose what they read and write. They keep up a reflective reading log. They also plan peer conferences where they help each other as they go through the pre-writing, composing, revising, and publishing cycle. Students regularly share their work with the whole group as well as with audiences outside the classroom. Since students usually make their own topic choices, they relate their learning to their concerns in life, especially in and through their reading response journals. Joan complements her workshop approach with novel studies that frequently relate to social studies themes. In this way, the class as a whole still addresses issues that benefit from sustained analysis.

Do you think Joan's language program is a balanced one? Why or why not? Which values do students learn in this program? Are there any values that you would give more emphasis? If so, how would you alter Joan's program? Do you agree with Joan that her program meets the goals of a Christian approach to education?

"In the beginning was the Word, and the Word was with God, and the Word was God. . . . Through Him all things were made" (John 1:1,3). Here the Bible uses a powerful metaphor for Jesus Christ: God's love and communication reach us through the Word that is Christ. Through that Word all things were made. Therefore God's gift of language also comes to us through God's love in Jesus Christ. God speaks to create. He speaks to rule and inform. He speaks to bless and to curse. And God expects us as His images to respond by speaking: Adam's first task was to name the animals. Students should become aware of the significance of the gift of communication, what its loss would mean, and nurture respect for language and a concern for integrity in its use (Smith 1991, 4-5).

Language is a beautiful and exciting gift of God. The Bible decries language that violates love, truth, or justice. The apostle Paul warns against unwholesome talk, adding that we should use language to benefit others and build them up (Ephesians 4:29). The Bible gives us norms for language use: truthfulness, considerateness, fairness, appropriateness, clarity, conciseness, aesthetic vitality. These norms provide a framework of responsibility and freedom within which we unfold and use language with gratitude and wonder (Smith 1992, 11-12). Regrettably, sin and ignorance often cause people to use language to remake the world in their own image, for their own self-interest.

Language arts curricula should help students use language function-ally and creatively to praise God. They use language skills to clarify their thought and to serve others. Language learning can contribute to building relationships in community, developing personal and communal percep-tions and insights, and obeying the four great Biblical injunctions. Students' experiences form the basis of language reception, understand-ing, and expression. They learn to listen thoughtfully, speak clearly, read critically, and write imaginatively. They should experience the delight of using language effectively and creatively in open-ended activities. As they do so, they should also experience how they can use language to become healing, reconciling agents in their communities.

Language learning takes place across the curriculum. It is a tool that is sharpened not just in the language arts time slot, but in all subject areas. The main goal of language studies, to learn to communicate effectively with others, is so broad that it almost defies description. Through speaking, writing, reading, and listening, students learn to conceptualize and respond to feelings and attitudes. They articulate and shape their experiences in their environments. They become committed to certain values. Language studies contribute to critical discernment and foster creative abilities.

The wide range and complexity of language studies makes it impossible in this section to do justice to the many complex issues. Language learning is fraught with controversy. This stems more from differences in philosophical orientations than from a knowledge of "what works." Indeed, the long-term effects of specific language arts ap-proaches are little understood. Research findings provide little guidance for language arts curriculum development (J. Langer and R. Allington in Jackson 1992, 716-17). Therefore I comment only briefly on a few issues teachers need to consider. You will find more extensive discussions in Bruinsma (1990), Bosma and Blok (1992), and the Society of Christian Schools in British Columbia (1994).

Some things *are* clear about language learning. Students learn language incrementally through interactive experiences in listening, speaking, writing, and reading. They learn more from using language for varied purposes and audiences than from specific skills taught out of context. The teaching of skills such as writing, vocabulary study, and spelling can be more effective in a relevant context. As they process language actively, students also develop interpretations and meanings. The "whole language" approach has incorporated these guidelines, but not without controversy.

The whole language approach holds that language is learned from whole to part. Its focus is language experiences that emphasize the meaning being communicated rather than skills. Teachers provide mean-ingful reading material, and encourage children to communicate their insights and discoveries both orally and in writing. Students read from a large variety of sources. This may include selections that contribute to a Christian worldview. Kindergarten children already become excited about their ability to communicate through writing. This comes about in part because teachers encourage them to experiment with emergent writing without at first demanding adherence to adult spelling and grammar conventions.

One problem with whole language is the demands it places on teachers as they provide personalized programs. Also, opponents of whole language claim that standardized test results have declined because of the newer methods. On the other hand, supporters say that such tests fail to measure the most important aspects of language growth (Willis 1993, 7-8). Some constructivist educators argue that children, as creators of their own meaning, must discover phonetic and spelling rules themselves. That has meant that some students even in higher grades do not know phonetic word attack skills and still "invent" their own spelling. On the other hand, programs such as the television-promoted *Hooked on Phonics* may help children become excellent decoders--but ones who lack comprehension and analysis skills.

More deliberative approaches can be used to avoid these shortcomings. Kindergarten teachers provide rich reading and writing experiences. They constantly demonstrate good reading by using a pointer while reading books to the class. They ask students to listen to recorded books while following along. Soon they also pair students to read to each other. They also methodically teach the principles of phonics and word attack, often in playful ways. They steer children toward adult spelling conventions as they become proficient in sounding out words and learning phonetic approaches through their own "invented" spelling. They recognize that different children benefit from different approaches. They also know that informal exploration, while meaningful and important, at some point needs to be complemented and followed up with specific instruction.

Fostering critically reflective habits of reading should complement decoding and comprehension. Already in kindergarten and grade 1 teachers can ask, "What do you think will happen next?" or, "What could Jennifer have done differently?" Later they can ask more probing questions, not only in language arts but all across the curriculum. Helping students develop and apply criteria and strategies for critical discernment encourages them to evaluate the worth and validity of what they read. Students learn to distinguish between fact and opinion, detect false claims and contradictions, identify the assumptions and biases of authors, and develop their own value commitments (R. Parker and L. Unsworth in Lewy 1991, 522).

Writing as process has become popular in classrooms, using a cycle of prewriting, drafting, editing, publishing, and presenting. A. C. Purves (in Lewy 1991, 532) claims that with this approach students may write only a fraction of what they are able to do. Also, students may practice writing without receiving any direct instruction. If teachers prompt students to write more and provide structured writing instruction, the workshop or process approach means students learn to think about and express their ideas well and often. This occurs much more in elementary than in high schools where the amount of writing declines sharply. There, regrettably, writing assignments most often require short, correct answers rather than a consideration or expression of views (J. Langer and R. Allington in Jackson 1992, 709-10; Gehrke *et al.* in Grant 1992, 73-74). Joan Konynenbelt's deliberative approach provides a balance between unstructured journal writing on the one hand and information-based short answers on the other.

Literature uses the lingual and aesthetic aspects of reality to catch and present the meaning of a slice of life. It is a human, imaginative, and symbolic response that expresses some vision of life's meaning. It affords the opportunity to interact with the great characters and interpreters of human life. Christian teachers allow students to enjoy the beauty, wonder, and vicarious adventure of literature. They also use it to influence their students' view of life. They help them discern the vision of literary works, understand it in terms of a Biblical worldview, and respond in a considered, personal way. This often requires a thorough consideration of a literary work's aesthetic and lingual characteristics as well as of its confessional stance.

Choosing what literature to teach is not always easy. The Ontario Alliance of Christian Schools (1990) says that Christian teachers should teach some literature written by Christian authors. If it is of good quality and sensitive to Biblical mandates, such literature nurtures a Christian vision of life. The Alliance adds, however, that teachers should also include significant literature written by others. It may sometimes contain language or situations that offend Christians. The basic criterion for its inclusion should be whether its teaching will affirm a structured and morally responsible world. Non-Christian works taught in the knowledge of faith can extend students' vision of reality and their understanding of and sensitivity to other people and other cultures. This also holds for film and media studies.

Through the study of foreign languages students develop an understanding of how people in other cultures live and express themselves. Students can become less insular and ethnocentric, and see how language and culture are interrelated. They gain insight into the factors that have shaped how we speak, think and live, and how languages obey certain laws. Sometimes economic competitiveness is stressed as a goal for foreign language study. While acquaintance with their language is helpful when dealing with people, a more basic reason for learning a language is that it enriches our perception and discernment of other cultures. Therefore such language teaching should include a critical awareness of the associated cultures. Foreign language knowledge helps Christians serve people in other cultures, and, of course, acquaint them with the Gospel.

■ React to two language arts units briefly described below. In what ways do the units reflect the guidelines of this section? Would you teach the unit? Why or why not?

»David Wu teaches a unit on Bunyan's *Pilgrim's Progress* to his grade 7 class. His theme is that God calls Christians to travel the road of discipleship with the promise of eternal life. He starts by asking students to consider characteristics of the Christian life. Students first work in pairs. They then design a questionnaire that they use to interview adults. The class examines the themes of suffering, despair, and temptation, finding parallels of the allegorical situations in modern life. Later, small groups of students write about how Bunyan contrasts good and evil, hope and despair, truth and deceit. At the end, students may choose their final mode of response. They may create and present a modern drama illustrating or comparing themes or characters from the novel. They may also create a mural of a modern Christian life. Other possibilities include writing an essay or song about the Christian life, or a pamphlet to explain the Christian life to non-Christians.

»The heart of Frank DeVries' grade 6 poetry unit is that each student makes a "beautiful, neat, phantasmagoric, and exciting" book of poems. The book includes eight poems chosen according to specific criteria, with students' reasons for the choices made. The students also include a review of a poetry book. Then they write about forty poems of nineteen specified different kinds. At the end, Frank asks his students to pick their four best poems. The students compile these and publish them as a book.

SOCIAL STUDIES

■ Use the examples below to reflect on two questions: What is the scope of social studies? Which values should it nurture?

»Betty Stark teaches a grade 3 unit, *How Have You Changed?* Most of her children's grandparents came to Canada with few possessions (from 19 different countries!). As her class investigates how their families and communities have changed, she weaves several themes into the stories: the importance of reliance on God, the meaning of joy and thankfulness, the need for patience, and the importance of selfless care for others.

»Wayne Lennea builds his middle school social studies course around several questions. In what ways is the common belief that governments can and should solve society's problems misleading? What is their role when they cannot legislate or impose morals and values? Also, is the prosperity of Western nations a blessing of God or the result of an imperial system that has caused hardship elsewhere in the world?

»Gwen Wray's grade 10 class includes several aboriginal Indian students. The class explores the roots of the problems facing Indian people today. They take a critical look at a range of materials: historical and recent articles, textbooks, tapes and videos, parts of Michener's *Centennial*. Students begin to see the complexity of the issues. They no longer simply blame problems on native people's own abuse and idleness, nor, on the other hand, just on white male oppression. Gwen asks what society can offer aboriginal peoples today. She has her students investigate how we can balance justice and responsibility in particular situations.

The heartbeat of social studies is cultural formation. Social structures depend on religious, ethical, jural, economic, and social beliefs. Social studies therefore includes content from history and geography and often also from anthropology, sociology, economics, and political science. Social studies sheds light on how the motivating ideas of groups of people have affected the development of communities and cultures. It explores how the dominant worldview of a culture—its beliefs, commitments, values, and dispositions—has framed and guided human endeavors.

Cultural formation involves all aspects of reality from the mathematical to the confessional. Interdisciplinary integral units therefore often are a good vehicle for teaching social studies. Social studies is so broad that its goals may duplicate the aims for schooling. "To impart knowledge, values, and skills needed for active participation in a democratic society" is so general that it helps little in designing a social studies program. To give social studies a clearer focus, the concept of cultural formation should be central. The main goal of social studies, then, is to help students understand and respond to the process of cultural formation, both past and present.

To meet this goal, social studies should help students observe and fathom their physical, aesthetic, social, economic, institutional, and religious environments and how they came about. How have humans used ideals, movements, and systems to affect cultural formation? How has the "spirit" of cultures resulted in diverse patterns of human activity? What are the basic beliefs, commitments, and values that undergird identities of individuals, groups, nations, and civilizations? (Society of Christian Schools in B.C. 1980). In short, social studies explores the factors that shape cultures, countries, communities, and individuals.

To do so, the curriculum needs to do more than impart information. It must help students consider the values that guide society, and encourage them to act on Biblically-based ones. Such social values include human dignity, mutual responsibility, economic fairness, and environmental integrity (Citizens for Public Justice 1993). For instance, human dignity means that all persons and their communities have the right to be treated with justice, love, compassion, and respect, and have the responsibility to treat others likewise. Mutual responsibility includes the principles that persons respect the law and that governments implement fair laws and make provisions, for instance, for stable family life. I have not included tolerance as a social value. Too often it is used as a club to pounce on those holding specific value positions. Christians love their neighbors regardless of color or creed but cannot tolerate dishonesty or cruelty or lack of respect.

Social studies is often linked to preparing students for active and responsible citizenship. But, as Ken Osborne points out, we should not confuse teaching for citizenship with teaching civics. Rather, everything that happens in school contributes to students interpreting and relating to the world around them, and thus teaches citizenship (Osborne in Erwin and MacLennan 1994, 417ff.). The whole curriculum should foster an active interest in the affairs of society and ingrain commitment to basic values, rights, and responsibilities.

The citizenship task of social studies is to have students consider human actions in social settings and, especially, in social institutions such as governments. Social studies contributes to students understanding their nation and the degree to which Charles Colson's four "myths" have influenced its development. This, in turn, prepares students for Biblically-based citizenship: they recognize the dead ends in our world and work for real change by demonstrating that God's justice can bring peace, well-being, and fulfillment (Koole 1990, 7).

The North American elementary social studies curriculum is usually an "expanding horizons" one. In kindergarten, children look at their personal environment (e.g., *God Made Me Special*). Successive grades branch out to neighborhoods, communities, states or provinces, the nation, and the world. This pattern, however, is not well-grounded (G. Marker and H. Mehlinger in Jackson 1992, 833). For instance, what fascinates young children are things foreign to their experience. They learn a great deal from units about Japan or Mexico if the content is concrete and embedded in stories. By contrasting life in such countries with their own, they learn to appreciate different cultures. At higher levels, adolescents would benefit from taking an in-depth look at their own community and how it functions.

Geography deals with how people use their physical environment to shape communities and society. It involves both environmental and social issues. The values of individuals and societies are important in explaining landscapes. Where, for instance, do communities build churches, parks, shopping areas, and industries? Why and how do they grow? There have been two main interpretations to such questions. The capitalist one is that unfettered entrepreneurship and the accumulation of personal wealth drives the economic engine. The Marxist one is that workers will be oppressed until the state on their behalf takes over the means of production and rewards all citizens equally.

An alternative Christian interpretative framework is that God created the world to enable humans to unfold reality's potential. The fall into sin led to selfish and sinful developments, including outrageous capitalist excesses and centralized Marxist oppression. Those who live in Christ resist such patterns of self-interest. They work toward justice and compassion, balancing rights and responsibilities. This interpretative framework does not give simple answers to complex problems. Nevertheless, it does shed light on issues in environmental studies, urban planning, and economic development at home and abroad (M. Bradshaw in Francis and Thatcher 1990, 377-81).

History investigates how humans have responded to God's call to care for and unfold the earth. Often, it tells a lamentable story. Yet its focal point, Christ's cross and resurrection, gives meaning and hope to life. In history, students learn how ideals and ideologies have shaped people and their institutions. They explore how beliefs, physical and social conditions, and institutions interacted as humans responded to God's mandates. They also begin to recognize that history itself is never neutral. To include or exclude events requires judgment. Students become aware that historians choose and interpret events to fit their guiding perspective. In high school students may be asked to compare different historical versions of events. They begin to use Biblical norms to interpret historical events.

To deal adequately with cultural formation, social studies includes more than geography and history. It also considers the roles of governments and citizens. It looks at how our economic system works and the increasing disparity between rich and poor. Christian teachers help students see that material prosperity does not define the quality of life. What are Christian responses to resource abuse, armed conflicts, poverty, and the population explosion? How can students contribute, even if in small ways, to restoring brokenness and despair?

Regrettably, many students find social studies unrelated to their experience and boring because of its detail and repetition (G. Marker and H. Mehlinger in Jackson 1992, 845). This is likely due to rote learning with little real pupil involvement. Yet social studies lends itself to diverse learning strategies: problem posing and problem solving, cooperative jigsaw techniques, simulation games, case methods, debates and panel discussions, drama and role play, and so on.

Chuck Chamberlin some years ago entitled a chapter on teaching social studies *Knowledge + Commitment = Action* (Parsons *et al.* 1983, 321ff.). Chamberlin described how primary students have influenced decisions of parks departments, how middle schoolers convinced a city to condemn and remove dangerous buildings, how high school classes participated in the hearings for a low rental housing proposal. Such commitment and action requires students to investigate problems, plan cooperatively, and extend their oral and written communication skills. This type of activity may be time consuming but is necessary if students are to become strongly committed to acting on their convictions and to take an active hand in cultural formation.

■ Selma Wassermann describes the use of the internment of Japanese-Canadians during World War II as a case study. The study deals with three "big ideas": society's paranoia and racist attitudes, the discriminatory policies of the Canadian government, and the way civil rights were stripped. Students read the narrative and in small groups discuss five provocative questions. After forty minutes of discussion, the teacher debriefs the case with the whole class, listening to and paraphrasing students' comments while zeroing in on the main issues. He avoids making value judgments, even about clearly racist attitudes. Over the next week, he introduces print and visual materials that supplement the original narrative. Students openly express feelings and insights. This allows the teacher to help them reevaluate their views (Wasserman 1992, 793-95, 800).

Think of an event or phenomena in social studies for which you could write a case. What would be its "big ideas"? How would you teach the case so that the students would remain involved and yet address issues that deal with important values?

RELIGIOUS STUDIES AND ETHICS

■ A pastor explained why he felt religious studies should not be included in the curriculum of a new Christian school. Teaching the subject is the task of the church, not the school. It would lead to controversies about doctrine in an interdenominational school. Most importantly, the school's Christian nature should be evident in its whole program. Teachers might become complacent and assume that religious studies gives the school its Christian character.

However, most Christian schools have argued that church education programs are too limited to do justice to Biblical-theological analysis and reflection. They use Biblical studies to explore basic Biblical motifs and themes. Should religious or Biblical studies be part of the curriculum? Why or why not?

The Bible functions in three ways in Christian schools. First, as the Word of God it gives basic perspective for life, and therefore for schooling. My understanding of Scripture undergirds my views of education, for instance. In devotions and chapels, the Bible's message also gives spiritual direction for being a committed, discipling, learning community. Finally, the Bible serves as the main resource for Biblical studies as a subject. Here students analyze and interpret its textual meaning, explore its cultural context, trace its themes, and discuss its implications for everyday life.

Faith and morality, of course, affect all of life and all of the curriculum. An important goal of social studies is to explore how basic faith commitments affect cultural formation. Religious studies and ethics focus more specifically on the confessional and ethical aspects of reality. They may include courses or units in world religions and church history as well as Biblical studies. Some high schools also offer a course or units on ethics.

Biblical studies uses the Bible as its main text even as teachers and students submit themselves to its authority as the trustworthy Word of God. The Bible is the story of a loving, faithful, and just God acting to redeem His people, a story that culminated in the death and resurrection of His Son Jesus Christ. It is also the story of God interacting with His people and calling them to faith response. God calls those renewed in Jesus Christ to be co-heirs and co-workers in planting signposts to God's Kingdom of truth and justice. Biblical studies deals directly with such Biblical themes and helps students explore and deepen their faith and commitment.

Biblical studies has three main goals. First, it enables students to experience the Biblical narrative as God's revelation of His plan of redemption. Through hearing and retelling the Bible narratives, students begin to experience God's power, anger, and mercy. They understand the Bible as the history of salvation in Jesus Christ, a history through which God calls them to repentance, faith, and discipleship. Second, Biblical studies helps students understand and interpret the Bible. Students investigate its literary forms, its cultural context, and its origins and translations. They tease out significant Biblical themes and practice techniques of Bible interpretation. Third, Biblical studies helps students apply the Biblical message to their personal lives and to situations in our culture (Society of Christian Schools in B.C. 1984, 4-5). The content of Bible books, as one teacher told me, can be "strong stuff"!

For younger children, Bible stories often speak for themselves. But Bible stories can be told in different ways. One teacher may tell the story of Isaac, Jacob, and Esau, for instance, by stressing that while Jacob did a wicked thing in lying to his father, afterward he became a good man who served God. Another may emphasize that despite human wrongdoing, God remains faithful to His promises. The latter points out that God uses even sinful situations to further His plan of salvation. The first teacher falls into the trap of reducing the richness of Scripture to the moral aspect of reality. The second acknowledges that while the moral dimension is important, the story of God's redemption in spite of human failure is the confessional crux of this event.

One danger of teaching Biblical studies in Christian schools is that we force faith and spirituality onto students. Students, particularly as adolescents, need to come to their own commitment. Teachers can help students read and interpret the Bible in a more meaningful way, but they cannot force them to believe it is the Word of God. Here as elsewhere, teachers need to foster an atmosphere of trust and care where students feel free to express their personal views. Teachers should make clear through their modeling that they base their whole life on their faith. Teachers' prayers and faith insight mean little to students if teachers do not apply Biblical holiness, compassion, and justice in their classroom dealings and in their everyday lives. Teachers should mention from time to time what impact their faith has on their personal lives and decisions.

While only Christian schools can teach Biblical studies in the way described above, schools in general need to pay renewed attention to the spiritual and ethical dimensions of human life. These aspects of life must again become components of the curriculum. A good example is a program of the Quebec Protestant (public) schools. It includes a module on knowledge of the Bible since "the Bible is not only the source of the moral and spiritual values of the Protestant tradition, but it is also the foundation of many values found in Western culture and civilization" (Comité Protestant 1992a, 14). The program includes an understanding of both Christian and other moral and religious traditions. It views topics such as human sexuality, the environment, peaceful solutions to conflict, and concern for the poor and vulnerable from the perspective of religious and spiritual values (Comité Protestant 1992b).

The ethical aspect of reality is dealt with to some degree in all subjects, of course. But at the senior secondary level it may be worthwhile to offer a separate ethics course, as suggested by the Quebec committee, especially in a time of ethical uncertainty and superficiality. We neglect the strands of life that provide its meaning and purpose at society's peril. The meaninglessness of our culture is the most serious disease of our times, and schools must do what they can to counter this hollowness.

■ To make the Bible speak to their own experience, Curt Gesch' grade 11 students paraphrased passages in Isaiah using modern examples. An excerpt from Raymond's work for Isaiah 11:1-9:

[God] will create a new earth where all is good,
and he will be happy with his people.
It will be a place where
the ivory hunter will live with the rhino,
the Iraqi and the American will be neighbors,
the Serbs and Croatians will live side by side,
and all will be brought together by a child. . . .
A child will play alone in the park and be safe,
and a child will not find needles in the grass. . . .
for the earth will be filled with the knowledge of the Lord.

In what ways does this type of assignment contribute the three goals of Biblical studies? Can you suggest other meaningful activities when studying a book like Isaiah? How can you help younger children apply the message of the Bible without reducing it to the moral dimension only?

SUBJECTS WITH APPLICATION EMPHASES

■ An Australian *World of Work* program has four strands. Classroom-based learning includes work-related studies and skills. School-based learning involves mini-enterprises and contact with resource people. Industry-based learning incorporates work experience and excursions to industrial and commercial plants. Community-based learning consists mainly of voluntary service. The program begins education for work early in children's schooling, integrating theory and practice. Also, it teaches personal skills and positive work attitudes in experience-based settings (Y. Dror in Lewy 1991, 799-800).

Should general vocation-related education be part of schooling for all students? If so, to what extent and at what age levels should schools teach more practical, applied content, and skills? How do you respond to the argument that with the workplace changing so rapidly, schools should use their limited time to provide a general education and leave it to employers to teach about work and vocational skills?

We often refer to school subjects with direct work or leisure applications as practical or vocational subjects. In some ways, this sets up a false dichotomy. For, what is as practical as being able to read or write? Or what is as work-related in many service-sector jobs as being able to do simple calculations? Can we really say that learning woodworking skills is more practical than learning interpersonal skills in cooperative learning situations? Conversely, what is as rooted in a thorough understanding of the dynamics of our culture and its values as learning about family management in home economics? Calling "practical" what involves hands-on activity is too simplistic.

All school subjects contain—or should contain—a mixture of more theoretical and more practical aspects. Some subjects do have more emphasis on direct applications than others. Those include, for example, technology education, home economics, computer literacy studies, and business education. The importance of these is not specific vocational training. That would be counterproductive with our rapidly changing technologies and work settings. Instead, such studies should include general social, technical, and business skills that benefit students whatever their future careers will be. They should also give students some insight into the world of work, career possibilities, and their inclination and aptitude for certain fields.

At the elementary level students should experience how using simple tools and processes in creative ways can enrich their lives. Students can recycle materials such as aluminum or make bird houses or ceramic pottery. They can design and build electrical alarm systems on boards. They can explore alternative ways of constructing buildings or heating them. They can make some items in an assembly line, then in small groups, and then by themselves, comparing the advantages of each. Through this, they get an intuitive feel for technology. They can begin to talk about the relation of technology to work and leisure and life-style values (Triezenberg 1982, T-4 and T-5).

In the middle grades many schools offer a wide range of short electives or "exploratories." Often schools use parents and other volunteers to teach short, practical courses. The range of courses depends on the expertise of teachers and volunteers. Many are work- or hobby-related and may include, for instance, various crafts, car and small appliance repair, drafting, food and nutrition, and first aid.

Such a broad scope of experiences broadens students' horizons. It may also lead, however, to a fragmented approach without clear goals. Ray Sutton designed a grade 8 lifeskills program with a focus on planning, making, and maintaining useful products related to a Christian life-style. He included a theme unit on "living more with less" in which students explore characteristics of stewardly living. How do we nurture people, cherish the natural order, nonconform freely, and do justice with our material possessions? What makes a "good" home? How can physical elements contribute to or detract from living harmoniously and soberly? What can we reduce, reuse, and recycle? Specific "exploratories" then relate to this introduction. They show how we can use our gifts in practical and creative ways to lead lives of obedience to God (Sutton 1981).

At the high school level, courses with a practical emphasis become more extensive. They include courses in family living, career planning, business education, technological education, and work experience. It can be argued that all students should take a course, or at least some units, in family living and career planning. Family living includes home management but also allows students to explore, within the framework of God's Word, the effect on families of redefined sex roles, two-career families, marriage arrangements and divorce, and so on. Also, in a restructured economy with much youth under- and unemployment, students need to analyze and experience how to use their gifts most effectively for a satisfying future career path. Work experience, even of short duration, enables students to analyze and discuss the nature of work and life on the job.

Thus far I have not mentioned computer studies. Word processing is a useful skill that can improve students' writing. Elementary school students should also begin to use data bases accessible by computer. But computers have limitations. Access to more information or more efficient mastery of skills does not always cause social progress. According to C. A. Bowers, computer studies also contributes to students believing they are autonomous, self-directing individuals. The technological-computer mind set assumes that all problems can be technologically fixed. Further, computers lead their users to reduce knowledge, meaning, and wisdom to "objective," discrete bits of data that can be recovered efficiently (Bowers 1988, 6-8, 33, 77). Having access to information is very different from dealing with it in a meaningful context, recognizing its significance, and using it responsibly. Computer studies should include a healthy dose of skepticism about the limitations and dangers of this technology.

Nevertheless, computers can be used to engage students in higher-order tasks, to solve complex problems, and to nurture artistic expression (Peck and Dorricott 1994, 12-14). Computers can enhance and extend the products students are able to produce. Students, in turn, are more motivated and take pride in their creations. Teacher Pat Sutton, for instance, has her grades 6, 7, and 8 students use computers to create projects on topics such as threats to the environment, rain forests, and endangered species. The students use their research to write text on the computer, organize it, use a "paint" program to draw a cover, import graphics and pictures from CD-ROM files, and print professional-looking products using color printers. All projects on one topic can be published as a book. Pat uses interactive programs and encourages open-ended creativity. Of course, this type of approach requires substantial investments in software, hardware, network link-ups, and teacher time.

■ List topics with an application emphasis that you believe should be included in the curriculum at elementary, middle, or high school levels. Which of these are currently not taught in schools with which you are familiar? If these topics were introduced, what parts of the curriculum would they replace?

■ Discuss the excerpts from the draft curriculum statement for technology of the Christian Community Schools in Australia. What are its implications for the curriculum at the level(s) you teach or plan to teach?

"Technology from a Christian perspective is the application of God's truth and principles to the created world in order to create processes and products that meet human needs. Some people say rather simplistically that technology is neither good nor evil, that it just depends on how you use it. While it is true that technology can be used for good or evil, its very existence will in itself change us, and the way we relate to others. Technology is not neutral. It can enrich life on earth but it can also become a god in itself, alienate people from each other, and ultimately destroy the earth.

"As technology becomes more complex, so do the issues of its impact on our existence. As Christian educators we need to be aware of the nature of that impact and the changes it may bring, and to respond to them in ways that are true to our understanding of what God has revealed in His Word. Students in Christian schools need to be encouraged to seek the 'wisdom that comes from above' regarding the use of technology.

"Modern technology is characterized by increasing complexity and rapidity of change. Technology also has a profound impact on the type and amount of work available. The creation of advanced technology is impacting on the natural environment in many ways and the students of today will have to face [related] local and global issues. Students will need knowledge and a value base from which they will make decisions about these issues. To be effective Christian citizens they will need to have an informed understanding of their expectations and of the consequences of continued technological innovation and development on society (including human relationships), their culture and the environment.

"The process of designing, making, and appraising is central to the study of technology. Students explore, apply, and develop materials, information, and systems. They integrate theory and practice, utilizing resources to solve problems. They learn to value practical and creative gifts for personal enjoyment, vocational purposes, and in the service of others. They learn to appreciate the importance of using materials wisely and responsibly, appreciating God's order and design in the systems we use. They learn to discern the positive and negative aspects of technology on the individual and society. They develop godly values in judging ethical and social justice issues raised by technology.

"As students explore the forms, functions, and performance of organizational, electronic, mechanical, structural, and information systems, they need to address issues such as the relation between a Biblical worldview and the technical culture of our day, the effects of computers, 'computer mentality' and a Biblical view of the person, social alienation caused by technology, technostress, technocracy as an idol, and the effects of technology on human creativity." (Clinton et al. 1993).

SUMMARY

A balanced curriculum includes content that deals with all aspects of reality. It is rooted, as much as possible, in students' own experiences. It often deals with situations that involve several aspects of reality, and does not neglect more practical applications. With a wealth of content possibilities, schools need to set priorities based on their mission and aims and on what they consider to be basic issues in the various subject areas.

REFLECTING

1. How would proponents of the four curriculum orientations described in chapter 1 differ in their choice of subject area content? How would they differ in organizing the curriculum?

2. Go back to the outline of a Christian curriculum orientation given at the end of chapter 2. In terms of what it says about curriculum content and what this chapter says about individual subject areas, which subjects currently in the curriculum would you consider most important? least important? How would the age level of students influence your answer?

3. Computer hardware and software changes so rapidly that as you read this, my descriptions may seem out-of-date. What type of computer-related learning have you experienced that you deem to be effective? ineffective? What steps should schools take to use current computer technology responsibly?

PART III:
Planning and Implementing Curriculum

Teachers can make a difference in the lives of their students. For curriculum plans to contribute positively to this difference, teachers must do more than justify their aims and values and know how to organize their curriculum. They must also use curriculum theory and their experience reflectively and effectively as they design and implement programs.

It is not enough for teachers to choose curriculum content with care. Think about how Jesus taught. He used diverse ways and means to meet people in their social and personal situation. He involved them. He challenged them to respond personally and genuinely to His teaching. His methods or pedagogy, even the way He lived, affected His "students" as much as the content He taught. Similarly, how teachers structure their teaching and learning affects not only how their students perceive content but also their attitudes and values. Teachers must consider how they can nurture responsible and meaningful personal and communal response. They must plan the pedagogical dimensions of teaching and learning. Pedagogy--how we go about learning in the classroom--is an integral aspect of the curriculum as students experience it.

Part III of the book, then, has four chapters. I first discuss the pedagogical contours of curriculum, including learning styles, phases of learning, and developmental layers of understanding. Chapter 8 describes the practical steps of planning classroom units. Chapter 9 looks at general models of curriculum planning, how elements outside the school affect curriculum, and curriculum implementation and evaluation. The last chapter briefly sums up the curriculum roles of Christian teachers in both Christian and public schools.

One key point that becomes clear time and again is that curriculum is never neutral. Previous chapters have shown that curriculum content and the way we organize knowledge is always based on a particular worldview. The discussions in Part III make clear that the pedagogy we use as well as the way we go about planning curriculum are also founded on specific and vested beliefs about education, and, ultimately, about life itself. A Christian approach will counter the individualism and lack of trust of our age.

Chapter 7
Pedagogical Contours for Curriculum

■ When I ask Susan Dick about her primary classroom program, she says little about content. Instead, she dwells on two aspects she considers more significant. First, she plans so that her children can celebrate their gifts. Second, she consistently stresses the importance of responsibility and accountability. Susan does carefully consider her unit themes and content. But she knows that the pedagogical aspects of her program affect her children at least as much as the content.

Susan makes sure, first, that all children realize their uniqueness. She affirms their gifts. She challenges them to develop and use them, even if at first they may fail. She encourages her students to compliment each other for their successes: "You sure read that well!" She uses mistakes as a launching pad for further learning. When children have not yet mastered an intellectual skill, she applauds their gifts in music or helpfulness. "Use your gifts positively and well," Susan tells them. "Then it doesn't matter how far you have developed in a certain ability."

At the same time, Susan makes her children accountable for their behavior and action. She often gives them choices about their tasks and where they sit. She steps in only when the children cannot handle their responsibility: "Do you think you should move to get your work done?" Disruptive children must apologize to the whole class. On specific days children complete their own daily time schedules. They plan their work for one or two open time slots for the day. They are responsible for their own progress. They regularly evaluate their progress through simple checklists and completions ("I think I can do better in . . . "). They also give each other feedback. Susan incorporates some cooperative tasks that encourage servanthood. They work with new mixed ability groups each month.

Susan goes further than finding methods that teach content effectively. She thinks of her class in terms of her overall pedagogy. That is, she considers how she can best meet the needs of all children in her care. She thinks deeply about how to interact with them so that they unwrap their gifts in a supportive context. She thinks of herself as a mentor who guides and enables her children to take on life's tasks with knowledge, insight, skill, and commitment.

Is it important to consider the pedagogical "contours" for curriculum? Why or why not? In North America, curriculum developers often pay little attention to pedagogy. What effect does that have on curriculum plans?

PEDAGOGY, LEARNING, AND CURRICULUM

The Christian educator Comenius (1592-1670) already recognized that pedagogy and curriculum were closely intertwined. His concern for experiential learning led him, for instance, to be the first to use pictures in textbooks and ask questions about them. But 350 years later many curriculum planners still overlook pedagogy, stressing content instead. They leave it to psychologists to determine how such content can be transmitted effectively. As Walter Doyle points out, problems exist with that approach. Pedagogy is not just a neutral pipeline for delivering content and is not limited to applying psychological theories (Doyle in Jackson 1992, 492-93).

Good teachers recognize that their pedagogy profoundly affects their curriculum-in-use. They plan programs that will bind their pupils and themselves together in common purpose. They take into account their knowledge of their children's backgrounds and emotional needs, of learning styles and developmental stages, and of human relationships. Also, their reflection about classroom interactions and situations (e.g., the nuances of verbal and body language) causes them to revise their plans constantly. Pedagogy involves more than efficiently processing content (Max van Manen in Pinar 1988, 444).

Good pedagogy also uses applicable learning theory conclusions. Glen Hass (1987, 183) gives a summary of such results. An atmosphere of openness, trust, and security fosters successful learning. Pupils learn best when teachers know them as individuals and when they identify with their teachers and peers. Obtaining knowledge for oneself often leads to better motivation, retention, and meaningfulness. Students transfer their knowledge to new situations most frequently when teachers help them generalize and apply knowledge. Finally, students learn to like learning from teachers who show a personal love for knowledge.

It is clear, therefore, that learning theories support my claim in chapter 4 that knowledge involves the whole person, the heart as well as the mind. How teachers relate to and engage a class affects students' attitudes and the quality of knowing. It also touches what knowledge they are willing to consider, endorse, value, and apply. The knowledge and resulting value commitments in a classroom where a teacher projects selfishness, frustration, or narrow-mindedness differ a great deal from one where the teacher communicates care, patience, or acceptance. Donald Oliver suggests that teachers should view teaching as "entering a shared moment with others" and "participat[ing] in an occasion . . . wherein there is both special human sensibility and a significant natural happening" (1990, 68).

In this chapter, then, I consider human qualities that shape such shared learning occasions. I discuss how curriculum planning needs to take into account the following pedagogical concerns: a Biblical view of persons, learning styles and phases of learning, developmental layers and the importance of story, personal response and service, and relationships in community. Separate books could be written on each of these topics! This chapter can only sketch brief outlines and give some classroom examples.

A BIBLICAL VIEW OF THE PERSON
AS IT RELATES TO LEARNING

As teachers we strive to be trustworthy guides for our students. We want to be present to our students in a sensitive yet influential way. We plan units and lessons so that they find learning meaningful. For this, we need to understand the nature of human beings and what implications that has for the classroom.

A Biblical view of the person holds, first of all, that students are images of God. That means that they stand in relationship to God. They reveal God as they live lives of loving service to Him and our neighbor. They image God as they carry out the four great injunctions. Therefore their heart commitment, whether to God or to other "gods" such as materialism or hedonism, affects their imaging, including their learning, attitudes, and values.

This means that our personal modeling and our planned learning must aim to foster commitment to God. Students, like all of us, are sinful and will try to be independent of God and those in authority. Sometimes we cannot reach a student no matter what we do; to do so requires a change of heart. However, our structures of learning can recognize the inherent dignity and worth of all and nurture mutual respect and order. If we do this, most students will try to fulfil their tasks lovingly, responsively, and responsibly. In this way they image God.

The Bible also makes clear that all people have unique gifts. All students are special, created with singular traits, gifts, and abilities that they unwrap in the classroom situation. We therefore plan diverse learning activities and encourage students to respond in unique ways. Learning thus becomes a personal occasion. It is rooted in students' own experiences. It involves telling stories, molding stories, transforming stories, and creating stories. It does so through thoughtfulness, playfulness, and creativity. Students develop their giftedness through different ways of knowing. Meaningful learning allows students to transcend content transmission and skill dexterity. They respond through developing, giving, and finding themselves.

At the same time, God created persons in relationship to His other creatures. We are gifted in order to contribute to the welfare of those around us. Our uniqueness is not an end in itself; it is a means to enrich the communities where God places us. Classrooms therefore must be places where students learn to bear each other's burdens and share each other's joys, and where they learn to work together for the common good. (For more detailed accounts of how a Biblical view of human beings frames learning, see Fennema 1977 and Van Brummelen 1992, 38ff.)

Students today face a different context from that of 100 years ago. The reasons for learning what we ask them to learn are often much more obscure, especially for adolescents. Combined with a lack of meaningful responsibility, this can make schooling a frustrating experience for them. For many years they depend financially on their parents, but when both parents work or only one parent lives at home they have fewer meaningful relations with adults. They tend to live and make important decisions apart from adults (Hass 1987, 118-19). Although their basic characteristics as images of God have not changed, we do need to stress, more than before, personal relationships and opportunity for meaningful responsibilities in our classrooms.

■ Peggy Barlow describes her experience of teaching *Pilgrim's Progress*. Describe how Peggy has grasped what it means to be present to her students as images of God.

»Frequently my teaching merely reflects the craftsmanship of my students, God's images. Our study of John Bunyan's *Pilgrim's Progress* exemplified this playful dynamic of our teaching-learning. Intending to counterbalance the grave truths of *Lord of the Flies* and the traditional essay assignment, I approached Bunyan's work from a more subjective and/or experiential framework, and, from the onset, my students intervened lovingly and creatively.

After photocopying engravings from my personal copy of *Pilgrim's Progress*, I used overheads (and Pachelbel's *Canon*). My students were to interpret what they saw and write in their response journals. Predictably, when students started to share what they had written, something happened. One moment they were reading, and the next they were up in front of the class using the transparency, explaining, and pointing. The only directive I gave was that they had to support their ideas by showing us details in the picture and from the book. They were doing that anyway! What had started out as a "set" ended up lasting an entire period, and I never "taught" at all. Students commented readily on each other's responses.

I watched, delighted, but no longer surprised. No wonder it is such an honor to teach these precious beings. . . .

The finale [of the unit] was an exam which I said they were going to enjoy. Incredulous, they tried to extract its contents. I only gave them one hint: "Here are some giveaway marks. Make sure you know at least eight characters and eight places in the allegory."

They smiled. "That's easy."

I smiled.

The test was writing a short story about a student and a teacher meeting in a cafe to discuss *Pilgrim's Progress*. (Next time, I will broaden the parameters and let the students create the situation.) I indicated some topics to be discussed but it was up to the students to create the story and the interpretations of the allegorical aspects of specific places and characters.

The test took just over two periods which meant that by the second class they would have been able to study further.

"Oh, we know what's on the test!"

Did it matter? Using a narrative format with expository overtones as they wrote their interpretations precluded the possibility of "cheating." Quality of thinking when it exists transcends quantity of information. A well-crafted insight exudes intellectual integrity. Paradoxical. Unconventional. NONSTANDARD.

TEACHER PLAY, therefore, transforms into STUDENT PLAY.

In the transcendence of storytelling, these students sit transfixed by their own knowledge and imagination, "both sides of the brain." They lose track of time. Affective, psychomotor, and cognitive aspects meld ethereal. Creativity reflects perhaps the quintessence of our former unfallenness, for, as God's images, we still create. God, our Creator, grants us merciful art.

This then is my cathedral. I sit and watch the students write. Ideas, like Impressionist tints, blur past, flowers of my garden.

LEARNING STYLES AND THE RHYTHM OF LEARNING

■ Doreen Fairweather builds trust relations with her grade 7s and 8s. For example, she eats lunch with a different student each day: "Once they let you in, you can get them to think about issues." She wants her class to function as a team where all feel accepted and free to share. She ensures that her students perceive how the content she teaches affects their lives. Her students may write, for instance, an account of a Bible story as if they were there, describing their feelings and reaction.

Doreen's novel studies help her students understand truth. She refrains from telling them, "This is the way it is." Rather, she asks many inference questions. One student's answer leads to other questions ("Do you agree? Why or why not? How does the Bible speak to this issue? How does this apply to you?"). She encourages her students to look at different sides of issues. They take and justify positions.

Doreen also constantly keys in to her students' different learning styles. She encourages them to respond using their specific individual gifts, whether that be through stories, poems, projects, mini-debates, posters, or music. In creative writing, Doreen provides "starters" suitable for different learners: for example, she shows pictures on the overhead, gives a pile of sentence fragments, or has students work in small groups for several minutes. Doreen sometimes discusses the giftedness of people portrayed in a novel. The students indicate the characters' personal traits and gifts on a color-coded wheel using the physical, social, intellectual, and emotional categories. Doreen does this deliberately to stimulate a metacognitive consideration of students' own gifts. Students make a similar wheel for themselves, reflecting about their own giftedness. A celebration of giftedness may complete this exploration.

■ After introducing the Renaissance, Leigh Bradfield gives his grade 8 students three periods to complete an assignment on art and the Renaissance. They first study, either individually or in small groups, an untitled pre-Renaissance art picture. They answer ten questions (e.g., "Is the person male or female? What expression is shown in the face? How would you improve this picture?"). They then answer the same questions for a post-Renaissance painting that most have seen before, the Mona Lisa. The students then use their answers and further research to draw three generalizations about art and the Renaissance. Afterwards, Leigh leads a class discussion and at the end tells students that the title of the first painting was The Virgin at Prayer. The class discusses whether there is anything specifically Christian about the Mona Lisa, and whether Christian artists necessarily paint Christian subjects.

The students' initial exploration and Leigh's disclosure lead to students using vocabulary words in sentences that relate to their study. They then apply what they have learned by drawing a picture of a girl praying that shows characteristics of post-Renaissance art. Leigh gives several reasons why this learning activity is effective. It starts with an intriguing puzzle; the students are curious about what the first picture portrays. They do much of the work themselves. There are no right and wrong interpretations. At the end, they respond personally and have a sense of accomplishment.

Note how Leigh deliberately plans for four phases of learning, each suitable for different types of learners. He sets the stage with open-ended exploration. The students' findings provide background for more formal disclosure through readings and class discussion. To ensure that the students grasp the key ideas they reformulate them in writing using related vocabulary. Finally, they apply their learning in a personal way. They draw a picture based on but extending their learning.

Being a meaningful pedagogical presence to your students means you care about them. Therefore you want to provide them with learning activities suitable for their various favored learning styles. It would be overwhelmingly complex to plan learning for all styles in each lesson, nor would that be desirable. All students should regularly have the opportunity to learn through their preferred style. At the same time, we need to stretch students' learning style preferences so that they gradually become more flexible. We should be aware of our learning style leanings to prevent overemphasizing those.

There are many ways to categorize learning styles. There are the left brain/right brain and the sequential/random, abstract/concrete distinctions. We also know that students may favor either visual, auditory, or kinesthetic means of learning. Other profiles show strengths in multiple intelligences or modes of knowing. Some learners like to learn by themselves, in small groups, or by relating to the teacher. Learners may favor a certain temperature, a degree of sound and light, and a time of day. Other categorizations relate learning styles to personality types. All these are also likely affected by a student's age, cultural background, and home environment.

At this point you could choose one schema and apply it rigidly, neglecting all others. Or you could throw up your arms in despair at the complexity of it all. But there is a better alternative, I believe. That is to relate learning styles based on psychological attributes to the natural rhythm of learning. Alfred North Whitehead (1929) describes that rhythm in terms of romance, precision, and generalization. Doug Blomberg uses the terms immersion, withdrawal, and return (Stronks and Blomberg 1993, 172ff.). Maria Harris (1987, 43) describes concrete experience, reflective observation, abstract conceptualization, and active experimentation. Here I summarize the four phase model I developed in *Walking with God in the Classroom* (Van Brummelen 1992 [1988], 50-58).

FOUR PHASES OF LEARNING

The model for learning presented here takes into account the rhythm of learning, students' different learning styles, and the learning theory conclusions presented above. It incorporates the learning style categorization developed by Bernice McCarthy (1990). The model involves four phases of learning: setting the stage, disclosure, reformulation, and transcendence. Each phase is well suited (though not exclusively) for learners with a particular learning style preference. The Ontario Alliance of Christian Schools, for one, uses the model in its curriculum development work.

The four-phase model of learning intends to help you plan a balanced curriculum, one that acknowledges that both you and your students are responsible and responsive images of God. Students need all four phases of learning for insightful, reflective, and committed response and action. Usually you move from *setting the stage* (*preparing*) to *disclosure* (*presenting*) to *reformulation* (*reinforcing*) to *transcendence* (*responding*). The transcendence phase may lead to a new "setting the stage" situation or problem.

Despite a natural rhythm, the phases do not always follow each other sequentially. At the beginning of a unit you may spend most time on "setting the stage" activities; at the end, on transcendence. In the middle of the unit a lesson may use only a minute or two to set the stage, with disclosure or reformulation taking up the rest. A grade 10 geometry unit may contain far more transcendence-type learning than one on simplifying polynomials. What is important is that each unit includes all four phases of learning, and, where applicable, that each major activity does also. You can use a variety of teaching and learning strategies in each phase.

The first phase of learning, setting the stage, makes use of students' experiential knowledge. It encourages students to enjoy, discover, imagine, brainstorm, ask questions and pose problems, search for relationships, and draw tentative conclusions. This phase of learning is a time for experiencing, exploring, and responding to real-life phenomena and imaginative cultural products ("immersion"). Teachers provide activities and make suggestions. Their main role is to encourage students to reflect on and extrapolate the knowledge they already have in nonthreatening ways. This phase stimulates and prepares students to become involved in the more formal and abstract disclosure phase.

Learners who are intuitors feel comfortable in this phase. They are the ones who need to experience situations concretely. They examine and reflect on its aspects and related perspectives in order to seek meaning and draw conclusions. They benefit from personal involvement and social interaction as they go about their tasks. They learn by asking and answering "Why?" questions about their experiences and reasoning inductively. They need their learning to be based on their personal experience and issues relevant for them.

The second phase of learning, disclosure, consists of precise, well-organized instruction. Here students withdraw from their concrete experience in order to unfold or disclose a topic in a carefully structured manner. This may be done through oral and audiovisual presentations, demonstrations, class discussions, small group tutoring by the teacher or fellow students, focused readings, and so on. This phase emphasizes careful conceptual development even as teachers continue to ask penetrating questions and actively involve students in developing a topic. Here teachers help students assimilate concepts, theories, and issues in a structured and meaningful way.

Intellectual or analytic learners delight and excel in the disclosure phase of learning. They prefer to perceive information abstractly and process it reflectively. They relish gaining detailed, precise knowledge. They learn by asking information questions ("What?") and by reasoning things out. They are interested in gathering, classifying, analyzing, and critiquing concepts, theories, and ideas. They find satisfaction in thinking through problems and issues and determining the validity of hypotheses and conclusions.

In the third phase of learning, reformulation, students demonstrate that they can understand, interpret, and use what they have learned in the disclosure phase. During this phase teachers ask interpretation and inference questions. They ask for specific reactions. They ask students to explain what they have learned and use it in simple applications. They use textbook questions, worksheets, journal responses, and various assignments to reinforce, strengthen, and sharpen what has been learned. Often teachers intersperse reformulation questions and activities with their disclosure.

CONCRETE EXPERIENCE EMPHASIS

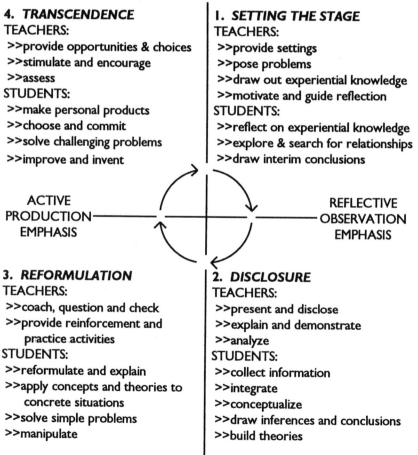

4. TRANSCENDENCE
TEACHERS:
>>provide opportunities & choices
>>stimulate and encourage
>>assess
STUDENTS:
>>make personal products
>>choose and commit
>>solve challenging problems
>>improve and invent

I. SETTING THE STAGE
TEACHERS:
>>provide settings
>>pose problems
>>draw out experiential knowledge
>>motivate and guide reflection
STUDENTS:
>>reflect on experiential knowledge
>>explore & search for relationships
>>draw interim conclusions

ACTIVE PRODUCTION EMPHASIS — REFLECTIVE OBSERVATION EMPHASIS

3. REFORMULATION
TEACHERS:
>>coach, question and check
>>provide reinforcement and
   practice activities
STUDENTS:
>>reformulate and explain
>>apply concepts and theories to
   concrete situations
>>solve simple problems
>>manipulate

2. DISCLOSURE
TEACHERS:
>>present and disclose
>>explain and demonstrate
>>analyze
STUDENTS:
>>collect information
>>integrate
>>conceptualize
>>draw inferences and conclusions
>>build theories

ABSTRACT CONCEPTUALIZATION EMPHASIS

THE FOUR PHASES OF LEARNING

Students who are implementers appreciate this phase of learning. They perceive information abstractly and process it actively. They are the ones who like to do well-defined, focused tasks, including drill and hands-on activities. They want to try out how they can use the concepts they have learned. They want to be actively engaged individually or in small groups. They learn by asking "How do I do this?" and using step-by-step procedures to solve problems. They make the material their own through reformulation activities, beginning to add something of their own and to use it in personal ways. If something works, they want to apply it, particularly in situations that they see as useful.

In the final phase, transcendence, students move beyond reformulation. Here theoretical reflection and practical application become reflective and innovative response. Students apply concepts and principles in their own unique ways, often in what for them are original situations. They develop personally meaningful products and choose responses that affect their lives. They commit themselves to certain values and courses of action. They explore questions about the meaning for themselves personally of what they have learned. They share in choosing, planning, and exhibiting their responses. Expressive representations and creative investigations may create new perspectives of seeing and responding to God's world.

Learners who are innovators do well in this phase. They perceive information concretely and process it dynamically. They like to make things happen, always seeking out possibilities for themselves. They use and apply what they have learned in creative and imaginative ways. They learn by asking and answering "What if I try this?" and finding out by trial and error. They enrich reality by animatedly trying out new possibilities. They take initiatives and risks, developing ideas on their own.

No learners, of course, fit anyone learning style category precisely. But most are stronger in one or two than in the others. Using the rhythm of the phases helps you maintain curricular balance. You will neither overemphasizes academic traditionalist content nor constructivist personal meaning making. It allows students to obtain knowledge for themselves and to respond by generalizing and applying it. Pedagogical tact and wisdom therefore suggests that you plan activities for all four types of learners, in all four phases of learning.

■ The following are two examples of lessons that used the foregoing model. Suggest the strengths and possible pitfalls of each.

»I am a Canadian, grade 7-8 (Arden Post, unpublished): The focus of this lesson is that being a citizen of Canada secures freedoms and demands responsibilities. For setting the stage, small groups brainstorm the meanings of citizen, citizenship, responsibility, and privilege. For disclosure group members read handouts entitled "The rights and privileges of citizenship" and "The responsibilities of citizenship." For reformulation, the groups discuss and list on a worksheet four rights and privileges and then four responsibilities. The group leader assigns one right and one responsibility to each group member. They take a few minutes to write individually what that particular right means and how they can carry out the responsibility. After sharing what they have written, the group selects one responsibility and makes a plan to carry it out or to help others carry it out (transcendence).

»Key themes in the Scriptures, grade 9-10 (OACS, 1994, 31-35): The focus of these two lessons is to identify and explore four key themes running through Scripture, viz., the kingdom of God, the covenant by which God relates to His people, the antithesis between the Kingdom of God and that of Satan, and the history of redemption focusing on the cross of Jesus Christ. For setting the stage teachers ask how students would envision an ideal world. They ask them to compare their responses with the first and last two chapters of the Bible. They then discuss the reality of our world, why bad and good things happen in our lives, and why tension exists. For disclosure, the teacher presents information about the four key themes, discussing how these apply to everyday situations. For reformulation, the students complete a chart on an activity sheet outlining different types of covenants. For transcendence students create a collage, design a symbol, draw a picture or write a play or poem to show how they as adolescents experience the antithesis between the kingdom of God and the kingdom of Satan at home, school, work, and play.

LAYERS OF UNDERSTANDING
AND THE IMPORTANCE OF STORY

■ You may be able to teach some unit topics successfully at various grade levels as long as you consider students' developmental levels. Discuss how you could teach a unit on China (or another culture) at the grades 1, 6, and 11 levels. How would the units differ? Are there any themes or objectives that would be the same? If so, how would your learning activities differ? Can any science or social studies topic be taught effectively at any grade level as long as you adapt the learning to that level? Why or why not?

Persons move through different developmental stages as they mature. A five-year-old acts differently than a fifteen-year-old when lost in a department store. A number of psychologists and educators have described different developmental phases and their implications for learning.

Psychologist Erik Erikson, for instance, describes eight psychosocial stages, each of which builds on the previous one. These are characterized by trust (from 0 months on), autonomy (12 months+), initiative (4 years+), industry and accomplishment (6 years+), identity (11 years+), intimacy (15 years+), generativity (18 years+), and integrity (45 years+). The development at each stage continues to exert an influence over the person's whole life span.

Erikson's schema is not a fixed formula. Maturational development differs from one person to the next. For curriculum planning Erikson's stages give several broad guidelines. When children enter school they are in a period of vigor, enterprise, and imagination. They need to explore and discover, to open up their world, to learn from structured play. Kindergarten and grade 1 children benefit from varied learning centers. Soon pupils enter a stage of industry where they appreciate executing and completing tasks. In this stage securing real achievement is important. Learning should help them develop a sense of accomplishment. This is the time when pupils are ready and often eager to learn many basic skills and concepts. As students reach adolescence, classrooms should allow students to establish and maintain a sense of identity. Often this is not an easy time. Here teachers continually try to balance the personal identity needs of teens with the need to keep their classroom functioning as a unit.

Erikson's stages give a general psychosocial backdrop for school curriculum. They are too broad, however, to give much specific help in curriculum planning. On the other hand, Piaget's preoperational (1.5-7 years), concrete operational (7-11), and formal operations (12+) stages focus narrowly on the development of rational thought. Followers of Piaget tend to focus only on the development of logical thinking. Often they neglect the fact that non-analytic types of learning are not only meaningful and enriching but also prepare students for more formal deductive thinking later (Egan 1986, 22-23). Young children can understand abstract concepts when we present them in concrete settings such as stories, for instance. Piaget's work is important in understanding how children develop their rational thought processes. But its application to school learning is limited mainly to the rational or logical mode of knowing.

Egan's primary layer of understanding

More helpful for curriculum planning are the first three of Kieran Egan's four "layers of understanding" (Egan 1988, 1990). These are primary understanding (up to nine years old); romantic understanding (ages 8-15); and philosophic understanding (ages 15-19). Egan uses the term "layers" rather than "stages" since students accumulate one layer on top of the previous one. The new layer does not replace the previous one but coalesces with it, giving deepened understanding and insight.

In early childhood, Egan (1988) argues, pupils take their surroundings for granted. It is difficult for them to take enough distance to deal intellectually with topics such as their families or neighborhoods. While learning should focus on basic concepts that make life meaningful, they do so most effectively through knowledge that expands their horizons. What intrigues them at this age is the distant, the remote, the imagined.

Moreover, education for young children is a serious adventure. Too often we trivialize it. When we design curriculum, *meaning* must be foremost in our minds. This is possible: children already know about joy and fear, hope and disappointment, and love and cruelty before they can perform concrete skills like riding a bicycle or skating. We need to teach fundamental meanings that help children make sense of their world. Children discover themselves, paradoxically, by focusing outward on the world and others (Egan 1988).

The medium that allows this to happen is the story, Egan continues. Children can understand abstract concepts and causality within the context of stories. The story is the best tool we have to communicate meaning and values. It blends events into a powerful unit that evokes children's affective as well as intellectual responses. The story carries forward real and imaginative possibilities that develop a sense of wonder and awe. It can give children intellectual and emotional security. Within the context of the story, children can understand the role in life of abstract concepts like power, ambition, greed, and punishment. The curriculum at this level is more a set of great stories to be told than objectives to be attained. The story needs prominence because it is fundamental to our thinking. It precedes literal reflection and the development of theories (Egan 1988).

What does this mean for curriculum in the early grades? It means that teachers need to be the principal story tellers of our culture, telling the great stories, for instance, of history and science. They tell (not just read) children powerful, dramatic, great stories, including the Bible stories that recount the story of God's dealing with His people. But more than that, teachers make units and lessons accessible and meaningful to children by using the main features of the story in their planning. In other words, Egan (1986, 1988) claims, teachers should design all units at this level so that they tell a meaningful story.

To do so effectively requires five steps. First, teachers identify what is important and affectively engaging about a topic. Second, they find "binary opposites" that best express and articulate the importance of the topic. Egan points out that children see issues in terms of opposites such as good and bad, love and hate, courage and cowardice, security and fear, and so on. (From a strictly logical point of view the "opposites" contrast but may not be antonyms.) Egan gives many examples: destroyer-helper (unit on heat); survival-destruction (North American Indians); practical visionary-conventionalist (flight); dominance-submission (our town or city); ingenuity-conventional dullness (subtraction); and freedom-tyranny (the Greeks and Persians) (Egan 1988, 118, 234ff.). The Bible shows, of course, that the basic antithesis is between the Kingdom of God (good) and the kingdom of Satan (evil).

Third, teachers use a pair of binary opposites to develop a story that reflects human hopes, fears, motives, dispositions, and beliefs. They choose content that dramatically develops the opposites in story form. Fourth, they resolve the dramatic conflict inherent in the opposites at the end of the unit. Finally, they evaluate whether the children grasped the unit's importance and learned its content (Egan 1988, 232-33).

Looking at primary understanding in this way helps us not to sell children short. We can teach them much about the meaning and purpose of life as long as we do so in a concrete story setting. We may question whether it is *always* possible or even desirable to teach topics of significance at this level as a story that resolves binary opposites. Some topics do not easily fit this pattern. Nevertheless, Egan's approach is a powerful one that we can often use effectively. Thomas Groome (1980) and John Bolt (1993) also describe the importance of the shared story in passing on our cultural memory, wisdom, and vision.

Egan's romantic layer of understanding

Egan's next layer of understanding is the romantic one (ages 8 or 9 to 14 or 15). He uses the term "romantic" because now a desire for adventure, imagination, and idealism dominate students. They enthusiastically explore the world and their experience in it. They are fervent in their quest for knowing about the extreme, the exotic, the distant. Detailed factuality and explanations of how things happen fascinates them. They like lists, tables, and formulas. They want to know about other styles of life and ways of living, both past and present, about the technology of familiar things, and about animal and plant life--especially if these involve the dramatic and unexpected. Teachers continue to stimulate wonder and awe, but now more by making the familiar strange (Egan 1990).

Gradually a more technical, non-narrative form of teaching becomes possible. But narrative involving a powerful affective component is still important. The central role of the story focused on binary opposites gives way, however, to narratives that provide a context for students deepening their understanding of the meaning and purpose of life. Students develop a rational grasp of detail and particulars within a narrative context. Transcendent human values such as goodness, vigor, resilience, and ingenuity replace binary opposites as the unifying threads for teaching topics. Units now focus on human motives, intentions, and emotions. By using concrete and disparate examples of ideas, students learn about justice, love, courage, grief, patience, authority, beauty, and altruism. During this layer we stimulate both the imagination and literal thinking (Egan 1990).

Egan's planning framework for the romantic layer starts by teachers considering which transcendent human values are central to a topic and can evoke affective images. They then choose content that stimulates romance, wonder, and awe about reality. They organize it into a narrative structure that shows human hopes, fears, intentions, and other emotions. They also make sure that students can pursue some aspect of the topic in exhaustive detail. They stimulate their imaginations and encourage them to see the topic in a wider context. A satisfactory closure at this level is one that opens other topics (Egan 1990, 257; Egan 1992, 94). Egan suggests teaching about geometry in terms of practical ingenuity; trees in terms of their faithful supportiveness of civilizations; government in terms of courage and generosity of spirit (Egan 1992, 120ff.).

We choose values for units that we consider important, and we may prefer ones that differ from Egan's. We may see trees, for instance, in terms of God's faithful provision for life on earth. We can certainly agree with Egan's main point that the detail and skill learning of the romantic layer needs to be grounded in significant values. This can often be developed best through a narrative approach, although the role of narrative is now less central than the story form was for younger children.

Egan's philosophic layer of understanding

The third layer of understanding Egan calls philosophic understanding (ages 14 or 15 to 19 or 20). Here students realize that all knowledge of the world and our experience is connected, and that they are part of a historical process. They want to understand and develop causal chains and networks. They redirect their intellectual attention from detail to general concepts in culture and human nature. They become interested in general questions of religion, anthropology, politics, economics, and psychology. They search for truth about how society functions and their role within the world. They are now ready to focus much more on general schemata and ideologies (Egan 1990, 176ff.).

Again, this layer does not replace the previous two. Students are still interested in the story. Reaching philosophic understanding does not negate the fact that the story of the holocaust or the discovery of non-Euclidean geometry or the alchemist's search for gold or an existentialist Franz Kafka novel will still captivate students' interest. Narrative is powerful in all layers. That is why in this book I deliberately use (real) stories of teachers and classrooms to introduce and illustrate issues in curriculum planning. But at the philosophic layer students move beyond narrative for the sake of the story, move beyond detail into drawing general conclusions. They want to explore and understand what caused these happenings. As teachers we now focus our planning on underlying questions and issues. We help students explore and draw conclusion about the meaning of knowledge for their personal lives and life in society.

A curriculum example

I want to conclude this section by describing (briefly) how we could teach the topic of transportation at each of Egan's three levels of understanding.

For the primary level of understanding (say, six-year-olds), you would first ask what is important about transportation. In our world, we cannot be self-sufficient. Therefore, we need ways to move ourselves and our resources from one place to another. Without practical, effective transport, we would have far fewer conveniences and would lead lonelier lives. Several possible binary opposite pairs come to mind: slow-fast, fear-hope, tradition-change, constraint-freedom, immobility-mobility.

You could, for instance, use the immobility-mobility contrast. Then you might construct the unit around the story of people searching for more mobility as they looked for more food and other resources. The story of Abraham shows how animals at first helped people move from one location to another. Ships and wagons made settlement possible for the pioneers. Trains, cars, and airplanes allow us to get from one place to another very quickly and use products from around the world. At the same time, such mobility has created problems: pollution, less neighborliness, more crime. You use many books that tell parts of the story of transportation. In your learning centers children experience and explore various means of transportation. You could conclude the unit by considering how people can use transportation to build community in responsible ways.

For the romantic layer of understanding (say, age 11), you would first identify the transcendent values central to transportation. Again, several come to mind: human curiosity and inventiveness, economic stewardship, and the need for governments to maintain peace and order and a sense of national identity. A unit could have economic stewardship (and its lack) as its main focus, with the other values playing a supporting role. In Canadian schools, the building of the first transcontinental railroad could provide the central narrative structure. A story of high drama, it involved the clash of native and western ways of life, human ingenuity in overcoming the obstacles of muskeg and mountain, the development of rich farmland (but not without questionable land specu-lation), and governments wanting to prevent an American takeover and quash rebellions. The railroad can be shown as Sir John A. Macdonald's "national dream," culminating with his wife riding on the locomotive's cowcatcher through the Rockies soon after the railroad's completion in 1886.

While the main narrative of the unit is the building of the Canadian Pacific Railway, the unit would be broader in scope. Some students could investigate the building of other famous railroads. Others may want to trace the development and impact of the automobile or airplane. The focus of such investigations could continue to be how such inventions and innovations originated in human curiosity and ingenuity, with their development spurred by both positive and negative economic factors. At the end, students could draw conclusions about the positive and negative impact of today's transportation systems on our communities and on the world.

Transportation taught at the philosophic level would take a different approach. Now the students might consider the transportation infrastructure of their nation, or compare that of their nation with a very different region of the world. Students would still investigate the specifics of transportation systems, but would use them to consider the underlying issues. In what ways do our lives depend on our transportation systems? What is the impact of the car on our communities and on our way of life? Transportation and communication have led to a "global village." What are the positive and negative effects? Is the so-called "information highway" replacing the need for some transportation infrastructures? Which modes of transportation will become less or more important in the future? Why? A theme needs to give focus to such explorations. One possibility might be how we can use our transportation expertise to build more humane, caring, responsible communities.

Note that learning in all three layers of understanding helps students consider and understand value questions. But the way we go about this changes as pupils mature. In the early years, we may juxtapose value-related binary opposites within stories and within units that have a strong story line. We consider what Egan calls transcendent human values from ages 8 or 9 to 14 or 15. We may build our units around them using narrative structures as a context for factual, technical, and imaginative explorations. During the philosophic years, we emphasize how causal relationships undergird the meaning and purpose of life. We help students to analyze truth and values and become committed to a principled way of life. Christian teachers have an important role to play during all three layers in nurturing meaningful response based on Biblical values.

■ Now go back to the unit you discussed at the beginning of this section. In view of Erikson's and Egan's claims about developmental levels, what changes, if any, would you make in your plans for the unit at each of the three grade levels?

LEARNING THROUGH PERSONAL RESPONSE

■ Marian Piekema builds personal response into her grade I units. She gives all children specific tasks. They know she expects all to make a contribution. In her introductory unit on the school her class interviews all members of the school's support staff: "In what way can we help you?" After telling Bible stories she asks, "Is there anything you wonder about?" Her children often bring up and talk about issues of life and death, heaven and hell, and so on. Her fall unit includes a scavenger hunt that includes the clean-up of a park.

In a unit on seeds, Marian emphasizes the theme that the cycle of life is God's plan, a plan that gives us a task. She includes many open-ended "personal response" activities: drawing and painting, making models of flowers and bees, putting up posters for recycle boxes, journal writing about observations of seeds or reaction to music, and so on. She also capitalizes on teachable moments; her class, for instance, writes a letter to the school custodian about sand that they had left in the classroom.

While the children's plentiful personal response nurtures their growth in attitudes and values, one question still troubles Marian. Genuine personal response, she believes, is important. Yet particularly at this level, she finds it difficult not to impose the response that she would like to see as a teacher. How do you strike a balance between eliciting genuine personal response and guiding students to responding as contributing members of the classroom learning community? Discuss this question for the age levels you teach or plan to teach.

As we have seen, a Biblical view of knowledge demands personal response. In the classroom, all four phases of learning elicit response from students. But the transcendence phase especially calls for unique, formative response. Here students use their knowledge, thought, and creativity to extend what they have learned. Here they make personal choices and act on personal values and commitments. To do so , however, requires that we have engaged them in their learning throughout all four phases.

Harvard's Vito Perrone (1994, 11-12) recently reported on research about elements that lead to students being engaged in their learning. Teachers were passionate about their work and about inventing rich class activities. Their topics evoked surprise and puzzling but intriguing questions. They gave students time to wonder and help define unit content. They supported different forms of expression and directions of investigation that interested students. The students created original products that they exhibited publicly. They knew that the results of their work were open-ended and not prearranged by the teacher. They *did* things such as writing letters or volunteering. Note that many of these elements come to the fore in the fourth or transcendence phase of learning.

How can you plan curriculum to foster meaningful response? Here are some specific suggestions:

1. Know your students and their context. Jesus Christ could speak with authority because He lovingly but with conviction and integrity addressed people in their particular situations. He did not force His views on his listeners; their response had to be genuine. He sought to influence but not to coerce or manipulate. Similarly, plan your curriculum to address the needs and understandings of your students in their particular context (Pazmino 1992, 125-131).
2. Give each unit a clear focus. Ask, "What do I want my students to take away? What are my most important goals? What are the powerful ideas around which I organize my unit?"
3. Involve the students in reflecting on and then choosing at least some unit content. For this, you can use the K-W-L strategy: what I **K**now or think I know; what I **W**ant to learn; and, at the end, what I **L**earned. These are often done in teacher-led group activities, in part so that as a teacher you can help students categorize what they know and address any misconceptions. Alternately, you can involve the class in mapping related subtopics of interest to them.
4. Use the results of #3 to make the students' prior and experiential knowledge a springboard for learning.
5. Do what you can to convince students that the knowledge, skills, values and dispositions you help them learn are useful inside and outside the school (Good and Brophy 1994, 425).
6. Plan the activities so that students have some choice and alternatives, especially with respect to student response. You can do this, for example, through learning centers and through individual and group assignments and projects that allow options.
7. Encourage students to relate their learning to their lives by thinking critically or creatively in application contexts, by solving related problems, and by evaluating their own learning (Good and Brophy 1994, 426).

Learning centers as mentioned in #6 provide pupils with active investigations of topics or problems. They can allow your pupils to pursue topics beyond what you do with the whole class. Design the centers so that pupils can take responsibility for their own learning and make significant choices. They can choose from activities suitable for different learning styles and different levels of difficulty, and whether to work alone or in pairs. You can also ask the students to participate in planning specific centers from time to time.

Note, finally, that response in learning also involves applying skills. Both intellectual and motor skills need to be reinforced through practice. This takes place especially in the third phase of learning. Students need to know how to calculate percentages, how to use a microscope, how to read a map, how to use a computer, how to construct a logical argument, how to write a coherent paragraph, and so on. Students do not learn skills thoroughly merely by using them in a meaningful context. We may introduce skills that way (phase 1). But then students need precise, structured skill instruction, and adequate reinforcement and drill. This takes effort. At times it may be arduous for both teachers and students. But this necessary part of learning must be built into each unit. Only then will students gain the mastery needed for applying basic concepts and skills proficiently as they respond to their learning in new settings.

LEARNING THROUGH SERVICE

One important kind of response is school and community service. Here students apply what they have learned. They also develop communication, problem-solving, and leadership skills. Students could, for instance, be peer tutors or buddies to younger children. In science, they can set up recycling projects, maintain a bird sanctuary, plant bulbs or trees, or raise salmon fry for release into a river and monitor its water quality. In social studies, they can advocate certain political decisions or actions or participate in hunger awareness events. In physical education they can supervise games or organize activities for the physically or mentally challenged. In Biblical studies or home economics, they can volunteer in hospitals and homes for the elderly. As part of woodworking, they can help with Habitat for Humanity projects. They can make art for a homeless shelter. They can write letters to editors or leaders in society. They can hold clothing and food drives for the disadvantaged or help in a food kitchen in an integrated unit such as *Am I My Neighbor's Keeper?*

To be effective as learning opportunities, we should coordinate such service learning with our curriculum units. We need to prepare students before their service. We encourage them to pose questions that they want to answer. At higher grade levels they might research the context in which they will find themselves. The service experience itself then leads students to reflect on their questions and their initial findings. They discuss and write about how society deals with related issues. They consider their role in promoting compassion, justice, and integrity. They develop a sense of responsibility. They begin to ask what they can do to make a difference. Especially in high school, where too often we cut off students from everyday life, service learning opportunities can be authentic experiences. Here students who may not do well in the classroom show and develop surprising ingenuity and responsibility (Diamond, 1993; Willis 1993; Woehrle, 1993).

■ Pacific Christian Academy has a service outreach program at different grade levels. The primary "Joy Makers" program intends to make children sensitive to the needs of those around them and reach out and assist wherever that is possible. They receive lessons on the needs of and care for elderly persons and how to respect them and share with them. Each Friday morning from October to May, a cross-grade team of students (one-third of the primary pupils) visit two senior citizen residences. Here they "adopt" a grandparent. They read books, sing songs, and share what is happening in their lives.

In grade 11 students may volunteer service in an overseas developing country. There they learn about the culture and the people and participate in a variety of service activities. Seven weeks of training precedes the two-month experience. During the training weeks students also begin the Christian perspective, English, and social studies courses they will finish while "in the field." The school combines these courses with training in cross-cultural communications, counseling, and missions and culture.

In what ways does Pacific's service outreach program reflect the guidelines for student response outlined in this section? How would you make the program an integral part of the curriculum at the levels that I have described? Can you suggest any improvements? What kind of suggestions for learning through service could you make for other grade levels?

LEARNING IN COMMUNITY

■ Loving and faithful relationships are a prerequisite for meaningful learning. Children need to be trusted and feel accepted. They need to know that people around them care for them, give them meaningful responsibilities, and at the same time hold them accountable. They need to sense that they are part of a community where people have pledged themselves to each other as they work toward a common goal. Below are six examples of how teachers work at creating classroom and school communities with such a pedagogical atmosphere.

»Karen Osborne's kindergartners and Paul Smith's grade 4 students are paired as buddies. Throughout the year, the older buddies help the younger ones to complete learning log pages "What I enjoyed doing this week" and "What I would like to do next week." The kindergartners make drawings about something they learned, dictating descriptions that their buddies write down. The bond that develops between buddies carries over into the playground and the general school atmosphere.

»Nigel, a boy who is profoundly multiply handicapped, is an integral part of Debbie Benson's grade 1-2 class. Nigel is assisted in classroom activities by classroom aide Dorothy Bartel. Although it is difficult to assess how much Nigel understands, the teacher and students assume that Nigel is taking it all in. Nigel has a student partner for all activities. Partners do their own work first and then do Nigel's work "hand over hand" with him. Students have learned to assist him with his lunch (he uses a gastronomy tube) and also by pushing him around in his wheelchair. Nigel has become a gentle friend to everyone. His class has become a developing, caring, and compassionate community in which students take responsibility for each other.

»Bertha Tiemstra uses collaborative learning about 15-20% of the time in her grade 4 class. She finds that such learning helps students listen to and understand each other, become more accepting of each other, and take more responsibility for their own learning. The content of her units also nurtures a sense of community. A unit on *Self and Others* includes discussions on how you can help or hurt friendships. Another stresses communal care for and use of resources, including the use of paper in the school. At the same time, she stresses individual accountability. She demands, for instance, that students do as well as they can in spelling and math drills and in the quality of writing in their journals.

»Hugo Vanderhoek uses collaborative learning extensively in his grade 6 language arts/art unit on comics. He applies, for instance, the "jigsaw" technique by which students first learn the features of different types of comics in an "expert" group. They then report back to their home group. Each student has a specific role as they work in a group: checker for understanding, encourager, recorder, taskmaster, gatekeeper, reporter, or "gofer." The students depend on each other but are also individually accountable for completing assignments. Hugo carefully teaches the necessary skills for working effectively as a group. Today he explains and monitors how to check for understanding and how to listen attentively. Each group gets cards with suggestions: make eye contact, ask questions such as, "Will you explain?," "What does that mean?," "What were your reasons?," and so on. In the debriefing Hugo not only sums up the main content points, but also reviews how the groups implemented these skills.

»Henry Bulthuis sponsors a peer support system in his grade 8-12 high school. Each year, he offers a 40-hour course to a group of about ten screened volunteers. The course is offered in the evenings, in addition to regular school work. Toward the end of the school year, the first task of the peer counselors becomes to orient a group of five or six grade 7 students who will enter the school in September. Then in September, the peer counselors introduce these new students to the school. The peer counselors meet with the group at least four times during the year ("How are things going?," "What kind of help do you need?"). They also act as "sounding boards" for students that want to talk with them. This may involve academic concerns, but more often relationships with peers, girlfriends/boyfriends, or parents. A survey has found that the program has resulted in a quieter and improved atmosphere in the school.

»West Edmonton Christian School defines spirituality in terms of rejoicing in being a Christian, standing up for Christ, talking openly about personal faith and what God has done for you, being compassionate and servant-like rather than self-centered. They build spirituality-in-community through prayer bulletin boards, staff devotions in the foyer before school in which parents and students may join, class and cross-grade devotions with small group prayer, and discussions in class and among staff at the end of every week to share joys and concerns.

The view that education makes students become autonomous, self-directed individuals is, at best, a superficial cliche and, at worst, a cruel sham. God created us in relationship with others. We are part of communities that share common understandings and beliefs. We are interdependent. We need each other. We enrich (as well as bruise) each other's lives. Successful learning experiences build on the qualities and capacities of particular cultures and on pupils' identification with others (Hass 1987, 183).

We want students to become more discerning and responsive. Schools nurture their abilities to think clearly, decide responsibly, and act wisely. But schools must also help them understand that functioning as dependable and trustworthy individuals involves being constructive community members. The culture and ethos of the communities of which they are a part have shaped them. They have benefited from being part of various communities. They also have a responsibility to contribute to them. The words "dependable" and "trustworthy" themselves imply the relationship of people to God, their fellow creatures, and the physical world. It is impossible to be autonomous; it is self-worship to think that it is possible to be autonomous.

A community is a group of people living and working together that shares a common past and present. A shared ethos and purpose make it possible for its members to participate in making decisions and becoming agents of renewal. Schools that function well as communities have a clear moral vision and adjust their structures and daily routines to reflect their moral aspirations and goals. They realize that common values provide cohesion for life in school and society. They also know that as "communities of memory" they need to tell the story of the community within its cultural setting. Such retelling (and honest assessment) leads to a common understanding. This, in turn, allows students to see themselves as cultural-social beings who realize that public good sometimes overrides personal short-term gain and may even require self-sacrifice (Bowers 1987, 138-43).

Christian school classrooms strive to function as covenant communities. That is, they "foster an environment where students and teachers take delight in being with each other and build relationships based on a general desire to be with and for others" (Stronks and Blomberg 1993, 110). Such communities do not promote and celebrate individual accomplishment as the sole standard of success. Nor do they sacrifice individuality on the altar of the corporate good. Instead, their shared vision charts a vision and framework within which students are free to carry out their personal role by unwrapping their individual gifts. Teachers and students accept and support each other in their respective tasks (Stronks and Blomberg 1993, 114). Classroom communities with an atmosphere of mutual concern and trust are ones where children learn to accept and use their abilities in relation to themselves and others. There they experience the joys and difficulties of working unitedly toward common goals.

John Van Dyk (1994) has described the characteristics of such classrooms. There is a sense of feeling and belonging. They have a safe, secure, accepting, and mutually supportive atmosphere. Differences in abilities and interests do not lead to competition or alienation but are accepted and encouraged. Students and teachers practice servanthood skills. They listen to, support, and forgive each other. They have abundant opportunity to exhibit the fruit of the Spirit: love, joy, peace, patience, kindness, goodness, faithfulness, gentleness, and self control. Every member of the classroom is part of every other member, with failure of one causing pain in the class and success leading to communal celebration. Above all, students and teachers share their gifts so that others may be blessed.

We will never reach this ideal, of course. But we can work toward it, also in our curriculum planning. Christian schools will make learning-focused classroom devotions, chapels, and assemblies an integral part of their curriculum. They will plan programs where students help each other (e.g., buddy systems and peer tutoring). They will plan the inclusion of challenged or minority group students so that all students feel enriched by their presence. They will avoid ability grouping and streaming that destroys community. Instead, classroom groups will be, as much as possible, heterogeneous and flexible. They will design units for classes with a wide spectrum of abilities so that all students learn a basic core, with optional activities catering to differences in abilities. They will plan to include collaborative (cooperative) learning structures on a regular basis. They will also choose unit topics that shed special light on what it means to live in community.

■ Linda Samland's school realizes the importance of building community as a basis for learning. It begins each day with the staff having devotions and communal prayer in the hallway. Often, some parents join in. The theme for the year is how we share our insights, gifts, and resources and thus care for each other. Cooperative classroom and assembly activities contribute to the school's being a caring community, as do special activities such as holding a cookie sale to buy Christmas gifts for poor people in the community. Even the choice of unit themes reflects this concern. A unit on "building" stresses that building is a creaturely activity where we work together to erect buildings and shape lives. But the school also emphasizes each student's unique gifts. It helps students see how God calls them as persons with special gifts to be important "puzzle pieces" in the Body of Christ. It provides different activities suited for students with different learning styles, and does so especially in encouraging students with special challenges.

Suppose you taught at a particular grade level in Linda's school. What specific things would you plan for your curriculum to implement and complement what Linda describes as happening in her school?

SUMMARY

Pedagogy and curriculum are closely intertwined. Not only will curriculum implementation be ineffective if we neglect pedagogy, but our decisions about pedagogy will affect the content and structure of our curriculum. As Lee Shulman puts it, "Pedagogical content knowledge is of special interest because . . . it represents the blending of content and pedagogy into an understanding of how particular topics, problems, or issues are organized, represented, and adapted to the diverse interests and abilities of learners, and presented for instruction" (Shulman 1987, 8). Pedagogical content knowledge is the specialty of teachers and makes meaningful classroom learning possible.

Most meaningful learning takes place in classroom learning communities with an atmosphere of openness, trust, and security. Such communities recognize children as responsible and unique images of God, yet who need structure and guidance because of sin. They provide activities to suit different learning styles. As they do so, they recognize the rhythm of learning: (1) experience-based exploration and investigation, (2) formal, precise disclosure, (3) reformulation and practice, and (4) more open-ended application and transcendence.

Teachers also need to take into account cumulative "layers of understanding": (1) primary understanding where children can learn much about life and its values through story settings, (2) romantic understanding where pupils enjoy mastering detailed content and skills within a value-based narrative context, and (3) philosophic understanding where students search for general causal networks relating to the purpose and meaning of life and their place in society. In all these layers, students' learning is enhanced through activities that cultivate genuine personal response and service opportunities.

REFLECTING

1. Ephesians 4:1-16 contains a vision of what a Christian community ought to be. Read the passage and comment on its implications for classroom learning and the curriculum. This passage leads Everding, Snelling, and Wilcox (1988, 434) to conclude, for instance, that classroom dialogue should involve all students, that evaluation should not foster competition for grades, and that flexible classroom arrangements should allow for seating in a circle and small group work. Do you agree that this can be deduced from Ephesians 4? Why or why not?

2. Choose a topic that could be taught, say, both at the grade 2 and the grade 6 levels. How you would teach it according to Egan's recommendations for the primary and romantic layers of understanding? How would you plan the unit to take into account different learning styles? personal response? service opportunities?

3. Collaborative or cooperative learning allows students to be actively involved in their own learning and also to learn to work with others. One pitfall that can easily occur, however, is that students "ride the coattails" of others and do not take personal responsibility for their learning. How can this be avoided? How often and to what extent would you use collaborative learning? Why? Does this depend on age levels and subject areas? In what ways?

Chapter 8
Planning Curriculum
for the Classroom

■ Principal Lloyd Den Boer had in mind at least three goals when he proposed a school-wide integral unit to his staff. First, he wanted to give his 400 K-7 students a meaningful learning experience, one that would bind them into a closer community. Second, he wanted to improve his teachers' curriculum planning skills. Those included, for instance, choosing curriculum topics for their significance and designing more non-print activities for various learning styles. Third, he hoped the joint planning would bring primary and intermediate teachers in closer contact in order to share their skills and insights.

Late in October Lloyd and a consultant drew up a proposal for a one week unit, with an open house celebration on a day during the following week. From 10:30-12:20 each day groups of cross-age students would investigate one of five topic strands. Students would return to their own classrooms in the afternoons. Each would serve as an "expert" in one strand, teaching others what they had learned. Lloyd's staff agreed with the proposal and considered topics ranging from food to democracy to media. Finally they chose oceans as the main topic.

The consultant came in for a Professional Development day in mid-November. He showed how the unit could help students explore and experience Christian discipleship. He stressed that it must be Christ-centered, community-connected, teacher-directed, and student-oriented. He helped teachers develop a thematic statement:

> The ocean is a large part of our created world, teeming with life. It reflects God's power and the diversity of His creation. He made it good, for our use and enjoyment. As stewards, we have a responsibility to care for the ocean. Where greedy people have misused and squandered this gift, we can influence decisions made about its restoration and maintenance. We base our hope in its ultimate renewal on our belief that eventually all things, including the ocean, will be made new when Christ returns.

Staff discussions led to five different unit strands: creatures of the sea, physical aspects of the ocean, using the sea, effects of the ocean, and exploration and transportation. After the PD day, some teachers had misgivings about the "jigsaw" approach. They preferred students to spend one day on each strand in rotation. Others felt that the strands were too abstract for young children. Lloyd called a meeting in late-November where a discussion on the two strand possibilities led to an 8-8 tie vote. After giving the staff the opportunity for more input, Lloyd decided to go with the original plan, but the strands could make their topics more concrete. That's how "using the sea" became "fishing."

Lloyd gave the five strand planning groups a time line. In the second week of December all strands would report on their general direction. In mid-January they would share their objectives; two weeks later, their activities. He also put out a short report on how to meet the needs of diverse learners, including special needs students. The learning assistance teacher provided lists of reading and writing activities suitable for different levels. Also, Lloyd gave out a planning chart on living things in oceans prepared by another school. It gave suggested activities in five developmental areas.

Teachers in the five strands set out to gather resources. They planned learning activities and assessment to fit the thematic statement. They assigned about sixty students ranging from grade 1 to 7 to each strand. Finally, the school launched the unit on February 21.

Those in the fishing strand visited a fishing village and saw a film on salmon fishing. In small groups, pupils made charts on what they knew about oceans. On Tuesday, Lloyd told them the "sad story" of the demise of the Atlantic cod fishery and its effects on the people of Newfoundland. He emphasized that God gave us resources that were decimated by international as well as local overfishing. After splitting into four groups, students completed a handout on Lloyd's story with their partner from another grade level. The pupils also worked on one of five projects, with the morning ending with a fish tasting party prepared by some mothers.

In general, activities geared to lower grade levels were successful. Students, for instance, appreciated picture books read by the teacher even if written for children several years younger than their own age. Older and younger buddies collaborated well on activities such as writing stories together using "ocean words." They had one pencil between them and were instructed to include setting, characters, a problem, a solution and an ending. Art and craft activities were effective because teachers geared them to a spectrum of age groups.

The unit, of course, was not without some glitches. Some grade 1s felt overwhelmed, particularly if their group met in a upper level classroom. Conceptual learning was effective for younger children primarily when it took place in story settings. Activities in more abstract strands often still related to fish, and when they didn't, sometimes perplexed the grade 1s and 2s. Teachers used the "jigsaw" approach in their own classrooms, but had not worked out this part of the unit as well as the rest. Some, for instance, just asked their students to share what they had learned in the morning session. Nonetheless, the unit created a real sense of community in the school, with younger and older students helping each other and feeling good about their interaction. The unit emerged as one of the highlights of the year for most teachers and students.

Comment on the pros and cons of planning a unit like this with a whole school. Consider how the teachers worked together, the cross-age groupings, the thoroughness and complexity of planning, and the "jigsaw" approach. One person reading about the unit commented on the valuable incorporation of Biblical values; another, that on the fact that the emphasis on life-related issues was too strong and that learning about the sea and fish is valuable in itself. What do you think? In what ways can Lloyd claim that "everything in curriculum that needs attention came out" because of this unit? What other themes would be suitable for such a whole-school unit? Give reasons.

THE TEACHER AS CURRICULUM PLANNER

Planning curriculum for your classroom is a complex task. To do so responsibly, you try to incorporate the contours of a Biblical worldview and its values. You keep in mind that knowledge reflects created reality but is not static; it includes personal response. You set priorities as you plan and justify your content and pedagogy. You include various modes of knowing and provide for diverse learners. You find a suitable balance among the aspects of reality while also enabling students to experience the integrality of knowledge.

In the past educational leaders often assumed that curriculum design should take place outside the school. They limited teachers' tasks to planning instruction effectively. They supplied teachers with ends (concepts and skills to be learned). Teachers were to plan only the means (instructional methods). In the 1970s and again recently with skill-oriented computer software, technicists tried to remove even the means from teachers. The resulting programs, sometimes labelled "teacher-proof curricula," minimized the role of teachers. Teachers were to be technicians who followed directions one step at a time.

Constructivists correctly reject such a technical approach to planning. They believe that teachers with their classes should generate their own programs. Besides, they should also develop their own expert knowledge base through action research. Action research is a process in which teachers, usually in small groups, look systematically and critically at what is going on in their school and come up with action proposals. Such action research helps teachers systematically review their teaching. At times it revises their personal theories of learning and transforms their teaching (K. Zeichner in Hollingsworth and Sockett 1994, 73ff.).

In practice, action research often requires teachers "to develop knowledge, undertake research, change, grow, reflect, revolutionize their practice, become emancipated, emancipate their students, engage in group collaboration, assume power, and become politically active" (J. Clandinin and M. Connelly in Jackson 1992, 377). As such, Clandinin and Connelly add, action research leaders in subtle ways impose their own ideas of schooling on teachers. Teachers want to be more than technicians, but also balk at action research projects that are time-consuming and come with built-in agendas. It is no wonder that teachers often have mixed attitudes toward involvement in curriculum development.

Nevertheless, as a teacher you are the real curriculum planner and change agent for your classroom. You want to be more than a technician who just follows a detailed teacher's guide. You want to plan your programs taking into account your view of knowledge, learning, and the meaning of life. You want to respond to the needs of your class. And if you are a Christian teacher you see yourself as a professional disciple whose "professing" leads you to implement programs based on a Biblical worldview. You develop your own framework and goals, perhaps in conjunction with the rest of your staff. Only then do you decide how published resources fit into your program.

Yet you find that you cannot design your whole program yourself. You are not an expert in all aspects of reality. You need the time before and after school not only for planning but also for setting up your room, evaluating student work, contacting parents, running off materials, and attending meetings. You do not have time for action research that involves much collaboration and follow-up. Yet you know that your decisions affect students' lives. If you take that seriously, you cannot but be a curriculum planner.

In practice, as a teacher and curriculum maker you gradually develop your own curriculum repertoire. Your school's grade coordinator or principal may provide feedback and assistance for your yearly and unit planning. You may sometimes benefit from planning a unit with some fellow teachers. You use and adapt materials from many sources as you plan your units. You also recognize that your school and education system expect you to teach certain content and skills. You do, however, have much freedom to fashion your own units and approaches. In the end, you yourself are responsible for what you teach and how you teach it. You want your curriculum repertoire to reflect your beliefs about education and suit your context and personal characteristics.

The curriculum model presented in chapter 9 also applies to your personal curriculum making. Certain groundings frame your planning. These include your worldview and values; what you believe about the nature of knowledge, the person, learning, and teaching; what you hold to be the purposes of schooling; and your educational and community contexts. You need to develop intents, design activities, and choose resources. You deliberate as you lay out, implement, and constantly evaluate your planning. You reflectively design your program, courses, units, and lessons.

Curriculum development depends on a complex array of factors. Your personal planning cannot fully consider all of these. Yet you should ask some key questions as you go about your planning. What do you want your curriculum to accomplish? How does your guiding vision of life affect your planning? What contextual factors do you need to consider? Which types of learning activities and resources fit your curriculum orientation? How will you monitor the effects of the implementation of your plans? You cannot directly consider all curriculum ingredients while planning a unit. But you regularly need to stand back and reflect on such questions.

Remember that there is no one proper starting point for curriculum planning. The model I discuss in chapter 9 purposely is a circular one. You do not use its components in a purely linear, step-by-step fashion. Your thematic statement and objectives can emerge from thinking about curriculum groundings in connection with a topic. Often, however, you already have in mind some activities or resources before you write your thematic statement. You may well revise the statement several times as you design a unit. In other words, you will go back and forth among the planning components before completing a unit.

Also, it is unlikely that you develop all your curriculum components from scratch. You use teacher resource units written by others. You collect suitable activities from colleagues, conference workshops, teacher's guides, and resource books. In mathematics, you may follow a resource guide or textbook quite closely. Here you may accept the authors' choice of content and plan mainly your pedagogy. In subjects where careful sequencing of concepts and skills is less vital, you choose topics within general school directives. You set your own objectives and content. You use school-supplied resource materials only when they fit your intents. Throughout your teaching career, as a curriculum decision maker you will design, adapt, and use curriculum plans.

■ "Personal and communal staff development are significant components of developing a school's vision, strengthening a community for learning, developing integral units, and reflecting on student learning" (Stronks and Blomberg 1993, 302). What kinds of initiatives should individual teachers take in this regard? small groups of teachers at one grade level or in one subject? the staff of a school as a whole? the principal? How often could a school launch an effort such as Lloyd Den Boer's?

FOUR STAGES IN CLASSROOM CURRICULUM PLANNING

Classroom curriculum planning involves at least four stages: (1) considering external program expectations or "frames," (2) planning a yearly overview, (3) designing or adapting units, and (4) planning day-

208 STEPPINGSTONES TO CURRICULUM

to-day learning activities or experiences.

Education departments and school boards specify certain expectations for your classroom teaching. Christian schools are usually not bound by government program guidelines. But those policies do often reflect societal expectations for schooling that you should heed. You also need to recognize the role of external evaluation programs and examinations. These usually constrain you more at higher grade levels.

Most schools provide you with curriculum guides that list topics and skills to be taught at various grade levels. Schools also frame your program by supplying certain class resources and textbooks. You may sometimes consider some directives to be too limiting, inadequate, or against your beliefs. In such cases you can try to change them for the whole school or seek exemption from them individually.

When you know the external frames for your program, you can design a yearly curriculum overview. List the topics you want to teach, both within specific subjects and ones that span several aspects of reality. Define basic goals for each topic. Indicate the principal content, skills, resources, and activities. Include field trips so that you can obtain timely permission. Also identify projects that require many library or other external resources. Finally, show how you will sequence the topics and approximately how much time you plan to spend on each. In designing your yearly overview, ask:

1. Does the plan account for school and community expectations? Does it fit students' previous school experiences and prepare them for what follows, with no undue repetition?
2. Does each major topic meet the criteria for curriculum choice and justification such as those given in the next section?
3. Does topic choice and time allotment reflect a balanced consideration of all aspects of reality? Do you provide for learning appropriate content and skills that foster desired values, dispositions and response?

As you designed your yearly overview, you likely already thought of many worthwhile classroom activities for your topics. But you need to do more intermediate planning to ensure that you meet your goals. Jumping directly from yearly outlines to daily planning leaves out the crucial step of developing detailed unit plans. Such plans usually include a thematic statement, objectives, classroom activities, resources to be used, a time schedule, and a plan for evaluating student learning (including the general contour of any tests). This chapter will consider each of these in turn.

You use your unit plan to do your daily planning. But do not use it as a formula from which you cannot deviate. You ask students for their input. Each day you reflect on their learning and response, and modify your plans to meet their needs. "Teachable moments" or student reaction may lead you to explore some unexpected tangents. You also consider the school's day-to-day rhythm. Special programs, unexpected events, hot weather, or restlessness before vacations may force you to alter your plans. If some activities drag on, shorten or delete others. As a responsive teacher-disciple, you constantly reflect on goal attainment, and adjust accordingly, even while activities are going on!

■Wilma Van Brummelen's yearly overview for her kindergarten class lists nine thematic units: creation, apples and fall, God made me special, nutrition and grocery stores, transportation, farms, Japan, honeybees, and water all around. For each, she provides a time span and suggests a field trip. Her transportation unit, for instance, takes place from January 4 to 28, with an all-day field trip to a market by bus, train, and ferry. She also gives a thematic statement for each unit. The one for her farm unit is as follows:

> God gave Adam and Eve the first farm in the world and called it the Garden of Eden. They could eat most of its food for nourishment and enjoy it. After sin came into the world, growing and sharing food with others became harder. With God sending Jesus to redeem us from our sin, we can again begin to understand and apply God's will for growing and using food to meet our bodily needs.
>
> Through food God gives us the nourishment we need to serve Him in the best possible way. Many different kinds of farms produce foods that provide us with a balanced diet. In this unit, we will discover God's gift of farms. We will explore how farmers grow plants and raise animals to supply our food. We will learn to appreciate and praise God for His bountiful creation. At the same time, we will realize our responsibility for sharing food with the hungry.

Wilma's outline also includes special celebrations such as the production of a Christmas pageant and Chinese New Year. She specifies her mathematics topics (e.g., sorting and classifying during four weeks in November). She gives her monthly literary themes as well as nine general and ten specific language development emphases (e.g., becoming involved in emerging reading and writing; letter recognition and recording). She details the nineteen types of learning centers she uses at various times of the year (e.g., work jobs, water table). She notes that in the current year she will provide more specific, hands-on science experiences in each unit. She also describes her "kindercooking" and buddy programs, and lists her major resources. Finally, she indicates eight personal development areas she emphasizes throughout (faith, moral, social, intellectual, language, aesthetic, emotional, and physical development).

You can design yearly overviews in different ways. Use one that helps you in your more detailed planning. Some teachers give a brief rationale for including a topic and then list the subtopics they will teach. Some detail skills for the whole year, while others prefer to do this in their unit plans. At higher levels, teachers may include a description and the overall objectives of a course, general instructional approaches, major assignments, and a description of student evaluation methods.

Are there any things you would add to or delete from Wilma's yearly outline? If so, what? For the grade level you teach or plan to teach, list the items you would include in a yearly overview. With two or three other persons, come up with a defensible list of topics you would teach. For one topic, write a sample description for inclusion in a yearly overview.

DESIGNING INTEGRAL UNITS

Designing and adapting integral units is probably the most significant stage of your curriculum decision making. More so than for yearly or daily planning, here you carefully consider your intents and establish how you will go about accomplishing them. It is especially when developing units that your general goals and views of content and pedagogy play a crucial role. Here you keep on asking yourself, "Where am I taking my students?"

An integral unit, as defined earlier, meets three criteria. First, it is *internally unified*. It has a thematic focus toward which you direct all thought and activity. You capture this when you formulate your intents in your thematic statement and objectives. Second, an integral unit is *externally consistent*. As such, it promotes your worldview, values, and goals for schooling. Third, where relevant, the unit includes those aspects of reality that may go beyond the main focus of the unit, thus encouraging students to address multifaceted problems and phenomena.

This section gives steps for planning an integral unit. Often you may not follow them in strict order. Also, the suggested method is not intended to be a rigid formula. Many teachers effectively use these steps, but others plan successfully in different ways. As I discuss the steps, reflect on the examples I give of units written by practicing classroom teachers. Then use the suggested steps to outline a unit topic you plan to teach at some point.

Selecting a unit topic

■ When Lloyd's school decided to teach a school-wide theme, the staff suggested many possible topics: aboriginal people, democracy, the desert, the environment, family, food, forgiveness, the Genesis flood, handicapped people, health, the ideal life, the media, oceans, outdoor education, salt of the world, and water. For most, the teachers also showed a web of subtopics. For example, for the food topic, the subtopics were growing food, preparing food (with botulism and the ideal pot roast as sub-

subtopics), marketing food, eating food (with table manners), fast food, fine dining (with French cuisine), and the cultural dimension of food.

With a small group, try to reach a consensus about which topic from the list you would favor as a school-wide one for either an elementary or a middle school. Give reasons for your choice. List the criteria you used to make this decision. Then draw a webbing diagram showing the subtopics you would include in the unit. Justify the inclusion of each subtopic.

In choosing topics, you can use the general criteria for curriculum justification given at the end of chapter 4. Here I repeat them in shorter form, adding some that apply specifically to selecting a topic. Apply these criteria to a unit topic you have taught, have seen taught, or plan to teach.

1. Can the topic enhance students' understanding of a Christian worldview and its values as these apply to their personal lives and to society?
2. Does the topic address significant issues? Does it acquaint students with their cultural heritage and traditions?
3. Is the topic too general, without a clear focus? Or too narrow, restricting substantial learning?
4. Can the topic maintain interest for diverse students? Can it encourage personal, meaningful response?
5. Can the topic include apt skill development in different modes of knowing?
6. Is expertise and are suitable resources available for an effective unit?

Topics can focus on important concepts (e.g., light, government), events (e.g., World War II, the 1960s), or problems or issues (world hunger, bioethics). Teachers sometimes choose topics that are interesting and accessible but superficial. At the primary level, for instance, I have seen topics like "the circus" or "balloons." The circus has little cultural relevance when compared with a topic such as life in a pond. "Balloons" lends itself to many interesting experiments but is unduly narrow. A topic like "our atmosphere" allows students to investigate broader concepts and issues while still learning from some balloon experiments. On the other hand, topics such as "change" and "ecology" are so general and rich that the resulting units may cover much ground but lack depth and coherence.

A topic has to be suitable for a particular class. Your class structure and make-up may eliminate some topics or suggest others. Sometimes your students lead you to take up a certain topic. You must also consider your students' age level. A topic such as whales is suitable for five-year-olds. Eleven-year-olds would still be interested in investigating whales. By now, however, they would benefit more from learning about groups of living beings interacting in a certain setting rather than considering just one species. So a study of how whales function could be one part of a more general unit on ocean ecosystems. Some topics that fascinate students at one age will not appeal to different levels. It would be difficult to interest kindergartners in a full unit on the solar system or on revolution. And high school students would balk at a unit that looks at neighborhood helpers or at apples and fall.

Of course, you can teach many topics meaningfully at many levels. Transportation is an example, as described in the last chapter. Similarly, a unit on families would be appropriate at the grade 1 as well as at the high school levels. Six-year-olds would learn how God intends families as places where they find love and security. That is not always the case, but families can work at restoring broken relationships. Concrete activities would bring out that unconditional love should be the foundation of all families, no matter what kind. They would also explore how to use their gifts to show love and empathy for other family members. The children might investigate their family ancestry. Making a family scrapbook might be an ongoing activity throughout the unit (Rau, Roseboom, and Zazitko 1993).

A high school unit on the family would have a similar theme. Now, however, students analyze the family and family roles in much more depth. They consider the interdependence of family members and the need for loving authority and mutual submission. They examine Biblical standards for marriage and family life, comparing them with current practices. They also investigate the joys and sorrows of family life (and of remaining single), the changes families undergo over time, and the causes and effects of family breakdown. One major activity might be a formal debate on "The present social problems relating to the breakdown of the family are the result of people discounting Scriptural norms for the family" (Maggs 1988).

Completing a planning chart

Before writing a thematic statement and objectives for a unit, you want to think about its scope. What concepts, skills, and values do you want students to learn? Making a webbing diagram can be helpful. For a primary unit on gardens, for instance, you may have main "spokes" showing physical resources, plants, weather and seasons, tools and equipment, gardening setbacks, and growing food. A "spoke" such as physical resources may have sub-spokes for air, soil, water and fertilizer, with some subdivided again. You can change this until you feel that the set of subtopics forms a manageable and unified whole. (Sometimes you may involve your students in making a webbing chart to see what they already know about a topic and what they would like to explore as part of the K-W-L strategy.)

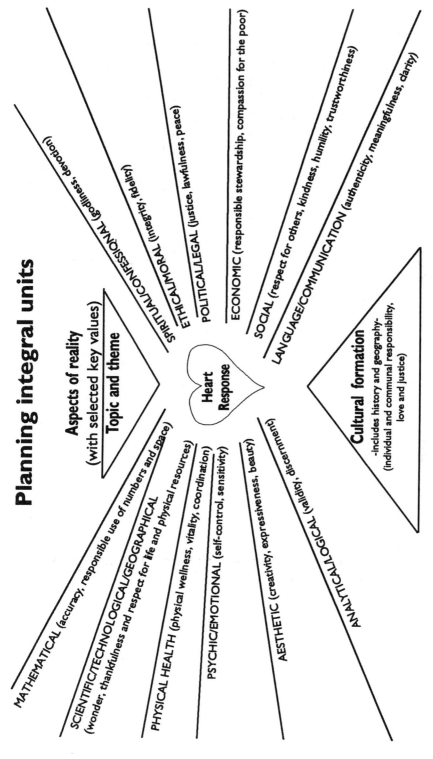

Planning integral units

Aspects of reality
(with selected key values)

Topic and theme

Heart Response

Cultural formation
-includes history and geography-
(individual and communal responsibility,
love and justice)

CONFESSIONAL (goodness, devotion)

SPIRITUAL/CONFESSIONAL (integrity, fidelity)

ETHICAL/MORAL (justice, lawfulness, peace)

POLITICAL/LEGAL (justice, lawfulness, peace)

ECONOMIC (responsible stewardship, compassion for the poor)

SOCIAL (respect for others, kindness, humility, trustworthiness)

LANGUAGE/COMMUNICATION (authenticity, meaningfulness, clarity)

MATHEMATICAL (accuracy; responsible use of numbers and space)

SCIENTIFIC/TECHNOLOGICAL/GEOGRAPHICAL
(wonder, thankfulness and respect for life and physical resources)

PHYSICAL HEALTH (physical wellness, vitality, coordination)

PSYCHIC/EMOTIONAL (self-control, sensitivity)

AESTHETIC (creativity, expressiveness, beauty)

ANALYTICAL/LOGICAL (validity, discernment)

Alternately, you may want to use an enlarged version of the "planning integral units" chart. This chart can be used in three ways. First, use the chart's suggested key values as a starting point to consider which ones you want to emphasize in your unit. Second, consider which skills you want students to learn and indicate them in the appropriate categories. Third, note some sample activities in relevant "spokes." All this will give you an idea whether your topic choice is a good one. It will also set the stage for writing your thematic statement and objectives. In short, use the chart for some initial brainstorming and planning.

Let me illustrate by looking at a primary unit on gardening, *How Does My Garden Grow?... God Makes It So!* (Chinnery et al. 1993). An initial planning chart would have noted the following values: thankfulness for God's provision for plant growth and the large variety of plants we have for food; careful and diligent workmanship; expressiveness and creativity in language, drama, art, music, and technical design; responsible stewardship of plants and related physical resources. Skills would be indicated in many categories: social (cooperation), language (listening, speaking, writing, learning vocabulary), analytic (alphabetizing, categorizing, inferring), aesthetic (singing, illustrating, dramatizing), emotional (persevering over time), physical (motor skills), scientific/technical (observing and recording, planting and growing, weighing using a simple balance scale, designing), and mathematical (graphing, estimating, patterning, adding). Indicating such key values, main skills and sample activities on a planning chart gives focus to your unit planning.

Learning experiences that might have been noted on the initial planning chart include (1) doing choral reading of paraphrased psalms, (2) dramatizing songs and story books about gardening cycles, (3) using a parachute game with vegetable names to improve large motor skills, (4) designing and planting a garden, (5) creating a new garden tool, (6) building and using a composting bin, (7) investigating the effects of light and water on plant growth, (8) estimating, counting, weighing, classifying, and graphing different fruits and vegetables, and their seeds, and so on.

Articulating intents: thematic statements and objectives

A thematic statement contains the key ideas that frame a unit's teaching and learning. It describes your overall intents. It indicates the main values, dispositions, and commitments you want to foster. It gives the major concepts and skills you want students to acquire and the creative experiences in which they will participate. You may want to list first some general themes that reflect your school's vision. Then you denote more specifically what you expect your students to learn in this unit.

Asking the following preliminary questions is sometimes helpful in the development of a thematic statement (the first three are based on Blomberg 1991, 9):

1. What is God's intention for the particular area of creation or society we will investigate? Why has God provided us with _____?
2. How has this purpose been distorted by the effects of sin? How has _____ deviated from God's original plan?
3. How does God want us to respond? Are there ways in which we can, through Christ's work of redemption, restore, at least in part, the love, righteousness and justice God intended for the world?
4. How can this unit's learning help to develop a deeper understanding of, experience in, and commitment to a Christian way of life?

The Valley Christian School in Morwell, Australia, asked these questions in planning a grade 1-2 unit on trees and forests. It used the creation story to determine that God created our environment with trees as an integral and necessary part. It then developed the paradox that a tree, created to sustain life, became the downfall of mankind, with resulting decay. "The soil became cursed and mankind throughout history has not taken sufficient care of our environment. Reckless destruction, pollution, erosion, food shortage, and extinction have been the results." It answered the third question by pointing to God entrusting the earth to our care and our responsibility to redress some of the mistakes of the past. In the unit the students are then made aware of (1) how we depend on trees; (2) how we have negatively affected trees and forests; and (3) how we can become better guardians and act responsibly in using forest resources so that the earth can continue to sustain human life (P. Brown 1994).

Objectives specify and extend your thematic statement. They have not been without controversy in education. At one pole are technicists who list detailed objectives not only for units but for each lesson. They insist on precise, pre-specified standards by which you measure whether you have reached your objective. They reduce education to learning tidbits of information and skill fragments. Their mechanistic view of the person easily leads to machinelike learning. Little sense remains of overall aims. They often neglect learning goals that are difficult to measure, important as they may be. Teachers object to the time it takes to develop such objectives. They point out that their activities themselves make clear their intents.

Educators at the other pole argue that objectives are superfluous. They hold that listing the key values you want to instill is all you need to choose appropriate and well-focused content and skills. True, spontaneous teaching is sometimes effective. If you seldom articulate your goals, however, you will likely not give enough attention to justifying learning activities as part of a balanced program.

Developing six to fifteen objectives for a unit helps you clarify how you intend to accomplish the intents expressed in your thematic statement. These may be categorized into three or four main objectives, each with several related sub-objectives. Your objectives delimit the scope of your unit's content. They provide a more precise framework and direction for your choice of learning activities, your selection of resources, and your means of student evaluation. They should not be so general that they just restate your thematic statement. But long lists of minute objectives are unnecessary. Either you neglect them or you lose yourself and your students in details.

Objectives have different emphases. A general objective emphasizing a value or disposition may have several sub-objectives. Sub-objectives may specify conceptual or skill learning, or describe problem-posing, problem-solving, or expressive and creative experiences that call for open-ended response. Worthwhile learning can take place during such experiences even when you cannot stipulate precise learning outcomes.

The best way to begin an objective is with an infinitive that gives direction in terms of student learning. This way you describe your intent and yet allow for personal student response. The implication of writing objectives in terms of "The student will . . . " is that students will exhibit only learning pre-specified by you as teacher. Write objectives in terms of student learning, not in terms of what you as a teacher intend to do. Your teaching is a means to an end. Your objectives should state your ends, your intended student learning. Possible infinitives include:

to acknowledge	to analyze	to apply	to appreciate
to assess	to celebrate	to compare	to construct
to contrast	to create	to critique	to define
to demonstrate	to describe	to design	to determine
to develop	to differentiate	to discover	to discuss
to distinguish	to enjoy	to evaluate	to examine
to experience	to explain	to identify	to illustrate
to imagine	to interpret	to investigate	to make
to observe	to plan	to practice	to present
to read	to relate	to respond	to review
to solve	to state	to survey	to trace
to understand	to use	to wonder	to write

Examples of thematic statements and sample objectives from four classroom units follow. The credit for the ideas goes to the teachers who developed these units. I take responsibility for some editing and for choosing a subset of objectives in each instance to conserve space.

GOD MADE ME SPECIAL -- Gr. K (Vonnie Roosendaal et al. 1985)

God created children as His unique images, called to redemption in Jesus. In this unit, children explore their uniqueness: their physical characteristics, senses, feelings, thoughts, creativity, talents, and actions. They consider how they are members of various groups and should relate responsibly to others in their family, friendship circle, classroom, church, and community. They examine how they need trust in God's love and care in order to apply such understandings fully.

This unit has three main objectives. They focus on faith and morals, on children's unique abilities, and on their relations with others. The second of the three objectives is:

2. To focus on our uniqueness as images of God:
   a. To investigate our physical characteristics and how we can use them.
   b. To explore God's design for and intended use of our senses.
   c. To consider the place and effect of our feelings, thoughts, and actions on ourselves, our friends and family, and God.
   d. To understand and experience how we can use God-given talents and creativity to serve God and our neighbors.

THE PIONEERS -- Gr. 4-5 (Christina Belcher 1988)

In past and present cultures, God has given people His mandate to live according to His will in a less than perfect world. Sin's entry into God's world produced individual and cultural consequences. Times and cultures may change, but the hearts of humans are sinful and remain so unless redeemed by God's transforming grace.
In this unit, the students will examine some early Canadian settlers, the pioneers. They will explore how vision and faith motivated them to immigrate and forge a culture in a new land. They will study how God's basic Scriptural truths about family, education, and community life directed or failed to direct their life-style. Finally, they will compare pioneer life to our current family, school, and social life in terms of the values by which people live.

Below are the three main objectives, but the sub-objectives only for the second one:

1. To investigate ways in which Ontario pioneers, like our present society, accepted or rejected God's plan for living as God's image bearers.
2. To explore and experience what it means to depend on God's natural world and on the family and community members He gives us.
   a. To investigate how pioneers used God's created reality as a beautiful and essential resource.
   b. To explore how God's purpose for the family unit was a necessity and blessing for pioneer settlements.
   c. To discover the gift of working with your hands as pioneers did in individual and cooperative ways.

      d. To develop an attitude toward work that is God-honoring and obedient to the principles of stewardship and service.
3. To explore how education reflects and contributes to a way of life that in different ways may either glorify or dishonor God.

TRAVELLING THROUGH THE TROPICAL RAIN FORESTS --
Gr. 6-7 (Fran Redekop and Gloria Strydhorst-Piers 1993)

The tropical rain forests are a breathtaking and incredibly beautiful part of God's creation. They provide a home for vegetation, animals and people, and supply us with many resources. A study of the tropical rain forests provides the class with opportunities to marvel at the Creator and His mighty acts of creation, and to respond to Him with in all their ways. It will, however, also challenge students with the effects of human sinfulness and call them to responsible action as stewards of God's world.

This unit has five general objectives as well as sets of objectives for each of its five parts. Below are the general objectives for the whole unit:

1. To develop an increased awareness and appreciation for the diversity and complexity of life in the rain forest, and to stand in awe before God who created and sustains all life.
2. To be mindful of our role as stewards in God's world, willing and able to do our tasks.
3. To enjoy and actively pursue learning.
4. To work responsibly and cooperatively as members in a community of learners.
5. To develop and use a wide variety of skills in a meaningful context.

The objectives for one section of the unit on *Those Amazing Animals* are as follows:

1. To become aware of and appreciate the diversity and beauty of rain forest wildlife.
2. To recognize and appreciate how the animals are especially designed to suit their environment.
3. To define the main characteristics of the six animal groups and classify rain forest animals accordingly.
4. To enjoy and appreciate works of fiction about various creatures of the rain forest.
5. To develop and use research skills within a meaningful context.
6. To respond creatively by making a mosaic and cooperating to write and publish two books about animals in the rain forest.

GEORGE BERNARD SHAW'S PYGMALION-- Gr. 12 (Mona Janz 1987)

God's gift to humans of the ability to communicate ideas can be used in powerful ways to teach, destroy, persuade, express feeling, attack or enlighten. Because "life and death are in the power of the tongue," students need to understand how literature can influence individuals and society. George Bernard Shaw's Pygmalion reveals how language affects people in almost all aspects of their lives (emotional, aesthetic, social, economical, political, and moral). In this unit, students will see how ideas can be presented dramatically in an enjoyable yet incisive way. They will deepen their appreciation of Shaw's play as they explore his dramatic techniques, use of myth, blend of comedy and didacticism, and his artistic purpose. The students will begin thinking about the power of language to effect changes in worldviews, values, and attitudes.

Objectives relating directly to the play:
1. To enjoy the play.
2. To differentiate between comedic and romantic genres of literature.
3. To understand how literature in general and drama in particular present ideas differently than speeches, essays, and letters.
4. To recognize that the play's dramatic techniques are inseparable from its content.
5. To examine and appreciate the use of myth in *Pygmalion*.
6. To recognize how *Pygmalion* fits into a historical and cultural context, and how it relates to contemporary culture.
7. To evaluate the moral consequences of Eliza's linguistic and cultural transformation.

Skill-related objectives:
1. To contribute worthwhile ideas to class discussions and activities.
2. To present a clear talk to the class on one aspect of the play.
3. To work and communicate effectively in a "lecture group."
4. To learn the importance of cooperation, sharing ideas, and account-ability when working in small groups.
5. To develop note taking skills and keep a record of lecture notes.
6. To prepare arguments for and participate in a formal debate.

Designing, balancing, and sequencing learning experiences

Every year I am delighted with the inventiveness of students in my curriculum course. Most have observed classrooms in action but have not yet taught. Working in small groups they come up with a wealth of possible learning experiences (or activities) on almost any topic. Some activities have to be modified to fit particular age levels. Others may not be structured tightly enough to suit some classes. Still others may take too much organization to please some teachers. When brainstorming with two or three others and using a planning chart to stimulate creative thinking, students as well as teachers come up with numerous worthwhile and useful learning experiences.

What is more difficult is to ensure that the experiences fit the intents of a thematic statement and the objectives. They must also suit the intended audience, and form a balanced unity. To do so, keep in mind certain criteria. Some apply to specific learning activities; others, to the whole set of experiences.

Questions to guide your thinking about specific experiences:

1. Does the experience contribute to your overall intents? Specifically, do its dispositions, values, concepts, skills, and creative and problem solving aspects flow out of the thematic statement and objectives?
2. Will your students have the prerequisite knowledge and aptitudes?
3. Is the experience at an appropriate level of difficulty and does it motivate your students?
4. Does the experience involve adequate student involvement and response, including, where appropriate, higher level thinking and transcendence?
5. Will the experience and its worth be clear to your students?
6. Will the experience work for your class? Can you adapt it for special needs? Does it anticipate critical points where students need help?
7. Are the skills of the activity clearly stated and taught in a meaningful context?
8. Will the required resources be available?

Questions for the set of learning activities as a whole:

1. Will your students grasp the unit's general aims? Did you sequence them so that they can follow the unit's "unifying thread," its direction, structure, and perspective?
2. Do the activities include a range of instructional possibilities? Did you include whole class, small group, individual, and center work? Is there a suitable balance of the four phases of learning? the modes of knowing? Did you provide for learners with different learning styles, at various levels of development?
3. Do the activities encourage conceptual and skill learning within a context of teaching carefully chosen values and dispositions? Do they include recall, skill reinforcement, interpretation, application, and more open-ended evaluation, problem solving, and creative experiences?
4. Do the activities include varied student products so that they can present their learning and understanding in different ways?
5. Are there introductory activities based on students' experiences that set the stage for the unit? Are there culminating activities that review and pull together the main themes?
6. Does your set of activities do justice to your thematic statement and objectives? If not, do you adjust these or revise your activities?

Providing what in the questions I call a "unifying thread" is important. Your thematic statement gives the unit its basic focus. But students may still experience the activities in a disjointed way. One unifying thread could be a problem that you or your students pose about the topic. Your activities would allow students to explore its complexity and gradually come to a fuller understanding of its resolution (or the irresolvable quandary it poses). Another thread could be a narrative format like that proposed by Kieran Egan (see chapter 7). You would design the unit so that students would trace the "story" of the topic (how it developed and where we are today), especially in terms of the unit's basic values. A third thread could use the basic theme or values of the thematic statement to look at different sub-topics. You would then consolidate the sub-topics and conclusions in your culminating activities.

Consider the unit on New World pioneers. One way to provide a unified sequence of activities is to ask students to consider the problem of creating a new life when a group of people arrives on uncleared land, with few resources. The unit would ask students to list and investigate the various problems pioneers would face, and discover ways to overcome them. A major part of the unit might be simulating the establishment of a pioneer community.

A second approach would be to develop a narrative approach. The unit's activities might recount the story of a family that faced and overcame challenges as it built life in a new community (preferably one familiar to your class). Students might consider themselves part of an imaginary pioneer family, with the teacher using "family case study situations" as starting points for research, projects, role plays, center work, and so on. The story line might contrast, for instance, personal resolution, family love, and community cooperation with physical hardship, disdain for Indian peoples, and economic greed.

A third approach would be to look at different aspects of pioneer communities: clearing land, providing food, building homes, family life, education, skills and crafts, community life, religion and faith. All these would be discussed in terms of how life-styles reflect God's norms for respecting physical resources, stewardship, peace, justice, love and devotion. The foregoing three approaches are not mutually exclusive. Many goals and activities would overlap. Yet each unifying thread provides a distinct focus of organization.

Finally, you need to decide a format for stating your activities. A popular three-column format has objectives and/or sub-topics in the first column, activities on the second, and resources in the third. Persons using the above "different aspect" approach often list sub-objectives at the start of each section. Then, without using columns, they describe the section's activities with the required resources. Use a format that will help your day-to-day planning. You usually list activities ongoing throughout the unit or done in learning centers separately at the beginning or end of a unit.

Planning a time schedule

You need to plan a time schedule for your unit. Decide, first, how much time you will spend on the unit each day of the week. Then decide from your yearly overview how many weeks you can spend on it. For the pioneer unit, for instance, you may decide to incorporate a great deal of language arts. Further, you may alternate your social studies-focused units with science-focused ones. In this case, you might set aside two hours per day for the unit for five weeks. The unit on Pygmalion, on the other hand, might take four weeks but be limited to the three or four periods per week available for English 12. Schools usually schedule cross-graded units such as the one on oceans for no more than one or two weeks; they demand much planning and day-to-day organization.

Most teachers find it helpful to develop an overall time chart or one for each week. Such charts give a planned schedule of activities. You may find you have to deviate at times, but then you can make a reasoned decision to make adjustments based on your circumstances. Without a planned time line, units tend to take more time than you intended. Then you may be forced to shortchange other important aspects of your program.

Selecting and using curriculum resources

Resources are valuable learning tools. The availability of resources will affect your choice of activities. You cannot teach a grade 6 unit on famous Christian leaders unless you have multiple copies of several biographies. You cannot effectively teach a unit on the use and misuse of statistics unless you have collected a number of case studies. You are more likely to teach research skills in a unit if your library has resources for the unit topic.

Resources should be used as *tools*, however. They should not determine the framework, content, and structure of your unit. As a teacher you set the direction and scope of your unit. Then you decide which resources will help you attain your objectives. As I showed in chapter 3, resources embody explicit and implicit values, both in content and pedagogical design. You may disagree with some of those values. That does not necessarily mean that their use cannot help you reach your goals. At some grade levels students benefit from considering, analyzing, and evaluating material with perspectives that differ from that of their teachers or their own. It does mean, however, that to make a responsible decision about their use, you have to become aware of the worldview and values promoted by any print, audiovisual, computer, and human resources that you may use in your class. Here are some questions you can ask:

1. What values, commitments, priorities, and goals does the resource state or assume? What does it portray as important in the way we live and view the world? Does it promote Biblical norms for ethical, economic, and family life? Does it deal with significant issues and do so fairly?
2. If the perspective of the resource differs from what you wish to promote, can you still use it? Why or why not? In what way(s)? If the perspective is similar to your own, does the resource stimulate thought about critical issues and not give glib answers to difficult issues?
3. How does the resource expect (or allow) learning to take place? Will it encourage thoughtfulness, creativity, problem solving, and personal response? Is it interesting and motivational? Does it develop skills in a meaningful context? Do the layout, illustrations, and special features promote meaningful learning?
4. Does the resource provide balanced and appropriate content, at a suitable level of difficulty? Does it endorse a balance of learning activities, with students able to take responsibility for their learning?

When you are aware of the strengths and weaknesses of the available resources, you can use them selectively and judiciously. Don't let your resources dictate an agenda at odds with your general goals. Also, use your position as a member of the school staff to be involved in evaluating and choosing new resource adoptions.

Planning student assessment and evaluation

Assessment means gathering information about your students' learning; evaluation means drawing conclusions and make decisions based on assessment. Teachers commonly use the term evaluation to include both aspects, and here I will also do so.

Your methods of evaluation affect teaching and learning. For instance, suppose a unit's main evaluation is a multiple choice test. Then the main goal of students will be to recall facts and concepts long enough to do well on a recognition test. On the other hand, the test may be a more open-ended essay type preceded by many self-, peer- and teacher-evaluated products compiled into a portfolio. Students will then work at processing, organizing, and presenting their research and thinking effectively. Evaluation affects curriculum more than we sometimes recognize.

You therefore need to consider evaluation as an integral part of your unit design. Evaluation is an undertaking that attaches value to certain types of learning. Since the results of evaluation affect students personally and often acutely, evaluation teaches them values and influences their attitudes to school and to life. Your evaluation methods and strategies should therefore promote the goals of your unit. They should encourage standards that are high but relate to students' individual abilities. Use evaluation to help students apply their God-given gifts responsively and responsibly. However, always stress that their inherent personhood and worth does not depend on how well they can do an assignment.

Evaluation should emphasize formative feedback. That is, evaluate student products and behavior in order to nurture and support them. The intent of evaluation is, first, to improve performance and encourage growth in different developmental areas. Students need correction, but it must be accompanied by encouragement, patience, and careful instruction (2 Timothy 4:2). That implies that evaluation should be done frequently, in various settings, using a range of methods. It may involve your informal observation and student self-evaluation of individual and group learning, evaluation of daily assignments and longer projects, exhibitions of student products, and tests. The evidence you collect should lead to discussions and conferences that help students make responsible decisions and choices about their learning.

Let me give an example. Sharon van Dijk's grade 2-3 unit on reptiles includes whole class activities such as reading non-fiction and fiction books about reptiles, responding to slides, making charts of reptile characteristics, teaching research skills, and dramatizing ways reptiles move. She also uses reading buddies and organizes a small group reptile project. Students keep an ongoing personal journal/chart, and make a poster on how they can be good caretakers of a chosen reptile. The six learning centers include research, composition, museum, computer, pattern and design, and creativity. Children complete at least one activity from each center, such as completing open-ended sentences ("If I were a . . . ," etc.), composing reptile resumes, examining slides, creating reptile pictures on the computer, and painting reptile habitats.

Sharon's evaluation is multifaceted. She keeps checklists to assess language arts skills. She records social and emotional development on "post-it notes" as children work at the learning centers. She also tracks daily progress by makings anecdotal comments on the learning taking place. She has conferences with several children. Here she checks comprehension and other items on her check list, and discusses personal goals and achievements. She gives written feedback to two or three children each day about their goals and progress. She listens to audiotaped readings the students have made, checking choice and difficulty of reading material and fluency. She collects and evaluates the children's work portfolios each week. She puts photographs of the reptile models students make in their portfolios. She uses six criteria to evaluate the group project (including research and cooperative skills).

Sharon also involves her students and parents in her evaluation. The students keep a goals booklet and complete "what I learned/what I did" sheets. She involves the whole class in completing "what I know/what I want to learn/what I learned" charts at the beginning and end of the unit. Each term, all children prepare a large envelope with sample work. They use these to self-evaluate and to recall and celebrate all they have learned over the past three months. Then with the teacher the students set new goals for the coming term. The work envelope is also sent home or used in student-led conferences. It includes this note to parents: "Please encourage _____ to discuss his/her work folder with you. Please write three positive things you have learned about your child from the enclosed work." Sharon asks parents to return the folder and completed note. She discusses these with the parents at parent/teacher interviews.

At higher grade levels examinations and tests play a more prominent role. They serve a purpose in encouraging students to review and understand course material. But parts of the test should be learning activities in themselves where students apply and evaluate what they have learned. Indicate in your unit what types of questions you will give and what weight you give tests in your total student evaluation.

ADAPTING UNITS FOR YOUR CLASSROOM

From time to time you will develop a totally new unit. This will happen particularly when your school decides to teach a cross-grade unit or when you plan a new topic for which few suitable references are available. You may want to teach a grade 2 unit on rocks and geology since this involves one of your special interests. However, no teaching materials may be available at that level. You may want to teach a collection of short stories that you chose as particularly suitable for your class, combining this with creative writing. Perhaps you want to study a major current event from another part of the world.

More often, however, you will adapt other units to fit your goals and purposes. You may even have two or three units available on a topic, some commercial educational materials, and a class set of textbooks with a teacher's guide that contains a chapter or two on your topic. In such cases, it is important that you first decide your own thematic statement, objectives, scope, and general approach. Once you have done so, you can then use your references to choose suitable learning activities, resources, and evaluation strategies. You keep in mind the make-up and chemistry of your class. You add your own activities where desirable, remembering your special needs students.

Let's consider the pioneer unit once more. You like Christina Belcher's perspective, with her emphasis on vision and faith as a basis for pioneer community life. You teach on the Canadian prairies, however. So you want to look at a pioneer community in your area around 1900. You take Christina's thematic statement but put more emphasis on the importance of community leadership as well as on farming as keys to understanding prairie settlement. You add an objective about farming.

Before you look at activities, you find a unifying "story line." If you don't know a personal story in your community, you could, for instance, use the (real) story of eighteen-year-old Irishman Ivan Crossley (Berton 1984, 114-156). Crossley was taken in by the promises of the Reverend Isaac Barr. Barr falsely claimed that settlers who joined him could look forward to a simple, easy farming life on a new colony around what is now Lloydminster. Timber would be readily available and fruit trees would grow. In the spring of 1903 Crossley and the other 2000 people who accompanied Barr had a long, difficult voyage in a converted troop ship from England to New Brunswick. A five-day train trip to Saskatoon and a 200-mile wagon trek to the new colony followed.

Crossley with a few friends claimed his 640 acre homestead. He built a sod hovel without windows for a house. His first crop of vegetables withered and died; like most other colonists, he lacked farming experience. He did everything by trial and error. He alternately broke ground, farmed, and took temporary jobs plowing for others and delivering winter mail. Yet despite inept leadership, lack of know-how, and a refusal to learn from non-British immigrants, Crossley and his fellow colonists succeeded. They persevered as they muddled through, though they knew how to run their Anglican church and literary and music societies better than their farms. Crossley's family prospered. Some of his descendents still live in Lloydminster.

Crossley's story (or similar ones for other ethnic groups) is readily available in books like Berton's. These provide a rich lode for a narrative approach to this unit. You can then still fit many of Christina Belcher's activities into your unit, albeit in a different context. The class could set up and operate a general store (as first set up by Barr as a cooperative venture). They could have a pioneer family and a pioneer school day. They could do research, analyze, and make maps at centers. They could investigate the treatment of native Indian people and other immigrant groups. They could survey their own family background to see if there were pioneer experiences in their families. They could consider why the role of the church was not as strong here as in some other colonies. Throughout, Barr's quest for power and profit can be contrasted with Crossley's reported honesty, perseverance, and loyalty.

In short, the original unit sets out a useful framework of intents and a source of possible activities. As a teacher, you can take the unit and convert it into one that fits your local situation. For more general topics such as science or novel study units, the adaptation might even be simpler—at least, if you agree with the basic intents. You will always find, however, that you need to make some revisions to make the unit one that you yourself can teach comfortably and successfully.

IMPLEMENTING CURRICULUM PLANS

As you implement your curriculum plans, you want to sustain progress toward your goals. You want to keep your students interested and responsive, make them responsible, and maintain high standards of work. For this, you need to reflect on your classroom dynamics on a daily basis. Use your daily lesson planning to make desirable revisions to your curriculum plans. Try to find the causes for student difficulties or lack of interest. Sometimes your plans or resources do not fit the nature of your class or its general aptitude. Your pacing may be too fast or too slow. The activities may not be suitable for late in the day or for the day before a long weekend. Even when you are meeting your goals, learning activities may have other unintended effects that you need to review.

I vividly remember simultaneously teaching a mathematics unit to two grade 10 classes, using a cooperative learning approach. With the one class this was a resounding success. They taught themselves a surprising amount of mathematics. They tackled difficult transcendence activities with enthusiasm. Students in the other class had similar mathematical aptitudes. Nevertheless, my approach floundered. Soon the students begged me to go back to a more traditional approach. While I didn't abandon my approach completely, I had to modify it substantially to meet my concept and skill goals. To this day, I do not fully know what caused the dissimilar reactions. But I do know that my daily adjustments in the two classes had to be quite different.

Sometimes curriculum adjustments cannot overcome more basic problems that need to be addressed: lack of order in the class or school, frequent external distractions, or a poor student attitude toward learning. But often you can bring about positive change by modifying learning activities, changing your sequence or time allocation, adding or deleting topics, and so on. While doing so, keep in mind your general goals and persist in doing what you can to have your students attain them. Ask your colleagues for suggestions and seek their advice before implementing new approaches.

INVOLVING YOUR STUDENTS IN CURRICULUM PLANNING

Try to involve your students in curriculum planning. This helps them to take ownership of their learning and encourages them to become responsible. Often the K-W-L approach works well. That is, you first ask students to list what they already know about a unit topic (K). This can be done by brainstorming relevant words or concepts. Student secretaries write them on pieces of cardboard. You then help the class sort them into categories, using the results to make a large webbing diagram. Then you ask students what they want to learn about the topic or wonder about (W). They could do so first in pairs, and then as a whole class. This results in a list of topics for investigation. You then revise your unit plan to include additional topics, perhaps as group activities or in learning centers. At the end of the unit, the class makes a chart listing what it has learned (L).

Also, regularly offer students choices or alternatives. At the kindergarten level, students can already choose learning centers themselves. You may have a few rules so that all students regularly attend the writing center and do not attend the same center two days in a row. You encourage responsibility by allowing students to make decisions about their learning activities. You also make some provision for the range of learning styles, abilities, developmental levels, and interests in your class. You foster accountability by involving students in setting learning goals. And you help them identify learning problems and possible solutions.

REVIEWING THE EFFECTIVENESS OF YOUR UNIT

It is important to evaluate your unit's effectiveness once you have taught it. You don't need high powered techniques. Some informal but honest reflection will help you improve the unit the next time you teach it.

Some teachers use a photocopied sheet with some questions to guide their thoughts and make some notes that they put with their unit materials:

1. CONTENT: Was the content appropriate, interesting, and worthwhile for the class? Did it contribute adequately to my goals? Were the resources relevant and suitable? Did the students respond personally and meaningfully to the content? Can they use what they learned?
2. INSTRUCTION: Which strategies were most successful? Which strategies did not work well? Did I provide enough variety to meet the needs of all my students?
3. STUDENT EVALUATION: Did the quality of the students' work meet my expectations? Did I use a broad enough spectrum of assessment strategies? Was the evaluation fair? thorough? Did my student evaluation, their self-evaluation, and parental feedback indicate that I met the unit's aims? If not, why not?
4. CELEBRATIONS: What things were particularly successful?
5. CHANGES: What changes should I make for the future?

At the end of the school year, you can complete an appendix to your yearly overview where you note modifications made or to be made, new sources, or things that were especially successful or need work. If filled out at the end of the school year, you won't forget them over the summer break.

SUMMARY

As a teacher you are ultimately responsible for curriculum planning and implementation for your classrooms. You prepare yearly overviews, unit plans, and day-to-day lesson plans. You use your beliefs and insights, but work within the framework established by school systems, your local school, and your parent community.

Your personal goals find expression particularly in the design of integral units. You can plan (or adapt) effective units in various ways. One such way uses the following steps (not always in sequential order!):

1. Select a topic.
2. Fill out a planning chart and use it to determine the main values, concepts, and skills you want your students to learn.
3. Articulate your intents (thematic statements and objectives).
4. Design, balance, and sequence learning experiences.
5. Select learning resources.
6. Plan a time schedule.
7. Plan student assessment and evaluation.

While teaching the unit, involve your students in planning learning experiences. Once you have completed the unit, review its effectiveness and note any improvements you want to make for the following year.

REFLECTING

1. Most principals require teachers to hand in yearly overviews at the beginning of the school year. Some also ask that they hand in unit plans before teaching them. Examine a yearly overview, if available, as well as one or two unit plans. What are their strengths and weaknesses? If you were a principal, what would you say to a teacher about the plans?

2. Find a teacher resource unit for a topic you may want to teach sometime in the future. After reading it, describe how you would adapt it to fit your own intents and situation.

3. Examine some textbooks and use the criteria in this chapter to determine their suitability and how you might make use of them in your class.

4. Talk to some teachers about their classroom curriculum planning. How much and what kind do they do? Are there any things they would like to do but don't have time for? In what ways have they found such planning rewarding? frustrating?

Chapter 9
Shaping Curriculum
Outside the Classroom

■ Political reasons prompt many curriculum decisions that are made outside the classroom. Consider Pennsylvania's proposal to teach students certain values as measurable outcomes.

Pennsylvania's State Board of Education sought to reverse declining levels of responsible, ethical behavior. It proposed to include a value component in the state curriculum. All students were to learn to appreciate other people and tolerate differences. One outcome was to be to show respect for the dignity, worth, contributions, and equal rights of each person. This core outcome was intentionally left vague so that local communities could set their own standards.

Community reaction was swift. Opponents accused the Board that its "respect for diversity" meant promoting alternative (e.g., gay) life-styles. They added that state-determined value outcomes should not be needed for high school graduation. At well-organized meetings, the Citizens for Excellence in Education said the Board's plan would force children to learn about New Age occult beliefs and homosexuality. It convinced many that the Board intended to seize the responsibility of teaching values from parents and churches.

The Board did not defend its proposal well. The public believed that the Board left its proposals and ways to measure outcomes vague so that it could impose its values on children. The pressure on politicians resulted in two items being removed from the Board's proposals: the value outcome and, wherever it appeared, the phrase, "attitude and behavior." (I have based this description on an article by J. McQuaide and A. Pliska 1994, 16-21.)

There are three issues you need to consider here. First, note the main curriculum "players." How did these players wield influence on curriculum policy? Which other players can affect curriculum guidelines? Why were principals, teachers, or students not much involved? Who should have the right to affect and set curriculum policies?

Secondly, who affects curriculum-in-practice (not just the policies)? Which players have strategic impact on the curriculum as experienced by students? Would the inclusion of the value component have made much difference in the classroom? Would not most teachers teach respect for diversity anyhow—and would those who do not be swayed by a policy? To what extent are teachers affected by top-down directives? Make a list of players that influence the classroom curriculum. Put them in order of most to least influence. Share your ordered list. How did you differ?

The third issue arises from the view I take in this book that all schooling teaches values. McQuaide and Pliska argue that Citizens for Excellence in Education won and the State Board lost. I believe that everyone, and especially the students, lost.

The opponents fought the battle on a wrong assumption: that teachers teach facts and skills but can avoid teaching values that relate to respect, tolerance, and equal rights. A more promising course of action might have been to involve the public and teachers in discussing the nature of respect, tolerance, and equal rights. That could have brought out that a Biblical conception of love is a sound basis for respect, that tolerance means little without a sense of responsibility and truthfulness, and that equal rights can function only where people exercise their personal and communal responsibilities on the basis of a shared value commitment. Such a discussion might have resulted in some state educators sensing the emptiness of how these terms are often used. Then, parents and teachers could work on a better curriculum proposal.

One of my assumptions here is that long-term curriculum change requires a change in community attitudes. Do you agree? Why or why not? Do you know of instances where groups have influenced public opinion and, as a result, curriculum policies? If so, how did the shaping of public values come into play?

Curriculum planning takes place at many levels. Governments set general policies. They develop curriculum guides and authorize or make available resources. They also often prescribe testing programs and school leaving exams. Professional groups make curriculum policy suggestions and develop resources. Publishers develop textbooks. To sell them, they consider state policies and teachers' likes and dislikes. Networks of schools, school districts, and local schools set up curriculum committees. Such task forces assess programs and recommend or develop more suitable ones. Curriculum planners make use of and consider what other groups have already done.

Planning groups tend to use models for planning that fit their curriculum orientation. In this chapter, therefore, I first present models for curriculum planning based on the four orientations of chapter 1. I then develop an alternate model that takes into account (1) the societal context of curriculum, (2) worldviews and basic values, and (3) how curriculum planning usually takes place. Next, I discuss the role of various curriculum "players." Finally, I describe curriculum implementation and evaluation.

EXAMPLES OF CURRICULUM DEVELOPMENT MODELS

Groups charged with planning school curriculum go about their work in different ways. Often, their approach itself contains the values of their curriculum orientation. Here I give examples of planning models commonly used by proponents of four curriculum orientations.

The traditional academic approach to curriculum development

As they plan curricula, academic traditionalists first focus on the subjects they want taught in school. Usually these include at least language and literature, mathematics, science, history, geography, a foreign language, and some fine arts. They then compose lists of content and skills for different grade levels. They may consider effective ways to teach students about their heritage, as well as how student testing can maintain high standards. Generally, however, this is less important than detailing content and skills. Until the 1970s, most curriculum guides resulted from this type of approach. Today, definitions of core curriculum still often list mainly subject content and skills.

The technical Tyler rationale

The late Ralph Tyler proposed a model or "rationale" used widely by persons in the technical orientation (Tyler 1950). It has affected the curriculum field in North America more than any other approach. Tyler's model pulled together a set of questions that until 1950 had seldom been addressed systematically:

1. What educational purposes should the school seek to attain?
2. What educational experiences can be provided that are likely to attain these purposes?
3. How can these educational experiences be effectively organized?
4. How can we determine whether these purposes are being attained? (Tyler 1950, 1-2).

Users of Tyler's rationale tend to overlook what worldviews mean for education. They seldom ask what kind of person students ought to become. Instead, they focus on the technical steps of curriculum making. They obtain lists of objectives from subject specialists, learners' needs, and conditions in society. Tyler believed that a comprehensive philosophy should be the basis for choosing objectives (Tyler 1950, 3, 10, 22-24). But in his model he used philosophy only as an after-the-fact "screen" to cut out undesirable objectives. This plus the assumption that knowledge is neutral means that Tyler's followers put value questions off to the side. They seldom even use the philosophic "screen." They fail to base their final set of objectives, and hence their learning program, on an explicit theory of education.

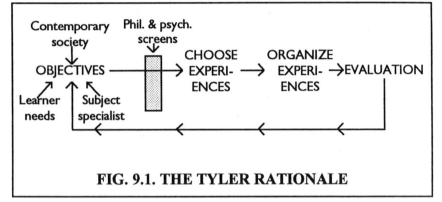

FIG. 9.1. THE TYLER RATIONALE

Tyler's followers use his model as a linear, technical model for curriculum planning. They split teaching into small, manageable "intended learning outcomes." For them, teachers are technicians who are to follow instructions for processing students efficiently. They focus on the best means to reach prespecified objectives. These objectives spell out narrow concepts and skills but often neglect important overall goals. Tyler himself held that objectives must indicate a change in student behavior that can be appraised. But later he became critical of how his followers' objectives were too specific, how they stressed behavior but neglected content, and how they paid little attention to choosing objectives (L. Sosniak in Anderson and Sosniak 1994, 118).

Students of Tyler developed Bloom's taxonomy of educational objectives with its cognitive, affective, and psychomotor domains. Tyler's followers therefore often use it in curriculum planning. The taxonomy correctly points to the need for different types of learning, at different levels of complexity. But its view of education is skewed. It holds that knowledge in the cognitive domain is objective. As we have already seen, however, you cannot teach a cognitive concept or skill without teaching inherent values as well. The taxonomy is also simplistic in its claim that cognition can be linearly ordered into recall, comprehension, application, analysis, synthesis, and evaluation categories. It also downplays the importance of creative expression, skills that are not psychomotor ones, and dispositions and commitments. It distorts or excludes goals like understanding, appreciation, and sensitivity. Indeed, its process-oriented approach may prevent students from getting a coherent view of the world (Edward Furst in Anderson and Sosniak 1994, 33).

Tyler's rationale also shortchanges how teachers actually deal with their classes. It fails to consider how they deliberate and negotiate as they plan and implement curriculum. It neglects the political realities of making curriculum decisions. By assessing only prespecified objectives, it overlooks the consequences of treating students in a mechanistic way. Tyler's rationale gives us a checklist of things that curriculum planners must do at some point. However, "there is no moral grounding for the Tyler rationale--no affirmation of basic beliefs, no reverence for life, no concern for compassion, or worrying about justice" (Macdonald and Purpel 1987, 183). As such, it falls short in providing a model for implementing the ideas of this book.

Joseph Schwab's deliberative "practical arts"

For Joseph Schwab (1978, 1983), either listing content topics or using the Tyler rationale is too simplistic. Rather than asking "What do we teach?" or "How can we meet our objectives?," Schwab calls for *understanding*. He asks, "What ought we to do?" How can we consider the moral, intellectual, and social basis, context, potential, and effects of the curriculum? How can we create programs that promote "right" action? For Schwab, curriculum planning involves reflection, considered judgment, practice, and response.

To bridge the common gap between theory and practice, Schwab suggests four curriculum planning components. These are not sequential steps but overlap with and enrich each other. First, planners consider which philosophical, ethical, and psychological theories they can apply to school settings. Second, they ready such theories for general use in curriculum planning. Third, they chart defensible directions for specific situations through deliberation. This process involves curriculum experts, teachers, and students. Finally, teachers and students put plans into practice. Schwab stresses that constant interaction is needed among all four components. Then the process can clarify values, intentions, theories, and practices. Theory will enhance practice and practice will also enlighten theory.

Schwab's process does not oversimplify how theory and practice interact. His approach involves cooperation among the various players. He takes into account the importance of teachers and students in their situations. Planners and practitioners use deliberation to clarify assumptions, values, intentions, and possibilities. How planners apply theories and research results depends on the situation. Schwab knows that his deliberative process--and hence curriculum planning--is complex. It is not linear. Often it may be difficult to choose among alternatives.

Schwab's model is not without its shortcomings. Its scope is vast and time consuming. Teachers are willing to work on curriculum projects for a year or so. But they do not want to "deliberate" continuously. More seriously, Schwab does not admit that the root meaning of curriculum lies in worldviews and convictions about basic values. He is too optimistic that diverse groups can forge meaningful consensuses acceptable to a broad spectrum of teachers. His deliberative process seems practical only if a common core of beliefs exists. Then, and only then, does it have much potential for curriculum planning. I use aspects of it in the model of curriculum planning I develop later in this chapter.

The critical theorists: curriculum as praxis

Critical theorists, like other constructivists, hold that to make sense of their world, humans *construct* their own personal social reality. Learning leads to meaning only when students actively reconstruct the world they live in. Most curriculum knowledge and classroom structures, according to critical theorists, hinder the political, social, and economic power of students. Therefore a basic curriculum question is, "How can the curriculum help students to free themselves from society's shackles?" To answer this question, critical theorists focus on what should count as knowledge and who should control it. They consider how students can be treated justly and develop critical consciousness that leads to real personal meaning (Beyer and Apple 1988, 5).

Curriculum, therefore, must begin with the interests and needs of students. Teachers facilitate students to reflect about and act in their world. They engage them in *praxis*, i.e., in critical self-reflection wedded with reflective action. In this way they can begin to reconstruct their lives and free themselves from oppression. Other than stating that teachers must work outward from learners themselves, they give few details about curriculum planning. Teachers must help students construct plans for learning in their own context. The very texture of day-to-day classroom relationships generates different meanings. To plan a curriculum beforehand would therefore make little sense.

Critical theorists have given valid critiques of schooling. They have, for instance, pointed out the oft-negative impact of the hidden curriculum. They have shown how dominant cultural beliefs affect textbooks. But there are at least three flaws in their approach. First, they frame issues and pose questions so that the social and political direction of the answer is already implied. Second, they refuse to grant that schools do enculturate students in some positive ways. Third, they fail to present useful alternatives. They do not make clear how praxis will function or how they will achieve emancipation other than by scrapping what is now in place. This is the case in part because teachers and students are to decide their curriculum collaboratively in their context.

The four models of curriculum planning that I have described are not the only ones. But most combine elements of these four. Kieran Egan's, for instance, uses deliberation to identify the importance of a topic and its related transcendent values. Egan rejects listing objectives in terms of behavior change. But he does use variations of Tyler's other three steps. He suggests we choose and organize learning experiences according to a story or narrative format (for younger students). His last step, like Tyler's, is to evaluate learning, albeit in terms of understanding and student engagement rather than narrow behavioral objectives (Egan 1986, 41; Egan 1992, 94).

■ Suppose you are asked to chair a curriculum team planning a new science curriculum guide for schools in your jurisdiction. Which of the four models would you prefer? Why? Which parts of the various approaches would you use? What would you do in your first meeting with the group?

A MODEL OF CURRICULUM PLANNING

I now describe a model that, I believe, more closely reflects how curriculum develops in practice. I see curriculum as a dynamic series of planned learning experiences. Teachers continually assess and revise and adapt their plans as they work with their students. This model for the process of curriculum has three concentric "wheels": the foundational frame factors on the outside, the program components in the center, and, in the middle, the deliberative process that allows for interaction between the two.

The lines of the model are broken ones because of the many interactions within and between the circles. For instance, how planners view knowledge affects their pedagogy as well. Also, planning and evaluation should take place together. Further, learning activities depend to some extent on the resources within reach and those, in turn, may affect the intents. Also, the social, economic, and political contexts of schooling will influence plans for learning. Beliefs about the purpose of schooling affects how planners implement and evaluate their work. In these and other ways the various program, process, contextual, and groundings elements interact in fluid and dynamic ways.

Note two points. First, there is no one proper starting point for curriculum planning. You cannot plan curriculum in a neat, step-by-step way. Intents, for instance, arise from groundings and contextual frame factors. But they also develop from potential activities and resources. Goals, activities, and resources often emerge together. Second, all those involved in planning can *directly* consider every aspect of the model. A curriculum specialist cannot take into account the features of a specific class. Teachers will seldom ask explicit questions about, say, the nature of knowledge. But teachers should know, be able to influence, and agree with the basic thrust of a program. Otherwise, plans will quickly founder when used in their classrooms.

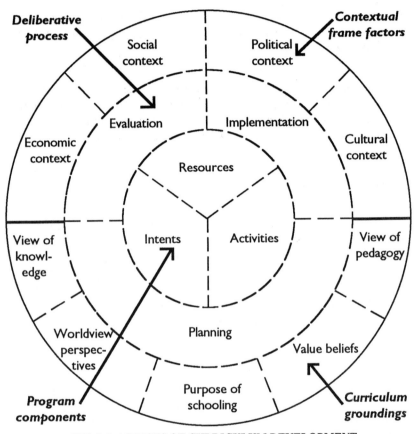

FIG. 9.2. ASPECTS OF CURRICULUM DEVELOPMENT

The model's outer circle shows the factors that frame curriculum planning. All who make curriculum decisions, from state officials to students, have beliefs about life and about education. They also work within a certain context. Answers to key questions frame their work. What is their guiding vision of life? What values are important in education? What are schools for? What is the nature of knowledge? How should they choose and structure subject matter? How do they view persons and what does that imply for curriculum planning? What are the economic, political, social, and cultural contexts that will affect what is possible? In this book I have already dealt with the Biblical groundings for curriculum. In the next section I discuss some of the contextual frame factors.

Discord about groundings can derail curriculum plans. I recall a department of education taking several years to seek public input for a new social studies program. But forums did little more than reveal conflicting views about the aims, and the nature of school knowledge. Some saw social studies as a way to transmit and explain historical information. Others, equally vocal, wanted it to be a workshop setting for democratic citizenship. Eventually, a frustrated top official scrapped the whole process. He appointed a small committee of like-minded educators who came up with a new program quickly and cheaply.

Curriculum planning teams seldom systematically delineate their views on groundings. Often their members are chosen to represent special expertise or different interest groups. No matter how appointed, they will have disagreements that will become clear as they develop program components. Some diversity can lead to healthy discussions and deeper insights. But unresolved fundamental clashes can stymie a project or lead to a curriculum that lacks a clear focus.

The innermost part of the model lists program components, i.e., the intents, activities, and resources (Werner and Aoki 1979, 7). Planners at some point must address the intents of their project. What should the proposed curriculum accomplish or achieve? What ends should be defined and selected? Intents are broader than objectives. They include both written and unwritten ones. An unwritten intent may be to reduce public controversy about a program or to raise the levels of math standards on an international assessment test. Written intents include statements of goals and thematic statements. Planners usually consider learning activities, resources, and intents in concert. Even if they first formulate goals, they will clarify and often alter them as they plan, implement, and evaluate learning activities and resources. The content, activities, and resources of final plans should be in accord with the project's intents.

Planners ask a number of questions that help them develop and choose activities and resources. How can we achieve our intents? Which content, skills, and expressive activities do we include? How do we structure, balance, and sequence them? Which resources do we choose and how should they be put to use? Are the connections among intents, activities, and resources logical and clear? Does the proposed program have a clear, unified focus? Answers to these questions, of course, depend a great deal on the planners' views of curriculum groundings.

The middle circle represents the deliberative process that links groundings and context with program components. Curriculum making involves three interrelated but distinct acts: planning, implementation, and evaluation. Here planners ask how they can coordinate and monitor curriculum planning. What factors do they need to consider and act on for successful implementation? How can they best meet their intents? What do they evaluate? How? Planning is never finished. Implementation and evaluation leads to more planning. Even government guidelines, once published, are interpreted, adapted, and evaluated both before, during, and after implementation. Teachers modify them for their own use, and may suggest future changes.

In short, when working on curriculum proposals, developers thinkingly or unthinkingly take into account their groundings and the project's probable context. They derive their intents, learning activities, and resources from a process of deliberation that includes planning, implementation, and evaluation. For meaningful curriculum development, planning teams need to consider carefully their views of the foundational frame factors before nailing down the intents, learning experiences, and resources for any proposed program.

> ■ You had your first meeting with your team to design a new science curriculum guide (see the end of the last section). Members disagreed about the worth of activity-based resources and the need to deal with social issues in science. You realize that these clashes about practical matters suggest deeper ones about the theoretical bases for science programs. You therefore explain what you mean by "groundings" and ask everyone to come prepared next time with a list of their "nonnegotiables" for science education. At the next meeting you will first have people share in pairs, then in groups of four, and finally as a whole group to see where consensus is possible and where irresolvable differences exist. Prepare the list that you yourself will bring to that meeting.

THE SOCIETAL CONTEXT OF CURRICULUM

Besides the basic beliefs of educators and their communities, the economic, social, political, and cultural contexts in which schools operate also frame school curricula. Large-scale projects consider only the broad strokes of such contexts. Individual schools and teachers use their local settings to adapt general guides or to make their own plans.

Let me give two examples. In 1993, Australia's political leaders realized that their nation's trade and business focus had shifted from Europe to Asia. They decided, therefore, that Asian languages would become compulsory in the schools, replacing German and French. For many Australians this was not easy. The psychological tie with Europe was still strong for many, and teachers needed to be retrained. But individual schools had no choice; Asian languages were to become a requirement for university entrance. Economic and political circumstances affected the schools' curricula.

General policies, however, may not fit local contexts. Then local schools or teachers alter or subvert the policies. Some years ago a department of education prescribed a values-based social studies program. Instead of stressing content, the program would help students make decisions on value-related social issues. Some years later, after almost all teachers reported they had implemented the program, researchers checked its effectiveness. In actuality, only a small minority of teachers used the curriculum in the way it was intended! One reason was that teachers felt the program lacked substance. Also, they could not see how to involve students meaningfully in an open-ended values clarification process. Moreover, they did not expect parental backing for the new program. So the teachers, while officially adopting the new program, stayed with more familiar approaches.

Four important societal frame factors are the economic, the social, political, and cultural contexts. First, the economic context affects curriculum. Ample funds for resources may enrich, for instance, the reading program. But restricted funds may limit programs. One school district faced with budget cuts decided to move all elementary music specialists into regular classroom positions. This not only decimated the music program, but many children were then taught by disaffected teachers. Another economic example involves inclusive education in which many children with special needs now attend regular classrooms. At first such students and their teachers received specialized help. But such help has now often been cut back due to economic pressures. In order to cope, teachers then may, for instance, cut special activities that call for personal exploration and response (setting the stage and transcendence).

Our current social context also affects the curriculum. In some locales there is a large number of dysfunctional families. In others the pursuit of dual careers may mean parents spend little time with their children. In such cases teachers may spend time on functions traditionally carried out by parents (e.g., providing meals, discussing everyday problems and values). They also may modify the "standard" curriculum to allow more time, for instance, for reading readiness in kindergarten and grade 1. To give another social context example, in racially diverse communities teachers may need to teach units on multiculturalism.

The socioeconomic background of students has an impact on the curriculum. Critical theorists have shown that both content and pedagogy in schools with a lower class clientele stress mechanical, rote learning in a setting that is strictly controlled (see, for instance, Jean Anyon in Giroux and Purpel 1983, 143-167). The same is true for low track high school classes that tend to attract students from lower socioeconomic backgrounds (Oakes 1986, 60-80). Curriculum differences with higher level classes are real and regrettable. Critical theorists claim that these are deliberate attempts to maintain class, racial, and gender differences. But a major reason, it seems to me, is that the family backgrounds of students affect how teachers can implement learning. At the same time, the assumed expectations that teachers have of their students also contribute to the differences. In this respect, homogeneous tracking affects the curriculum negatively for weaker students and ones from lower socioeconomic backgrounds.

The political context also affects curriculum. Politicians are swayed by public opinion. Public concern for higher standards may lead politicians to set competency exams at different grade levels (although these often affect only minimum and not general standards). They also may bow to public pressure on contentious issues such as textbook content. Politicians may also have their personal agendas. A minister of education authorized the *Year 2000* program (see chapter 1) largely because, as a teacher, he had successfully used its approaches when he taught grade 9 math. A recent attempt to begin a "traditional" school within a public school district was passed by a four-to-three vote on a school board split between right-wing and left-wing views. But after the next election the vote could be reversed.

Finally, our cultural context affects education. North American society, for instance, has a strong streak of anti-intellectualism. Many people value experience over theoretical thought. Achievement in school counts less than in other cultures. Businesses, for instance, pay little attention to high school transcripts when hiring. In the U.S., few students take rigorous courses like senior algebra or physics. Only the top colleges have strict entrance standards. Parents value academic progress less than Japanese ones. As a result, American schools cannot offer a program that is as intellectually demanding.

North American individualism also puts a stamp on school curricula. The notion that persons should look out mainly for themselves without regard for others affects how parents evaluate their students' progress in school--and what pressures they put on schools. People no longer value a shared ethos or a sense of a community where people support and care for each other. Curriculum guides and textbooks often promote the concept that persons can and should decide their own values. School-based planning must counter such general trends by emphasizing respect, caring, responsibility, trustworthiness, and fairness.

The cultural context also has some positive consequences for school curricula. School programs today avoid blatant racial and sexual stereotyping. They also take up environmental concerns. Further, as public opinion increasingly favors choice in education, public school boards more often allow schools to operate special programs. In my community, for instance, that includes a fine arts school, French and Japanese immersion schools, and fundamental schools that stress traditional education and Judeo-Christian values.

The main point of this section is that schools are part of society and reflect what is going on in it. More than we often realize, the demands of our social, economic, political, and cultural contexts shape our programs.

■ Your meeting to discuss the groundings of the science curriculum went well. The group agreed that learning about the applications of science and technology should be an important part of the science program. It also reached a consensus that science education should involve, as much as possible, a problem-based approach.

A lively discussion took place on how much of this would actually be possible. One person pointed out that elementary teachers often have little training in science, and are not willing to take much time to plan hands-on activities. The expectations of colleges, another said, force secondary teachers to teach theoretical rather than relevant science. Moreover, added a third, parents and school board members seem more concerned about language and math basics than about science. Therefore they are reluctant to make enough funds available for science materials.

The group decided to poll a sample of teachers to find out their views and constraints. You agreed to draft the section of the poll dealing with the context of teaching science. As a first step, list the relevant contextual factors, with ways in which each might affect the science program.

PLAYERS IN THE CURRICULUM FIELD

■ Your science planning committee also decided to seek input from curriculum "players" who are not teachers and yet may affect the design or success of your science program. You therefore divided your committee in groups of three. You asked each group to make a chart showing (1) the types of people your team should consult, (2) how they may affect the written and experienced curriculum, and (3) how you should seek their input and advice. Prepare a sample chart with these points.

For successful implementation, curriculum planners must consider the beliefs, values, positions, and roles of curriculum "players." These players include students, teachers, administrators, parents, interest groups, school boards, government officials, and professional organizations. Planners also must heed the personal needs of students, teachers, and supervisory staff, and how they interact. In this section I discuss the roles of various curriculum players. In the next I look at the dynamics of curriculum implementation.

Curriculum players exercise authority and influence in different ways. Teachers adapt, plan, and implement programs that directly affect and guide students. Governing bodies, central offices, umbrella organizations, and school administrators institute policies and provide teachers with curriculum support. Other interest groups share their insights with those charged with planning and implementing curriculum. Usually most are motivated by a desire to promote students' welfare. They want their influence to help students become more knowledgeable, perceptive, responsive, and responsible persons.

Teachers make most of the vital curriculum decisions behind the closed classroom door. The resulting experienced curriculum may or may not correspond to top-down directives or the policies set by the school (Richard Clark in Tanner 1988, 186-87). Teachers wield much power in deciding their pedagogy, content choice, activities, and resources. They are well-educated professionals who tend to make their own decisions. They also seek their students' advice, or, at least, are sensitive to their reactions (How did you feel about . . . ? What would you like to know about . . . ?) Giving students a sense of ownership in their own progress improves the learning atmosphere.

At the school building level the curriculum players include teachers, coordinators, and department heads, principals, and parents. Coordinators, department heads, and principals stimulate teachers to set and choose school-wide curriculum guidelines and resources. They also help groups of teachers set priorities for school-wide curriculum work and plan jointly-taught units. They react to teachers' yearly overviews and specific units. The effectiveness of a school's curriculum planning often depends on the leadership of one or more curriculum "catalysts." That may or may not be the principal. Schools implement and maintain their educational focus and quality only as long as an internal leader with a compelling educational mission and the support of the school community acts as an effective change agent (Van Brummelen 1989, 32-34; 1993, 14, 26).

The Bible assigns first responsibility for educating children to parents. Governments have become the agencies that raise and distribute school tax funds. As such, they have taken on a prescriptive role in setting curriculum policies. It is neither necessary nor desirable, however, for governments to do more than ensure that schools enable children to function well in society. That is, they should set minimum standards and see to it that all schools provide a safe and secure environment. Local parent groups that set policies will have a stake in the quality of education offered. Such groups could be geographical communities or ones with common interests. When parents agree with a school's vision and keep closely involved, the resulting esprit de corps often fosters a good educational climate. Parents who together with teachers build a unified vision for the school affect the quality of education much more than would top-down regulations.

Parents have a stake in the education of their children. Today parents are well-informed, willing, and able to contribute to school policies. Schools do well to seek parental input on major curriculum decisions.

They may use parent advisory committees or education committees with parent members. Generally, schools benefit from parent communities that feel ownership of the school. In the 1970s I was the curriculum coordinator of a system of four schools. We introduced a family life education program, then very controversial, without any objections or complaints. The main reason was that we fully involved parents in planning and setting up the program. The program, updated several times, still functions today.

Interest groups that include but go beyond parents also affect school curriculum. Religious groups have influenced the use of textbooks. Business interests have tried to influence schools to raise reading and writing standards as well as foster personal traits such as dependability and teamwork (Pratt 1994, 43). Language interest groups have sought immersion programs. Others have lobbied to establish fine arts or Montessori schools. Political pressure groups may, of course, run counter to what most educators believe to be important. Some may push for higher standards in the basics, with accountability through regular testing. Educators may respond that schools teach basics well but need to do more to meet emotional and social needs.

Wise school leaders listen carefully to community concerns. They try to build a consensus before making important decisions. Sometimes radically different views make that impossible. In most English-speaking jurisdictions, public school leaders strive for educational conformity. I believe they would serve democratic interests in a pluralist society more by encouraging tax-funded alternative schools. The interest communities supporting such schools could be based on pedagogical, cultural, or religious beliefs and values. Such alternatives would allow for more curricular diversity. Parents, interest groups, students, and teachers would feel they have a stake in such schools.

School boards set policies that affect curriculum. They approve statements of philosophy. They set subject time allotments. They make program decisions (e.g., to expand or reduce the art program). They decide on testing programs. They select major resources. In public systems, school boards often feel caught between government agencies and teacher unions. As a result, they often react to situations rather than proactively setting out curriculum directions. Public school boards and regional organizations of Christian schools often employ curriculum consultants. Their roles are most effective if they stimulate local curriculum planning. Such consultants can make or break top-down policies. They can, for instance, set the agenda for professional development and make decisions about resource allocation.

Central education agencies at the state, provincial, or national levels have several curriculum roles. According to Susan Lusi (in Elmore and Fuhrman 1994, 124), staffs of such agencies need a shared set of beliefs, values, and purpose to be effective. This is difficult to achieve when they often have 1,000 or more employees. Yet they often mandate subject content, high school graduation requirements, minimum time allotments, and testing programs. They also may provide financial incentives to encourage, for instance, teaching English as a second language or piloting new programs.

These central agencies also develop curriculum guides and assessment programs. Curriculum guides may contain a bare listing of course content, or give detailed content and skill requirements, or provide conceptual maps for big ideas and approaches. In all three cases, evidence suggests that teachers typically interpret the guides to justify their current practices. Teachers also often are unsure how to change to implement new frameworks. In short, the influence of curriculum guides is seldom strong (A. Porter, J. Smithson and E. Osthoff in Elmore and Fuhrman 1994, 161).

Testing programs begun by regional authorities have an impact on curriculum mainly when tests are "high stake," i.e., when they have important consequences. Test results affect teachers' curriculum only when they have a direct bearing on the future of students and the status of teachers. In the American Advanced Placement Program, for instance, exam content in effect becomes the curriculum since good results lead to college credits. The same is true for high school leaving exams used to decide university entrance. Whether other testing programs mandated by central agencies affect the curriculum likely depends on the degree of follow-up by individual principals.

Tests can have unexpected results. Some American states have instituted minimum competency high school graduation tests. As a result, more students take remedial mathematics, often taught through mechanical drill. In states without such tests, more students have enrolled in advanced math courses. In other words, the tests have had a limiting influence on the type of math taken, especially by students of average ability (A. Porter, J. Smithson and E. Osthoff in Elmore and Fuhrman 1994, 157; D. Cohen and J. Spillane in Grant 1992, 16-19).

Politicians set policies that affect the curriculum. They deal with large educational budgets and react to parental pressures. One Canadian provincial cabinet some years ago took a personal hand in approving the main reading series used in public schools. More commonly, ministers of education or state superintendents will ask legislators to approve changes in high school graduation requirements, testing initiatives, or major new programs (e.g., drug or consumer education).

General policies intended to set a direction for educational programs seldom live up to politicians' advance billing. To be successful, they need to be compatible with the structures and *modi operandi* of schools. They must be workable and not raise undue negative reaction. They must call for incremental rather than wholesale change. They must be implemented in a climate of accommodation where both teachers and the public are willing to give their support (Walker 1990, 420-430). It is uncommon for all these conditions to occur simultaneously. The *Year 2000* program described in chapter 1, for instance, was quite successful at the primary level. There it received the backing of parents and teachers because it boosted teachers' current practices. The plans for higher grade levels, however, ran counter to the views of many parents and teachers. Mostly, they were scrapped.

I will mention some other curriculum players only briefly, mainly to stress the complexity of curriculum decision-making. Professional groups like the National Council of Teachers of Mathematics through its resources and recommendations affect the thinking of curriculum planners. When textbook publishers win central adoption in states like Texas or California, they have much impact on classroom curriculum. Curriculum specialists in college faculties of education serve regularly as consultants to curriculum planning and assessment teams. Particularly in the U.S., courts make decisions that affect, for instance, choice of textbooks or the inclusiveness of education. Foundations may influence curriculum by funding certain education projects. Finally, the media not only reports but also sways public opinion and student attitudes and behavior. It thus indirectly affects curriculum policies and practices.

- The players in curriculum policy setting, planning, and implementation form a complex network. Are there players not mentioned in this section? If so, who are they and what is their role and influence? Now go back to the chart you made at the beginning of this section. Are there any changes you would now make? Is it possible to seek too much input when designing a program?

THE DYNAMICS OF CURRICULUM IMPLEMENTATION

Curriculum plans often sit on shelves without being implemented. There are many reasons for this. Grandiose plans may clash with the limited expertise or time of teachers. Many teachers prefer a conformist role or lean toward curriculum inertia. Curriculum innovations require teacher change and signal more work, strain, and fatigue. Teachers therefore need to be convinced that there is a clear payoff. Even then, barriers may remain. There may be a lack of clarity about the new initiative. Teachers may be uncertain about the outcomes. They may feel a perceived or actual lack of time, knowledge, skills, or resources. Schools may not want to open themselves to criticism from public interest groups.

No simple formulas exist to bring about curriculum change. Effective implementation depends on matching the features of the innovation with its context. What are the needs of and benefits to students? How committed are school personnel and what are their strengths? What are the school's current programs? What resources are available? Below I describe some key factors necessary for successful implementation. I use the conclusions of Michael Fullan (in Elmore and Fuhrman 1994, 186-202); Ornstein and Hunkins (1988, 223-48); Pratt (1994, 326-40); J. Snyder, F. Bolin and K. Zumwalt (in Jackson 1992, 402-35); Walker (1990, 246ff., 383); and Werner (1983, 120-24).

Curriculum proposals imposed on schools from the top down have a poor record in improving education. But neither has school-based curriculum reform been often sustainable over a period of time. Michael Fullan, a foremost researcher on educational change, has concluded that "in the mid to long run, there can be no district development without school development, or school development without district development" (Fullan in Elmore and Fuhrman 1994, 198). For Christian schools, the word "regional service organization" replaces "district." In other words, an ethos of curriculum collaboration must exist between central administrators and local schools and teachers. Central coordinators provide essential stimuli and support for change. Left by themselves, local schools seldom maintain change. They benefit from being part of a network of schools that implements new programs. Top-down and bottom-up strategies need to be coordinated (Fullan 1994, 186-202).

The support of central administrators is necessary but not sufficient for successful implementation. Wide-ranging consultation needs to establish a climate of trust and relate the innovation to the mission and vision of the school. Teachers, administrators, and parents must believe that the project meets local needs that benefit students. They must understand fully the rationale, goals, and central features of the proposed change. The principal needs to support the initiative, as does an effective in-school leader-facilitator (not necessarily the principal). The change needs district and local advocates who can deflect controversy. Planners need to build in evaluation procedures that monitor the effects of the change.

Teachers must sense how an innovation matches their own curriculum orientation (if it doesn't, it is unlikely to succeed). Teachers must become genuinely committed to and take ownership of the planned change. They should be involved in reviewing, exploring, and evaluating plans and recommended resources. They need systematic in-service training and support. Without adequate knowledge or skills, teachers seldom make intended changes. They should participate in frequent formal and informal consultations and decision-making. Supportive feedback and help with unexpected problems should complement their practice. They must feel free to learn from their initiatives and possible failures, and to make revisions for their own situation. They need adequate human and material resources for the change. They themselves can ease implementation by convincing students that the change will benefit them, and by getting their cooperation.

It takes time to convince people of the value of curriculum change. It takes even more time to orient teachers and get them ready to implement a new program. Substituting one textbook for another or revising an English course to include more writing is not all that demanding. Implementing a new program that requires major restructuring or a value reorientation is far more time-consuming. For that, a local staff may need a year or more of discussion. This is true especially if they first review the current program and consider several alternatives. A year of pilot implementation and two or three years for full implementation may follow initial deliberation. If the initiative is a major one, it may be the only curriculum innovation a staff can address in a school year. Staffs should therefore set goal and time priorities for their planning. It is easy for principals and coordinators to ask teachers to address too much at once, or to forget that effective and long-lasting curriculum change is usually limited in its scope.

Curriculum planners should be aware of both benefits and costs of curriculum initiatives for individual teachers. Decker Walker (1990, 408) includes as benefits renewed enthusiasm, greater self-esteem and status, professional contact and involvement, and more teaching satisfaction. There also are costs, however. Curriculum change takes time and effort. It involves risk of failure and embarrassment. Also, less satisfaction in teaching may result if the proposed changes do not work out. Some initial resistance is therefore normal. Planners help to overcome this by giving first-hand information about the project, suggesting how teachers can implement programs to fit their individual styles, and facilitating early success (Walker 1990, 410).

There is, finally, a dilemma embedded in the conditions for successful implementation. Teachers usually implement change only when they believe it to be worthwhile. But some will not accept its benefit until they themselves experience it. They will not try until convinced and they will not be convinced until they try. Some will change their minds if they hear that other teachers whom they respect have used the approach successfully. Curriculum planners, however, will not be able to convince all teachers of the value of a change. Planners may decide not to force strong opponents to make the change; antagonist are unlikely to implement it in the way planners intend.

The book *A Vision with a Task* (Stronks and Blomberg 1993) discusses in detail how schools can generate intentions and implement programs that realize its vision.

■ In the last section you identified curriculum players and their roles as you dealt with them as a science curriculum revision committee. Plan a three-year strategy that would help bring or keep the players "on-side" as you develop and make plans to implement the new program.

CURRICULUM EVALUATION

Curriculum evaluation assigns a value to a school's or school system's curriculum. It assesses the worth of a program, a course, a unit, a pedagogical approach, or the intents of any of these. It does so in terms of the school's mission and aims. Curriculum evaluation should consider the actual effects of a program, whether intended or not. Its purpose is to use findings to make decisions. Such decisions take into account the beliefs held about curriculum groundings, the goals of a school, and the implementation context.

Curriculum evaluation differs from but overlaps with student evaluation. Its focus is on the general impact of a program, rather than on the outcome for individual learners. Teachers may use the results of a test to help students overcome personal weaknesses (student evaluation) but also to find out the success of a particular approach (curriculum evaluation). They may also use systematic observation to be able to help students' individual progress during conferences (student evaluation). An analysis of the observations as a whole also may lead, however, to curriculum revisions to improve overall learning (curriculum evaluation).

No easy formulas exist to judge the value of an educational program. Evaluation takes place before, during, and after the planning and implementation process. Evaluators question, observe, and analyze program groundings, intents, contexts, planned and actual learning activities, resources used, and effects on other programs. What makes evaluation even more complex is that evaluators (whether teachers or program planners) have a personal stake in the success of a program. They may find it difficult to take distance and be impartial. Yet they are most familiar and in the best position to evaluate a program in a particular setting. External assessments such as those designed by departments of education are more impartial but draw only general conclusions. They may, for instance, assess the abilities of grade 7 students to solve math problems. Their conclusions may lead them to recommend general program revisions. They cannot, however, give the best way to teach problem solving to a particular student or class.

The type of curriculum evaluation used depends on the curriculum orientation of the evaluators. Academic traditionalists use the results of content and skill-based tests to decide whether groups of students are making satisfactory progress with a certain curricula. Evaluators in the technical orientation devise instruments that include tests, inventories, and check lists. Then they gather and analyze data using suitable statistical methods. They interpret the data in terms of the initial behavioral objectives. They base their advice on the discrepancy between the objectives and actual results. Once their recommendations are implemented, the cycle is repeated.

Note that both the academic traditional and technical evaluations emphasize quantitative data. Such data sheds light on student success in learning specific content or skills in a particular program. The evaluation is limited in scope, however, in that it does not concern itself with how the program affects the type of person the student is becoming.

Evaluators in the deliberative and constructivist orientations, on the other hand, believe that qualitative evaluation is essential for a complete picture. Elliot Eisner, for instance, recommends a process of educational critique that yields a rich subjective description of how students experience curriculum. Evaluators observe school life, the tone of learning, the quality of student work, how events arose and affected the participants, and the subtleties of individual situations (Eisner 1979, 190-260).

This type of evaluation has four interrelated steps. First, observers consider the question "What is happening here?" Second, they describe the situation as accurately as they can. Third, they interpret what they observed in terms of worldview and contextual criteria. Finally, they draw conclusions about the quality and merit of what they observed (Doll 1989, 269). Critical theorists use similar steps but their interpretations emphasize socioeconomic aspects much more than Eisner.

The advantage of a deliberative approach to evaluation is that it sheds light on a curriculum's overall impact. It addresses more basic educational concerns than would a purely quantitative appraisal. The disadvantage is that the criteria used to decide which observations are noteworthy and how to interpret data not only differ from one person to the next but often remain implicit. Resulting reports may say as much about evaluators as about the program being evaluated.

Balanced and thorough curriculum evaluations use both internal and external evaluators as well as both quantitative and qualitative data. One aspect of such an evaluation is teacher self-evaluation of a unit as described in the last chapter. Evaluations of new programs take place during a program's development, while it is implemented, and after its conclusion. Finally, large-scale projects may use a meta-evaluation to assess the evaluation process itself in terms of its effectiveness.

Curriculum designers constantly evaluate the products of their thinking and planning in terms of their beliefs about education, their curriculum intents, and other programs with which they are familiar. Are the intents clear for teachers and students? Do the content, recommended resources, and pedagogical strategies match the aims of schooling? Do they match the context in which teachers will implement the program? Does the program meet quality and quantity standards? Evaluators use answers to such questions formatively to improve the program.

Most evaluation takes place informally and internally at this point. But plans are also often sent to external appraisers for reaction and input. A group of teachers may ask their principal to give feedback on a unit plan. Large-scale programs may ask external teachers or experts to answer questionnaires about program drafts or to meet with the planners to discuss reactions. For Christians it is important that such evaluation goes beyond the feasibility of the program but includes a foundational analysis. What keys to understanding the world does the curriculum use? In whom or in what does it suggest students put their trust? What does the curriculum presume and endorse about truth and basic values?

Evaluation continues to take place during implementation. Reflective teachers constantly assess the effects of a new approach as they teach. New programs intended for groups of schools require more formal evaluation at this stage. Pilot testing often gives positively skewed results since it tends to include enthusiastic volunteers. Field testing in a representative sample of classrooms yields a more accurate assessment of a program's qualities. Such field testing can uncover unexpected results or problems. It gauges student and teacher reaction, and provides input for improving the program before it is widely shared.

In short, evaluation during the implementation stage is formative. It involves students and teachers as well as planners or evaluators designated by them who advise as they observe and collect data. Evaluation strategies include informal and formal observation, interviews, checklists and rating scales, teacher and student self reports, and achievement tests. Evaluators ask questions about ease of implementation, classroom climate, teaching strategies, distribution and use of resources, student learning, student involvement and interest (including those with special needs), balance of learning activities, teacher reaction, sufficiency of in-service training, and so on.

Curricula are also evaluated after their implementation. This may occur after the first general tryout or after several years of use. Early after-the-fact evaluations may still be formative. Later evaluations are more summative. They describe the program's general impact, perhaps with recommendations to revise it or to develop a new program.

Large scale evaluations involve both foundational analysis and assessment of observable features. Is the program in harmony with current beliefs about curriculum groundings? What effects does the program have, not only in terms of cognitive knowledge and skills, but also in terms of values, dispositions, and commitments? What are the program's strengths and weaknesses? Do the results justify the cost in time, emotional investment, and money? What impact does the hidden curriculum have on the program? How do results compare with those of other programs? Often university specialists in measurement and evaluation head teams that evaluate a large scale program. Persons with vested interests in a program may see such external evaluations as a threat. Evaluators are therefore careful to build a positive climate. They solicit the cooperation of teachers and students and make regular progress reports.

Schools that want to use the results of such evaluations must first ask in what ways the evaluators' beliefs about education match their own. They may disagree with advice because of a different perspective about the aims of education. Some years ago, for instance, a government-sponsored evaluation in my jurisdiction showed that the attitudes to science of Christian school students was less positive than of their public school counterparts. A closer analysis revealed, however, that the problem was not the students' attitude but the bias of the test questions. Christian school students had been discerningly negative in their reaction to statements that claimed, for instance, that science is a key to solving the world's problems.

■ The science curriculum committee that you head has available to it the results of a major curriculum evaluation conducted at the grades 7 and 10 levels by your department of education. While it concluded that science education is generally satisfactory, it also points to some problems that you need to address (these are the actual problems listed in the 1991 evaluation of British Columbia's science curriculum):

»a slight but significant decrease over the last five years in student performance in science, most noticeably at the grade 4 level (from 64.2% to 60.9% correct on 48 common items);

»a marginal general scientific knowledge at the grades 4 and 7 levels;

»a perceived weakness in the development of rational thinking skills in science;

»a concern about students' abilities to recognize and describe different points of view in socioscientific issues;

»a pattern, in many classrooms, of science teaching that does not engage learners;

»a concern about the amount of class time devoted to science, particularly at the lower grades; and

»a concern regarding the [low] number of students with positive attitudes toward a career in science (Bateson *et al.,* 1992, 11, 80).

How would the availability of this report affect your committee's planning? How would you make use of the above results?

■ You have asked a subcommittee of your science curriculum committee to plan a curriculum evaluation for your new program as it is developed and implemented. Make a one-page outline of such an evaluation plan.

SUMMARY

Curriculum planning takes place at many levels: national, state or provincial, regional, school, and classroom. How groups or individuals go about such planning depends on their curriculum orientation. Academic traditionalists may list content and skills. Proponents of the technical orientation most often use a variation of the four-step Tyler rationale: find objectives, choose learning experiences, organize the experiences, and evaluate success in attaining the objectives. Deliberators get theoreticians, curriculum specialists, teachers, and students to interact and clarify how theory and practice interact to develop an acceptable program. Critical theorists ask questions that relate socioeconomic concerns to curriculum.

A more realistic and usable model of curriculum development first recognizes the groundings and contextual factors that frame curriculum development. It allows the proposed intents, activities, and resources to emerge together as developers go about their planning, evaluation, and implementation. The contextual frame factors that planners need to consider include economic, social, political, and cultural ones. They must also take into account a great diversity of curriculum players such as students, teachers, parents, interest groups, central state authorities, and professional organizations.

The most promising approach to curriculum implementation involves catalysts external to the school working closely with local schools. For a new program to succeed, teachers must be involved in making decisions and feel ownership. They also must accept the worldview, values, and aims of the program. Curriculum evaluation is a necessary aspect of curriculum improvement. It is an ongoing process that starts during the development process, and continues during and after implementation. Such evaluation needs to go beyond assessing whether a program's objectives have been attained. It must assess a program's total effect in terms of a school's mission and aims.

REFLECTING

1. As the new principal of a school you face a visit by a Department of Education external evaluation team early in November. Almost immediately upon your arrival in the school, you submitted the school's mission statement and philosophy, as well as yearly course outlines and sample student evaluation products. After its visit, the team points out some strengths and weaknesses in your school's program:

   »the teaching approaches are well executed but one-sided, emphasizing teacher presentations, discussions, and individual student work;

   »the general school atmosphere is positive and enhances the school's stated wish to help students become respectful and responsible citizens;

   »the school is not as successful in its goal to enable students to use and develop a diversity of gifts. Little experimentation takes place in science classes; the art program consists of half hours of haphazard activities at the end of the week; students have little opportunity for personal response; and teachers do little to provide for special needs except where aides are available for students with severe handicaps.

   »the school has a top-notch library but it is not well used. The school's textbook and audiovisual resources are adequate but outdated in social studies.

   »the school maintains solid academic standards, but little formative student evaluation takes place in the writing program.

   You know that your teachers have been quite comfortable with their programs. Some older ones will be reluctant to spend time reviewing programs and introducing changes. Yet you believe that such a process will reinvigorate the staff, and you are glad that the team's observations confirmed your own. Outline a process that (a) tries to get the staff onside, (b) sets priorities among issues that need to be addressed, and (c) begins to plan and implement improvements.

2. Models help us focus on the essentials of a process, but they are metaphors that also constrain. Compare the strengths and weaknesses of the Tyler rationale with the model of curriculum planning presented in this chapter.

3. If someone asked you to list the three or four key questions you would ask when evaluating a program, which ones would you list?

Chapter 10
The Teacher's Role
in Curriculum

■ Over a ten year period, English teacher Naomi White taught a future evangelist, a boxer who was to lose an eye in a brawl, two boys later convicted of theft and murder, and a student who now "beats his head against a padded wall in the state asylum." She remarks, "I must have been a great help to these pupils—I taught them the rhyming schemes of the Elizabethan sonnet and how to diagram a complex sentence" (White in Harmin and Gregory, 1974, 84).

No doubt, Naomi White taught her students a great deal more. But reflective teachers do question the short- and long-term effects of their teaching. Sometimes they feel caught between opposing forces. They want to plan hands-on science programs that also deal with social issues but can't find enough time to prepare. They know that statistics is more important than simplifying polynomial expressions, but they must prepare for a district-wide math exam that excludes statistics. They realize the need to foster open-ended response but their strenuous class dynamics makes it undoable. They teach for commitment to a positive way of life but find that family and peer influences undermine their attempts.

Teachers fall short of their ideals. That should not surprise them. Nor should it discourage them as long as they try to plan and implement curricula that deal meaningfully with significant content and issues. Their programs can help many of their students grow toward responsible maturity and commitment. They can nurture students' insights and gifts so that they learn to balance independence with personal and communal responsibility. Teachers sometimes despair when they focus on students they cannot seem to reach, or whose later lives display little of their influence. But they do affect the lives of many students positively, often more than they realize.

Let me give an example. Teacher Curt Gesch published excerpts from answers to essay questions in his exams. Sarah describes how her grade 10 short story unit taught her to be more sensitive to people around her. She ponders why teenagers, herself included, often act erratically: "We run on emotion most of the time, and sometimes the emotion is due to fear of what the family will think, our friends' reactions, and all in all the people around us." Sheryl tells about the five most important things she learned in grade 12. She became appalled at social injustice in society today by studying the Biblical prophecy of Amos and the book *Black Like Me*. She learned how human sin demands discipline. She discovered that work is a gift from God, and that leisure time is time for "re-creation." Finally,

Hemingway's *The Sun Also Rises* was her springboard for reviewing how others and she herself search for meaning in life. Sheryl concludes that "although there is always room for more knowledge, I am grateful for what I have learned so far" (Gesch 1993c).

I regularly ask groups of college students about teachers who made an impact on their lives. Usually they first talk about the types of persons those teachers were: their unconditional love, their genuine desire to bring out the best in their students, their superb helpfulness with both academic and personal concerns. Often, however, students also will begin to see how those teachers planned and structured curricula to fit their beliefs about what was important for their students. And the curriculum shaped their thinking, usually incrementally over a period of time.

Think back to your schooling. Can you think of cases where the content and structure of the curriculum made a difference in your life or the lives of your classmates, either positively or negatively? What does this imply for your curriculum planning?

In this book I have shown that all curricula have a worldview foundation. I have outlined what I believe to be the consequences of a Biblical worldview for school programs. In this chapter I want to make three concluding points about the implementation of these ideas.

First, all teaching involves initiation into distinct patterns of behavior and thought. As such, it unavoidably encourages commitment of one kind or another. Teachers need to live and nurture commitments that are clear and defensible. Second, teachers in Christian schools may and should boldly initiate students into the Christian tradition. They also deal honestly, however, with the shortcomings of that tradition and present other belief systems fairly. They enable and allow students to freely make well-founded personal commitments as they mature. Third, public schools are not and cannot be neutral. Yet they must serve all segments of society. Christian teachers in the public school may not proselytize and must present different points of view fairly and sensitively. Yet their curricula can without apology reflect those aspects of the Judeo-Christian worldview and its values that society still accepts as universal principles.

TEACHING FOR COMMITMENT

Critical theorist Michael Apple (1983) argues that most teachers do little more than execute top-down prescribed curriculum directives and plans as they teach. As such, he claims that as deskilled technicians they think little about the effect of their curricula. Consequently, their teaching perpetuates the current economic and political hegemony. That is, the "official" curriculum teaches students to become committed to the dominant cultural values and class structures.

There are many exceptions to Apple's broad generalizations, and I disagree with his political agenda. Yet one of his main conclusions is an important one. The curriculum, Apple holds, is never a neutral instrument. Usually it serves up a superficial liberalism that leads to ethical and social starvation. That is why, Apple concludes, teachers ought to change their curricula and use them as pedagogical tools for cultural change.

Some critical theorists do precisely that—in public schools. Barry Kanpol (1993, 203-211), for instance, describes three studies where teachers strayed from the "official" curriculum and taught the value commitments of critical theorists. In one school a sexual assault issue became the basis for a grade 8 unit on race and gender rights. In another, a grade 4 teacher taught a global education unit that dealt with the importance of creating community and resisting individualism even when people's customs and habits differ. In a third school, the English as a Second Language curriculum emphasized the problems of the marginalized in society. Teachers used societal conflicts to stress the need to question hierarchical authority. In all cases the curriculum led students to consider the teachers' moral and social inclinations. In short, as the teachers taught with commitment, they taught for commitment.

Christian views of righteousness and justice differ from those of most critical theorists. If Christians in education take seriously the teachings of Jesus, they will, however, like the critical theorists, teach with and for commitment. They are images of God who responsively and responsibly plan units and courses that are framed by a Biblical worldview. Their belief in Biblical love and justice cannot but affect how they plan and implement their program.

That does not mean Christian teachers put children into narrow Christian straitjackets. Prejudice and intolerance contradict what Jesus stood for. Christian teachers want their students to develop critical discernment. For this, students need a knowledge base that they apply to a variety of questions and issues. Gradually teachers help and stimulate their students to make prudent commitments on which they base personal and communal decisions.

As Elmer Thiessen shows, nurturing children into critical reflection, open-mindedness, and normal rational autonomy is impossible without first initiating them into a stable and coherent tradition (1993, 141-43). All traditions inevitably include faith and commitment. These, indeed, form a necessary framework for developing critical faculties. Therefore, we need to dare teach for defensible commitment and "spare our children and students the hell of non-commitment" (Thiessen 1993, 277). Christians do not need to apologize for teaching commitment to the self-sacrificing love, righteousness, and justice of the Christian faith.

To teach a "value-less" or "objective" curriculum that supposedly leaves teaching for commitment to the home has one of several results.

First, students may without much thought accept the dominant material-istic, self-centered values of our society. Second, they also may learn to believe that objective concepts and skills are more important than values. They then accept that the structures and patterns of our culture are neutral, and that their particular choice of values and commitments is not all that pivotal. Or, third, they may accept the values of the models that mean most of them in their lives—their parents, their peers, or media or sports heroes.

Schools, especially Christian ones, owe their students more. Chris-tian faith has a great deal to say to society about love and compassion, about justice and truth, about rights and responsibilities. Christian teachers cannot and do not demand students to commit themselves to specific beliefs and values. But they can teach students that commitment to defensible beliefs and values is crucial in their lives. And they can also show that the Christian faith, despite the shortcomings of its followers, provides a sound basis for a just and compassionate society.

TEACHERS AND THE CURRICULUM IN CHRISTIAN SCHOOLS

In this section I summarize what Elmer Thiessen has written about Christian nurture in his book, *Teaching for Commitment* (1993, 245-267). I apply his conclusions to Christian school curricula.

Thiessen shows that every child is necessarily initiated into a particular religious (or irreligious) tradition. He argues that the role of schools to systematically initiate students into their human inheritance is not only desirable but necessary. When young, children need to feel secure and at one with a stable and coherent primary culture. In a society that increasingly excludes religion from that tradition, Christian schools initiate children into their Christian inheritance. Much early initiation takes place through stories. And Bible stories "provide children with the necessary tools for further growth and development in the area of religion" (249).

But, Thiessen continues, Christian schools must do more than initiate. Their goal is also to guide students into normal rationality and autonomy. While absolute independence is impossible and freedom occurs within a certain context, students with a stable initiation base are in the best position to achieve personal identity and appropriate autonomy once they reach adolescence. Especially at that age teachers must respect the freedom of students to affirm or deny their Christian heritage, and avoid unwarranted indoctrination. Schools "should attempt to foster both growth in rational groundings of Christian convictions and honest and serious grappling with doubt, questions, and objections to Christian convictions" (Thiessen 1993, 263). They should therefore also discuss alternate religious and philosophical belief system, Thiessen concludes.

Now it may not be easy for teachers in Christian schools, especially in middle and high schools, to keep initiation and growth toward normal autonomy in balance. On the one hand students crave the stability and coherence that sensitive and tactful initiation can give. And many parents who enroll children in Christian schools like "safe" climates. But on the other hand, students need to develop their critical and creative faculties to make their own decisions. They also need to learn to deal with the consequences of such decisions.

All this means that Christian school teachers need to give students curricular room to examine various views and to formulate their own, especially when they become adolescents. Teachers should challenge students not to give easy or pat answers to difficult issues. They should present non-Christian beliefs and positions honestly and fairly. They should admit that Christians do not have all the answers to social and moral problems. They should admit that they themselves have questions about, for instance, why God allows so much suffering to take place. They should show how God's common grace gives both Christians and non-Christians insights and abilities to create worthwhile and salutary books, economic theories, works of art and music, and technological breakthroughs. They should help them discern the strengths and weaknesses of such phenomena as well as of positions taken by both Christians and non-Christians.

Christian school teachers need to remember three key points as they plan their classroom curriculum. First, they must boldly initiate their students into their cultural and Christian heritage, using, for instance, the curriculum guidelines of this book. Using a supposedly "neutral" curriculum to which they add a course in religious studies and occasional value discussions is not sufficient. At best that initiates students into a dualistic view of the world where Christian faith is a private concern that has little to do with the warp and woof of life in society. Second, Christian school teachers must encourage students to grow in normal rational autonomy (i.e., in being able to think critically and discerningly, recognizing that such thinking always takes place within the bounds of faith commitments). For this, genuine and honest response in the transcendence phase of learning is particularly important. Third, such teachers need to teach with commitment if they are to teach for commitment. Their commitment must affect the way they make decisions in the classroom, the way they structure their classroom, the way they assess student learning—and the way they plan curriculum.

CHRISTIAN TEACHERS
AND THE CURRICULUM IN PUBLIC SCHOOLS

Public school teachers face a dilemma. On the one hand, by law they must remain religiously neutral and their curriculum must be secular. Such laws and regulations intend to ensure that public schools can serve all sectors of our pluralistic society. On the other hand, few teachers want to reduce their teaching to the lowest common value denominator. Most primary teachers, for instance, want to initiate their students into standards of behavior that reflect respect and tolerance. Most teachers choose literary selections that illustrate or promote discussion of values they hold to be important in life. Teachers recognize that their role includes encouraging commitment to a set of basic values without which society cannot function.

Most educators and parents still hold to universal value principles rooted in the Judeo-Christian tradition. The moral education framework of the Association of Supervision and Curriculum Development published in *Educational Leadership*, for instance, recommended that public schools should teach students to respect human dignity, care about the welfare of others, integrate individual interests and social responsibilities, and demonstrate integrity (ASCD Panel on Moral Education 1988, 5). In an article on ethics without indoctrination in the same issue, Richard Paul indicated that essential moral virtues that public schools must teach include humility, courage, empathy, integrity, perseverance, and fair-mindedness (Paul 1988, 15).

Significantly, Thomas Lickona's writings on character education in the public schools quickly became popular in the early 1990s. Lickona shows how religion has always been a crucial moral force in American life. American social reform and civil rights leaders, for example, were motivated by the deep religious belief that we are all equal in the sight of God who calls us to live in harmony and justice (Lickona 1991, 40). Lickona then builds a case for teaching respect and responsibility in public schools. Respect, based on the Golden Rule (''do unto others as you would have them do to you'') includes respect for other humans, for the whole complex of life, for authority, and for property. Responsibility means that we help rather than hurt others, that we are dependable, and that we keep our commitments. He shows how honesty, fairness, tolerance, prudence, self-discipline, helpfulness, compassion, cooperation, courage, and ''a host of democratic values'' stem from respect and responsibility. People may disagree about the application of these values in specific situations. But, Lickona adds, almost all teachers and parents will readily agree with this basic common moral ground (Lickona 1991, 43-47).

It is morally indefensible for a Christian teacher to use the public school classroom as a forum for evangelism. When you sign a contract to teach in a public school, you agree to teach a curriculum that is suitable for all children, no matter what their background. You may not promote or encourage commitment to a specific religion inside your classroom. Yet your curriculum cannot but foster a certain view of life, a certain set of values, certain dispositions and commitments. For the Christian teacher the basic common moral ground outlined by Lickona is a good starting point.

How, then, as a Christian teacher in the public school, can you plan a curriculum that is suitable for a system that must be fair to all religious (and nonreligious) positions, and yet fits your beliefs? First, choose content that helps students to function well in society and contribute to it. Such content should call for personal response and encourage thinking about the nature and purpose of life. The content also should lead to discussions about what Egan calls "transcendent human values." You can keep in mind the subject area goals discussed in chapter 6. Secondly, your pedagogy can reflect the implications of a Biblical view of the person as described in chapter 7. Again, your teaching should lead to students' personal response in a way that is appropriate for their age level.

Christian faith has been one of the foundations of western culture for many centuries. You can acquaint students with that heritage, especially in social studies and literature. To function meaningfully in our culture, students must know its roots. In a public school situation, you also should teach about other religions. It is important that your teaching demonstrates the importance of faith in life. Students should begin to realize how beliefs affect actions and historical developments, both positively and negatively. They also should learn that religion is the key to understanding a culture, whether that be Hinduism in India, or Islam in Saudi Arabia, or Roman Catholicism in Quebec, or Calvinism in the Netherlands.

Richard Edlin (1994, 213-214) gives the example of how in high school he was taught the English Civil War as if it was a political event with political intrigue where faith was irrelevant. In college he was taught it as a social event that exemplified the working-class struggle of the period. Edlin then adds how as a Christian teacher you can give a less distorted perspective by showing how it was a war about basic religious beliefs and their application to individual liberty. The central players were motivated mainly by key religious questions. That is something you cannot neglect if you are to give a fair interpretation of history.

As a Christian teacher, you should be balanced in your approach. You may show how the influence of the Roman Catholic church brought about a more stable and peaceful community in Quebec in the 18th century than anywhere else in North America. Or you may discuss how love and compassion motivated most Christian missionaries of aboriginal people. But you must not neglect how churches have sparked bitter religious strife, and how missionaries in their attempts to convert people also imposed Western cultural imperatives, sometimes with negative effects.

You can easily use the planning sheet in chapter 8 for planning units. The only values on the sheet that you cannot promote in a public school situation are godliness and devotion in the spiritual-confessional dimension. And you would be remiss not to teach *about* godliness and devotion when discussing, for instance, why the Pilgrims came to America or why the theologian Bonhoeffer involved himself in an attempt to kill Adolph Hitler.

You also can readily adapt the unit examples in chapter 8 to public school classrooms. *God Made Me Special* becomes *I Am Special*, with an emphasis on children exploring how their uniqueness helps them function as responsible members of their families and communities. Most of the activities of the pioneer unit would remain the same, although discussions of community and family life would consider values in a more general way, without reference to "God's basic Scriptural truths." With minor adjustments that delete explicit references to Christian faith, the tropical rainforest and *Pygmalion* units are also suitable for public school situations. Note that I can make these claims because on the whole society still in principle favors Lickona's basic common moral ground-- even where it is not practiced.

One question that Christian teachers in public schools sometimes ask is whether it is right for them to talk about their own faith and moral commitments. Philosopher Mary Warnock gives a helpful answer to this question. She says that those who advocate neutrality in teaching do so for two reasons. First, they want to avoid indoctrination. However, she adds, they usually apply this term only to the ideas of those with whom they disagree. Second, they want students to be able to draw their own conclusions from their own investigations. But learning would be too complex if students were to investigate everything fully. Students cannot evaluate the validity of all evidence or even understand the sources.

Warnock next shows that it is impossible to be neutral in teaching. Already our selection of content is biased by cultural assumptions and our view of what is important. Besides, she says, neutral teachers would seem remote to their students. They would also implicitly teach that any value position is as good as any other–a value position in itself. Since teachers will always go beyond teaching "facts," they shirk their duty if they do not give their own views and opinions. Such views, including moral beliefs, do not have to be prejudices. Teachers can and should show how they base their own conclusions on evidence. They must present various positions evenhandedly and leave students free to exercise their own imagination and judgment. But as leaders in argument they must be non-neutral. That is the only way to be sincere and get students to think about what is right and wrong. Interpretation enters any meaningful argument. Good teachers hold and express and defend moral views (Warnock in Hare and Portelli 1988, 177-186).

As a Christian teacher in public schools, in other words, you must be careful that your curriculum presents a diversity of views on crucial and controversial issues. You need to present such views fairly and equitably. You should give students full freedom to consider and adopt points of view that differ from yours. But not to indicate your beliefs and your reasons for them at appropriate points sells your students short. First, your beliefs will implicitly color your teaching. It is only fair that students, especially adolescents, are aware of your predilections. Second, your students need models in life who demonstrate that beliefs are important and have consequences. Third, students often ask teachers questions that they can discuss honestly only if they relate the issues to what they believe.

I recognize that teachers who take their beliefs seriously will still face problems. Critical theorist Barry Kanpol recommends that teachers turn from the official curriculum in order to promote their own cultural or political agenda. Teachers can usually follow the "standard" curriculum, however. They can plan meaningful units within it that meet, for instance, most of chapter 4's criteria for justifying curriculum decisions.

At a deeper level, however, a common curriculum becomes increasingly problematic as our society becomes more pluralistic. I agree with Barry Kanpol, for instance, that it is important to address the plight of marginalized people around the world and in our own communities. But I also know that Kanpol and I would have difficulty putting together a unit that would satisfy us both. For one, my Biblical view of authority and freedom differs from the left-wing views he implies in his article (Kanpol 1993, 213-14). A curriculum that is not superficial and yet satisfies people with opposing views on such issues as the nature and purpose of life, the concept of progress, or the role and task of governments is usually unachievable.

Regrettably, the current structure of schooling ignores the fundamental diversity of our pluralistic society. Although the Bible makes clear that education of children is primarily the responsibility of parents, the trend in most Western nations has been to centralize schools under state control. This has resulted in a homogenized curriculum. By avoiding central value questions the curriculum alienates especially those students whose parents or who themselves reject the dominant values of our society. The only long term solution that recognizes diverse faith commitments is that governments allow the operation of tax-maintained alternative schools whose curricula reflect the worldviews of their supporters. True democracy not only tolerates but welcomes diversity, also in school curricula.

REFLECTING

1. Define what it means to teach for commitment. How can a Christian school curriculum promote commitment without undue indoctrination taking place?

2. Rewrite Paul Still's criteria for justifying curriculum decisions (chapter 4) so that you could use them for planning public school programs. Choose a curriculum topic and apply the revised list of criteria.

3. "A curriculum must include a diversity of value positions without promoting any particular one." How do you react to this point of view?

Bibliography

Adler, M. 1982. *The paideia proposal*. New York: Macmillan.

Aikenhead, G. 1980. *Science in social issues: Implications for teaching*. Ottawa: Science Council of Canada.

Alexander, J. 1993. *The secular squeeze: Reclaiming Christian depth in a shallow world*. Downers Grove, IL: InterVarsity.

Anderson, L. and L. Sosniak. 1994. *Bloom's taxonomy: A forty-year retrospective*. Ninety-third yearbook of the National Society for the Study of Education, Part II. Chicago: NSSE.

Apple, M. 1983. Curriculum in the year 2000: Tensions and possibilities. *Phi Delta Kappan* 64(5):321-26.

ASCD Panel on Moral Education. 1988. Moral education in the life of the school. *Educational Leadership* 45(8):5-7.

Bateson, D., G. Erickson, P. J. Gaskell, and M. Wideen. 1992. *British Columbia assessment of science provincial report 1991*. Victoria, B.C.: Ministry of Education.

Beane, J., C. Toepfer, and S. Alessi. 1986. *Curriculum planning and development*. Boston: Allyn and Bacon.

Beisner, E. C. 1993. Justice and poverty: Two views contrasted. *Transformation* 10(1):16-22.

Belcher, C. 1988. The pioneers. Unpublished social studies unit.

Berton, P. 1984. *The promised land: Settling the West 1896-1914*. Toronto: McClelland and Stewart.

Beyer, L. and M. Apple (eds.). 1988. *The curriculum: Problems, politics, and possibilities*. Albany: State University of New York.

Bishop, S. and J. Carpenter. 1993. Constructivism: An introduction and critique. *Spectrum* 25(2):147-158.

Blomberg, D. 1991. The integral curriculum. *Christian Educators Journal* 31(2):6-13.

Bolt, J. 1993. *The Christian story and the Christian school*. Grand Rapids, MI: Christian Schools International.

Bonhoeffer, D. 1954. *Life together*. San Francisco: Harper and Row.

Booth, J. (ed.) 1985. *Over the mountain*. The first of two grade 3 reading anthologies in the *Impressions* readers. Toronto: Holt, Rinehart and Winston.

Bosma, B. and K. Blok. 1992. *A Christian perspective on the teaching of reading*. Grand Rapids: Calvin College.

Bowers, C. 1987. *Toward a post-liberal theory of education*. New York: Teachers College Press.

Bowers, C. 1988. *The cultural dimensions of educational computing*. New York: Teachers College Press.

British Columbia Ministry of Education. 1977. *Guide to the core curriculum*. Victoria, B.C.

British Columbia Ministry of Education. 1990a. *Intermediate program: Learning in British Columbia: Response draft*. Victoria, B.C.

British Columbia Ministry of Education. 1990b. *Primary program: Foundation document*. Victoria, B.C.

Brooks, J. 1990. Constructivists foring new connections. Educational Leadership 47 (5): 68-71.

Brown, P. (ed.) 1994. Trees and forests. A grade 1/2 resource unit. Morwell, Australia: Valley Christian School.

Bruinsma, R. 1990. *Language arts in Christian schools*. Grand Rapids: Christian Schools International.

Buytendijk, F. 1922. *Beschouwingen over enkele moderne opvoedkundige denkbeelden* [*Reflections about some modern educational ideas*]. Groningen: Noordhof.

Chinnery, J. et al. 1993. *How does my garden grow? . . . God makes it so.* A primary unit. Langley, BC: Society of Christian Schools in British Columbia.

Citizens for Public Justice. 1993. Public justice: Six guidelines. *The Catalyst* 16(8-9):3.

Clinton, L. et al. 1993. *Curriculum statement: Technology*. Consultative draft. Wentworthville, Australia: Christian Community Schools Limited.

Clouser, R. 1991. *The myth of religious neutrality*. Notre Dame: University of Notre Dame Press.

Colson, C. 1993. The enduring revolution. Templeton address at the University of Chicago, reprinted in *BreakPoint with Chuck Colson* (October 1993).

Commité Protestant. 1992. *Protestant educational values*. Sainte Foy, Quebec: Gouvernement du Quebec.

Commité Protestant. 1992. *Protestant moral and religious education program: Advice to the minister*. Sainte Foy, Quebec: Gouvernement du Quebec.

Council for Basic Education. 1991. Standards: A vision for learning. *Perspective* 4(1):1-5 and enclosed chart.

Curriculum Development Centre. 1980. *Core curriculum for Australian schools*. Canberra.

Davies, P. 1983. *God and the new physics*. New York: Simon and Schuster.

De Moor, A. (ed.). 1992. *Living in hope: Teacher resource manual*. Grand Rapids: Christian Schools International.

De Moor, S. (ed.). 1994. *Now you are the body of Christ*. Edmonton: CSI District 12 (forthcoming in several volumes).

Dengerink, A. 1987. *Reflections on the arts: A study guide*. Toronto: Institute for Christian Studies.

Diamond, D. 1993. How to develop volunteerism in students. In *Tips for principals* (April). Reston, VA: National Association of Secondary School Principals.

Doll, R. 1989. *Curriculum improvement: Decision making and process*. 7th edition. Boston: Allyn and Bacon.

Driver, R. 1989. The construction of scientific knowledge. In R. Millar (ed.), *Doing science: Images of science in science education*. London: Falmer.

Edlin, R. 1994. *The cause of Christian education*. Northport, AL: Vision Press.

Egan, K. 1986. *Teaching as story telling*. London, ON: Althouse Press.

Egan, K. 1988. *Primary understanding: Education in early childhood*. New York: Routledge.

Egan, K. 1990. *Romantic understanding: The development of rationality and imagination, ages 8-15*. New York: Routledge.

Egan, K. 1992. *Imagination in teaching and learning: The middle school years*. London, ON: Althouse Press.

Eisner, E. 1979. *The educational imagination: On the design and evaluation of school programs*. New York: Macmillan.

Eisner, E. (ed.) 1985. *Learning and teaching the ways of knowing*. Eighty-fourth yearbook of the National Society for the Study of Education. Chicago: University of Chicago Press.

Ellul, J. 1981. *Perspectives on our age*. Toronto: Canadian Broadcasting Corporation.

Elmore, R. and Fuhrman, S. (eds.). 1994. *The governance of curriculum*. Alexandria, Virginia: Association for Supervision and Curriculum Development.

Erikson, E. 1963. *Childhood and society*. New York: Norton.

Ernest, P. 1991. *The philosophy of mathematics education*. London: Falmer.

Erwin, L. and D. MacLennan (eds.). 1994. *Sociology of education in Canada: Critical perspectives on theory, research, and practice*. Toronto: Copp Clark Longman.

Evans, A., R. Evans, and W. Kennedy. 1987. *Pedagogies for the non-poor*. Maryknoll, NY: Orbis.

Everding, H., C. Snelling, and M. Wilcox. 1988. A shaping vision of community for teaching in an individualistic world: Ephesians 4.1-16 and developmental interpretation. *Religious Education* 83(3):423-438.

Fennema, J. 1977. *Nurturing children in the Lord*. Phillipsburg, NJ: Presbyterian and Reformed.

Fowler, S. 1991. *A Christian voice among students and scholars*. Potchefstroom, South Africa: Potchefstroom University for Christian Higher Education.

Francis, L. and A. Thatcher (eds.). 1990. *Christian perspectives for education*. Leominster, U.K.: Gracewing.

Freire, Paulo. 1970. *Pedagogy of the oppressed*. New York: Seabury.

Gardner, H. 1993. *Multiple intelligences: The theory in practice*. New York: BasicBooks.

Gesch, C. 1993a. *Putting creeds to work*. Telkwa, BC: Eskerhazy Publications.

Gesch, C. 1993b. *Teaching aids for the conservation and outdoor recreation education course*. Telkwa, BC: Eskerhazy Publications.

Gesch, C. 1993c. Selections and highlights from English 10 and Bible 12 examinations. Distributed, respectively, as *Powerful stories... Sensitive readers... and Studying God's Word: Light for our path...* Smithers, BC: Bulkley Valley Christian School.

Giroux, H. and D. Purpel. *The hidden curriculum and moral education: Deception or discovery?* Berkeley, CA: McCutchan.

Glasser, W. 1992. The quality school curriculum. *Phi Delta Kappan* 73(9):690-694.

Good, T. and J. Brophy. 1994. *Looking in classrooms*. Sixth edition. New York: HarperCollins.

Goudzwaard, B. 1984. *Idols of our time*. Downers Grove: InterVarsity.

Gow, K. 1980. *Yes Virgina, there is a right and wrong!* Toronto: John Wiley.

Grant, G. (ed.) 1992. *Review of research in education*, Vol. 18. Washington: American Educational Research Association.

Greenberg, B. and J. Brand. 1993. Channel One: But what about the advertising? *Educational Leadership* 51(4): 56-58.

Greene, A. 1984. Helps for preparing a statement of educational objectives for schools. Seven-page paper. Seattle: Alta Vista.

Greene, A. 1990. *Thinking Christianly: New patterns for new people*. Seattle: Alta Vista.

Groome, T. 1980. *Christian Religious Education*. San Francisco: Harper & Row.

Grundy, S. 1987. *Curriculum: Product or praxis?* New York: The Falmer Press.

Gutek, G. 1988. *Philosophical and ideological perspectives on education*. Englewood Cliffs: Prentice Hall.

Hall, D. 1986. *Imaging God: Dominion as stewardship*. Grand Rapids: Eerdmans.

Hamming, C., H. Van Brummelen, and P. Boonstra. 1984. *The story of numbers and numerals*. Grand Rapids: Christian Schools International.

Hare, W. and J. Portelli. 1988. *Philosophy of education: Introductory readings*. Calgary: Detselig.

Harmin, M. and Gregory, T. 1974. *Teaching is . . .* Chicago: Science Research Associates.

Harris, M. 1987. *Teaching and religious imagination*. San Francisco: Harper & Row.

Hass, G. 1987. *Curriculum planning: A new approach*. Fifth edition. Boston: Allyn and Bacon.

Hauerwas, S. and J. Westerhoff (eds.). 1992. *Schooling Christians: "Holy experiments" in American education*. Grand Rapids: Eerdmans.

Haynes, C. 1993. Beyond the culture wars. *Educational Leadership* 51(4):30-34.

Hirsch, E. 1993. The core knowledge curriculum--what's behind its success? *Educational Leadership* 50(8):23-30.

Hirst, P. 1974. *Knowledge and the curriculum*. London: Routledge & Kegan Paul.

Hollingsworth, S. and H. Sockett (eds.). 1994. *Teacher research and educational reform*. Ninety-third yearbook of the National Society for the Study of Education. Chicago: NSSE.

Holmes, A. 1983. *Contours of a worldview*. Grand Rapids: Eerdmans.

Holmes, M. 1992. *Educational policy for a pluralist democracy: the common school, choice, and diversity*. New York: Falmer.

Jacobs, H. 1989. *Interdisciplinary curriculum: Design and implementation*. Alexandra, VA: Association for Supervision and Curriculum Development.

Jackson, P. (ed.). 1992. *Handbook of research on curriculum*. New York: Macmillan.

Janz, M. 1987. *George Bernard Shaw's Pygmalion*. An unpublished grade 12 English unit.

Kanpol, B. 1993. The pragmatic curriculum: Teacher reskilling as cultural politics. *The Journal of Educational Thought* 27(2):200-215.

Kilpatrick, W. 1992. *Why Johnny can't tell right from wrong*. New York: Simon and Schuster.

Klein, G. 1985. *Reading into racism: Bias in children's literature and learning materials*. London: Routledge and Kegan Paul.

Kliebard, H. 1975. The rise of scientific curriculum making and its aftermath. *Curriculum theory network* 5(1):27-38.

Kohlberg, L. 1971. Stages of moral development as a basis for moral education. In Beck, C., B. Crittenden, and E. Sullivan, *Moral education: Interdisciplinary approaches*. Toronto: University of Toronto.

Koole, R. 1990. *Christian perspective for teaching social studies*. Edmonton: CSI District 11 Association.

Kuhn, T. 1970 [1962]. *The structure of scientific revolutions*. Second edition. Chicago: University of Chicago.

Kuyper, A. 1991 [1891]. *The problem of poverty*. Edited by J. Skillen. Grand Rapids: Baker.

Lasch, C. 1984. *The minimal self: Psychic survival in troubled times*. New York: Norton.

Leming, J. 1993. In search of effective character education. *Educational Leadership* 51(3):63-71.

Lewy, A. (ed.) 1991. *The international encyclopedia of curriculum*. Oxford: Pergamon.

Lickona, T. 1991. *Educating for character: How our schools can teach respect and responsibility*. New York: Bantam.

Lickona, T. 1993. The return of character education. *Educational leadership* 51(3):6-11.

Lucas, C. 1976. *Challenge and choice in contemporary education: Six major ideological perspectives*. New York: Macmillan.

Luke, C. and J. Gore (eds.) 1992. *Feminisms and critical pedagogy*. New York: Routledge, Chapman, and Hall.

Lundin, R. and S. Gallagher. 1989. *Literature through the eyes of faith*. San Francisco: Harper and Row.

Macdonald, J. and D. Purpel. 1987. Curriculum and planning: Visions and metaphors. *Journal of curriculum and supervision* 2(2):178-192.

MacIntyre, A. 1982. *After virtue*. Notre Dame: University of Notre Dame.

Maggs, D. 1988. *The family*. An unpublished senior secondary unit.

McCarthy, B. 1990. Using the 4MAT system to bring learning styles to schools. *Educational leadership* 48(2):31-37.

McLaren, P. 1986. *Schooling as a ritual performance*. New York: Random House.

McQuaide, J. and A. Pliska. 1993. The challenge to Pennsylvania's education reform. *Educational leadership* 51(4):16-21.

Nadeau, R. and J. Desautels. 1984. *Epistemology and the teaching of science.* Ottawa: Science Council of Canada.

National Association of Secondary School Principals. 1993. Science/technology/society-addressing the real problems in science education. *Curriculum report* 22(3):1-4.

Newbigin, L. 1983. *The other side of 1984.* Geneva: World Council of Churches.

Newbigin, L. 1986. *Foolishness to the Greeks.* Grand Rapids: Eerdmans.

Newbigin, L. 1989. *The gospel in a pluralist society.* Grand Rapids: Eerdmans.

Oakes, J. 1986. Tracking, inequality, and the rhetoric of reform: Why schools don't change. *Journal of education* 168(1):60-80.

Oliver, D. 1990. Grounded knowledge: A post-modern perspective on teaching and learning. *Educational leadership* 48(1):64-69.

Ontario Alliance of Christian Schools. 1990. Literature in the Christian school. *High school digest* 1(5):1.

Ontario Alliance of Christian Schools. 1994. *Thy will be done: Old Testament studies, Unit One.* Draft edition. Ancaster, ON.

Ornstein, A. and Hunkins, F. 1988. *Curriculum: Foundations, principles, and issues.* Englewood Cliffs, NJ: Prentice-Hall.

Oser, F., A. Dick and J. Patry (eds.). 1992. *Effective and responsible teaching: The new synthesis.* San Francisco: Jossey-Bass.

Owens, V. 1983. *God spy: Faith, perception and the new physics.* Seattle: Alta Vista College.

Palmer, P. 1983. *To know as we are known: A spirituality of education.* San Francisco: Harper & Row.

Parsons, J., G. Milburn, and M. van Manen (eds.). 1983. *A Canadian social studies.* Edmonton: University of Alberta.

Paul, R. 1988. Ethics without indoctrination. *Educational Leadership* 45(8):10-19.

Pazmino, R. 1992. *Principles and practices of Christian education.* Grand Rapids, MI: Baker.

Peck, K. and D. Dorricott. Why use technology? *Educational Leadership* 51(7):11-14.

Pentecostal Education Council. 1991. *A vision for educational excellence.* Windsor, Newfoundland: Pentecostal Assemblies Board of Education.

Perrone, V. 1993. How to engage students in learning. *Educational leadership* 51(5):11-13.

Phenix, P. 1964. *Realms of meaning.* New York: McGraw-Hill.

Pinar, W. 1988. *Contemporary Curriculum Discourses.* Scottsdale, AZ: Gorsuch Scarisbrick.

Poincaré, H. 1956. Mathematical creation. In James R. Newman, *The World of Mathematics,* Vol 4, 2041-2050. New York: Simon and Schuster.

Postman, N. 1993. *Technopoly: The surrender of culture to technology.* New York: Vintage.

Pratt, D. 1994. *Curriculum planning: A handbook for professionals.* Fort Worth, TX: Harcourt Brace.

Price, D., J. Wiester, and W. Hearn. 1986. *Teaching science in a climate of controversy.* Ipswich, MA: American Scientific Affiliation.

Purpel, D. 1989. *The moral and spiritual crisis in education.* Granby, Massachusetts: Bergin and Garvey.

Rau, S., L. Roseboom, and M. Zazitko. *The role of the family.* Langley, B.C.: Society of Christian Schools in British Columbia.

Redekop, F. and G. Strydhorst-Piers. 1993. *Traveling through the tropical rain forests.* An intermediate unit. Langley, BC: Society of Christian Schools in British Columbia.

Reynolds, W. 1989. *Reading curriculum theory: The development of a new hermeneutic.* New York: Peter Lang.

Roosendaal, V., A. Straforelli, and J. Vanderzwaag. 1986. *God made me special.* An integrated kindergarten unit. Langley, BC: Society of Christian Schools.

Scheffler, I. 1958. Justifying curriculum decisions. *The school review* 66(4):461-72.

Schlipp, P. (ed.). 1970. *Albert Einstein: Philosopher scientist.* La Salle, Illinois: Open Court.

Schwab, J. 1978. *Science, curriculum, and liberal education: Selected essays, Joseph J. Schwab.* Edited by I. Westbury and N. Wilkof. Chicago: University of Chicago Press.

Schwab, J. 1983. The practical 4: Something for curriculum professors to do. *Curriculum inquiry* 13(3):239-265.

Shapiro, B. 1993. Interpreting the world: Artistic and scientific ways of knowing. *English quarterly* 26(1):26-29.

Shulman, L. 1987. Knowledge and teaching: Foundations of the new reform. *Harvard educational review* 57(1):1-22.

Simon, S., L. Howe, and H. Kirschenbaum. 1972. *Values clarification: A handbook of practical strategies for teachers and students.* New York: A & W Publishers.

Sizer, T. 1992. *Horace's school: Redesigning the American high school.* Boston: Houghton-Mifflin.

Smedes, L. 1983. *Mere morality: what God expects from ordinary people.* Grand Rapids: Eerdmans.

Smith, D. 1991. Language, God, and man. *Language matters* No. 1:3-5.

Smith, D. 1992. Language, God, and man #3. *Language matters* No. 3:10-12.

Smith, F. 1990. *To think.* New York: Teachers College Press.

Society of Christian Schools in British Columbia. 1980. *Social studies handbook.* Langley, B.C.

Society of Christian Schools in British Columbia. 1984. *Biblical studies handbook.* Langley, B.C.

Society of Christian Schools in British Columbia. Forthcoming. *Language arts handbook.* Langley, B.C.

Son, B. 1993. Uniqueness of Christ and social justice. *Evangelical review of theology* 17(1):93-109.

Spencer, H. 1911. What knowledge is of most worth? In H. Spencer, *Essays on education.* London: J.M. Dent and Sons, 3-44.

Steensma, G. and H. Van Brummelen (eds.) 1977. *Shaping school curriculum: A Biblical view.* Terre Haute, IN: Signal.

Stronks, G. and D. Blomberg (eds.). 1993. *A vision with a task: Christian schooling for responsive discipleship.* Grand Rapids: Baker Books.

Sutton, R. Suggestions for a "lifeskills" program. Curriculum Resource Bank paper. Langley, BC: Society of Christian Schools in B.C.

Sweller, J. 1988. Cognitive load during problem solving: Effects on learning. *Cognitive science* 12(2):257-285.

Tanner, L. 1988. *Critical issues in curriculum.* Eighty-seventh yearbook of the National Society for the Study in Education. Chicago: NSSE.

Thiessen, E. 1993. *Teaching for commitment: Liberal education, indoctrination, and Christian nurture.* Montreal: McGill-Queen's University Press.

Tomlinson, P. and M. Quinton (eds.). 1986. *Values across the curriculum.* London: Falmer.

Triezenberg, H. (ed.) 1982. *Principles to practice.* Third edition. Grand Rapids: Christian Schools International.

Tyler, R. 1950. *Basic principles of curriculum and instruction.* Chicago: University of Chicago Press.

Van Brummelen, H. et al. 1985. *Science,* a component of the SCS-BC *Curriculum handbook.* Surrey, BC: Society of Christian Schools in British Columbia.

Van Brummelen, H. 1986. *Telling the next generation: Educational development in North American Calvinist Christian schools.* Lanham and Toronto: University Press of America and The Institute for Christian Studies.

Van Brummelen, H. 1989. *Curriculum: Implementation in three Christian schools.* Grand Rapids: Calvin College.

Van Brummelen, H. 1990. Tolerance in public and religiously based schools. *Ethics in education* 9(4):8-11.

Van Brummelen, H. 1991. The world portrayed in texts: An analysis of the content of elementary school textbooks. *The Journal of Educational Thought* 25(3):202-21.

Van Brummelen, H. 1992 [1988]. *Walking with God in the classroom.* Seattle: Alta Vista.

Van Brummelen, H. 1993. Effects of government funding on private schools: Appraising the perceptions of long-term principals and teachers in British Columbia's Christian schools. *Canadian Journal of Education* 18(1):14-28.

Vandenberg, D. 1988. Knowledge in schooling. *Phenomenology + pedagogy* 6(2):63-78.

Van Dyk, J. 1994. The multifunctional classroom: Pipe dream or possibility? Discussion paper. Sioux Center, IA: Dordt College Center for Educational Services.

Vitz, P. 1986. *Censorship: Evidence of bias in our children's textbooks.* Ann Arbor: Servant.

Walker, D. 1990. *Fundamentals of curriculum.* San Diego: Harcourt Brace Jovanovich.

Walker, D. and J. Soltis. 1992. *Curriculum and aims.* Second edition. New York: Teachers College Press.

Walsh, B. and J. Middleton. 1984. *The transforming vision: Shaping a Christian world view*. Downers Grove, IL: InterVarsity.

Wassermann, S. 1992. A case for social studies. *Phi Delta Kappan* 73(10):793-801.

Werner, W. and T. Aoki. 1979. *Programs for people: Introducing program development, implementation, and evaluation*. Vancouver: Centre for the Study of Curriculum and Instruction (University of British Columbia).

Werner, W. (ed.). 1983. *Program implementation experiences: Cases from British Columbia*. Victoria and Vancouver: British Columbia Ministry of Education and Centre for the Study of Curriculum and Instruction (University of British Columbia).

Whitehead, A. 1929. *The aims of education and other essays*. New York: Macmillan.

Willis, S. 1993. Learning through service. Association for Supervision and Curriculum Development *Update* 35(6):1-8.

Wittrock, M. (ed.) 1986. *Handbook of research on teaching*. Third edition. New York: Macmillan.

Woehrle, T. 1993. *Growing up responsible*. Educational leadership 51(3):40-43.

Wolters, A. 1985. *Creation regained: Biblical basics for a reformational worldview*. Grand Rapids: Eerdmans.

Wolterstorff, N. 1976. *Reason within the bounds of religion*. Grand Rapids: Eerdmans.

Wolterstorff, N. 1980. *Educating for responsible action*. Grand Rapids: Eerdmans.

Wolterstorff, N. 1983. *Until justice and peace embrace*. Grand Rapids: Eerdmans, 1983.

Woods, J. 1982. *Looking at the consumer*. Toronto: Gage.

List of participating teachers

The response of teachers and schools to my request for curriculum examples was deeply gratifying. The response was so great that I was unable to visit all of the schools that volunteered. I thank everyone for their willingness, and especially those teachers who shared with me what was happening in their classrooms. I have regained a deep appreciation for the many capable, committed, and innovative classroom teachers. I also appreciate principals and others who arranged for my visits to their schools. Below I list the teachers with whom I met, plus several who allowed me to use their written curriculum plans. I have tried to be complete; however, my apologies to anyone whom I inadvertently left off the list. Due to the many examples I experienced, I was unable to use all of the examples directly in this book. Each one, however, contributed to my insight into what is going on in schools and classrooms.

Abbotsford (BC) Christian Schools: Rick Binder, Rita Bot, Henry Contant, Lloyd Den Boer, Janet Hitchcock, Kathy Huizing, Clarence Janzen, and Anna-May Taekema.

Bulkley Valley Christian School, Smithers, BC: Curt Gesch.

Covenant Christian School, Edmonds, WA: Elaine Brouwer.

Credo Christian Elementary School, Langley, BC: Hugo Vander Hoek.

Delta (BC) Christian School: Frances Redekop.

Duncan (BC) Christian School: Susan Dick, Glenda MacPhee, and John Zuidema.

Edmonton (Alberta) Christian Schools: Dorothy Bartel, Debbie Benson, Carrie Chassé, Alisa Ketchum, Joan Konynenbelt, Anthony Looy, Doug Monsma, Marian Piekema, Bertha Tiemstra, Derk Van Eerden, and Stuart Williams.

Highroad Academy, Chilliwack, BC: Wayne Lennea, Betty Stark, and Gwen Wray.

Kelowna (BC) Christian School: Bruce Hildebrandt, Doug Sader, and Paul Smith.

Langley (BC) Christian School: Paul Still and Wilma Van Brummelen.

Leisin, Switzerland: Mona Janz Stuart.

Nanaimo (BC) Christian School: Anna Barber and Donna Ferguson.

Pacific Christian Academy, Surrey, BC: Ruth Frith and Pat Sutton.

Pacific Christian School, Victoria, BC: Peggy Barlow, Leigh Bradfield, Henry Bulthuis, Berta Den Haan, Frank De Vries, Inge Maier, and Merlie McGee.

Richmond (BC) Christian School: Gloria Strydhorst-Piers.

Timothy Christian School, Owen Sound, Ontario: Christina Belcher.

Torbain Primary School, Scotland: Emma Johnstone.

Valley Christian Community School, Morwell, Victoria, Australia: Phillip Brown.

Vernon (BC) Christian School: Doreen Fairweather, Linda Samland, and Elco Vandergrift.

Watson Groen Christian School, Seattle, WA: Lavonne Roosendaal.

White Rock (BC) Christian Academy: David Wu.

Index